Middle Tennessee
1775–1825

WITHDRAWN

Middle Tennessee
1775–1825

PROGRESS AND POPULAR DEMOCRACY
ON THE SOUTHWESTERN FRONTIER

Kristofer Ray

The University of Tennessee Press • Knoxville

Copyright © 2007 by The University of Tennessee Press / Knoxville. All Rights Reserved. Manufactured in the United States of America. First Edition.

Frontispiece: "The State of Tennessee." From Samuel Lewis Atlas, 1817. Library of Congress.

Portions of chapters 1, 2, 3 and 5 previously appeared as "Political Culture and the Origins of a Party System in the Southern Ohio Valley: The Case of Early National Tennessee, 1796–1812," *Ohio Valley History* 4 (Winter 2004): 3–26. It is reprinted by permission of the University of Cincinnati, the Cincinnati Museum Center, and the Filson Historical Society.

Portions of chapters 1 and 2 previously appeared as "Land Speculation, Popular Democracy, and Political Transformation on the Tennessee Frontier, 1780–1800," *Tennessee Historical Quarterly* 61, no. 3 (Fall 2002). It is reprinted by permission of the *Tennessee Historical Quarterly*.

This book is printed on acid-free paper.

Ray, Kristofer.
  Middle Tennessee, 1775-1825: progress and popular democracy on the southwestern frontier / Kristofer Ray.— 1st ed.
     p. cm.
Includes bibliographical references and index.

ISBN-13: 978-1-57233-597-4 (hardcover: alk. paper)
ISBN-10: 1-57233-597-1

1. Tennessee, Middle—Politics and government—18th century. 2. Tennessee, Middle—Politics and government—19th century. 3. Political culture—Tennessee, Middle—History—18th century. 4. Political culture—Tennessee, Middle—History—19th century. 5. Democracy—Tennessee, Middle—History—18th century. 6. Democracy—Tennessee, Middle—History—19th century. 7. Progress—History. 8. Economic development—History. 9. Tennessee, Middle—Economic conditions—18th century. 10. Tennessee, Middle—Economic conditions—19th century. I. Title.

F442.2.R39 2007
976.8'02—dc22   2007002617

For Bob

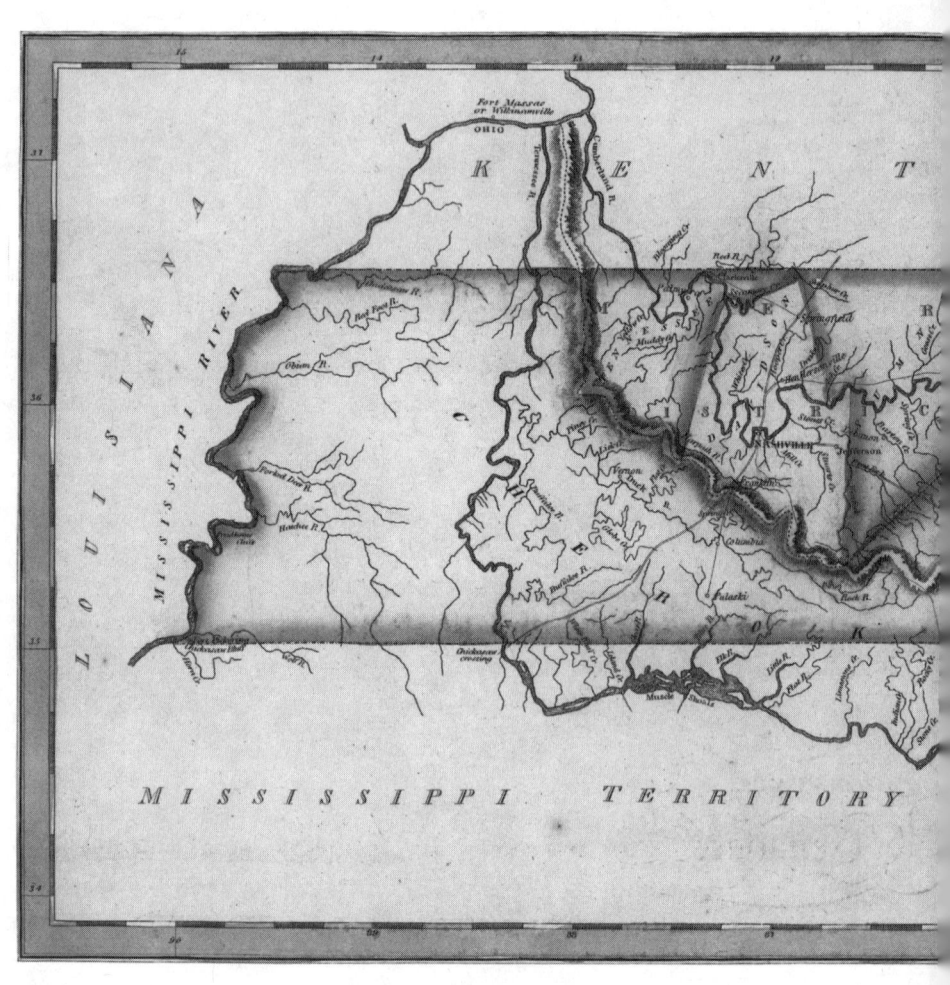

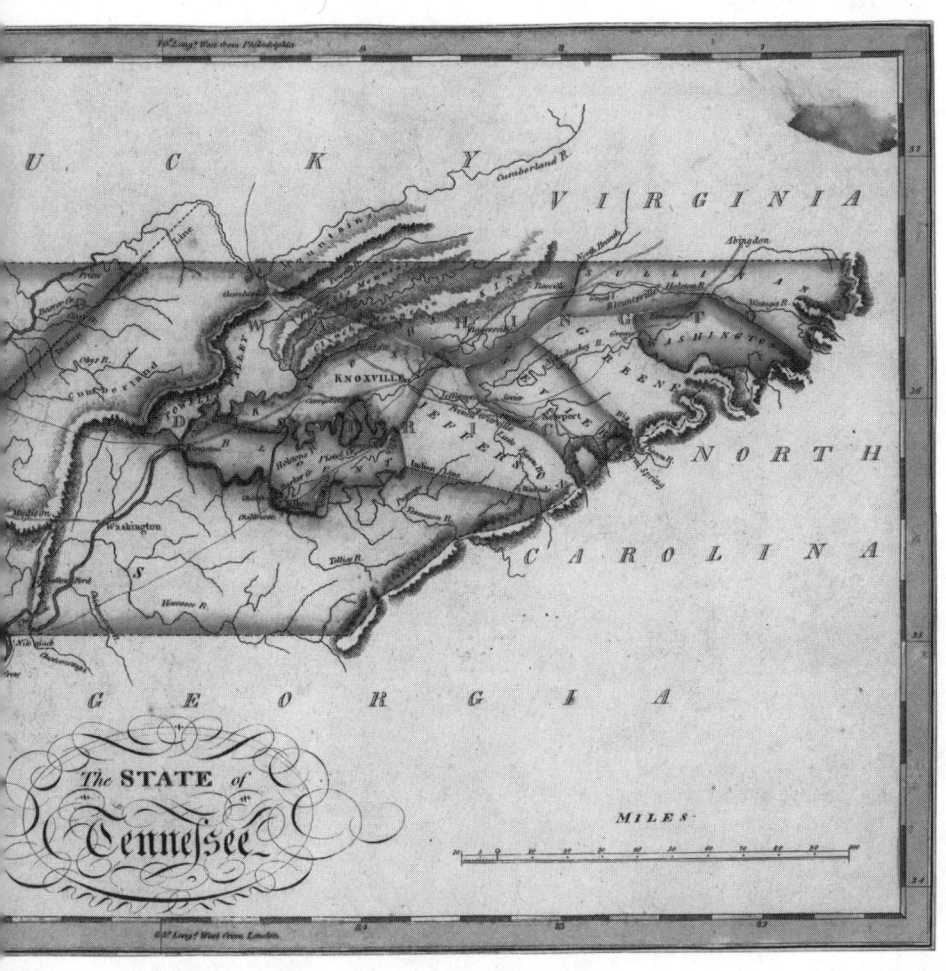

Contents

Acknowledgments	xiii
Introduction	xvii
1. Land Speculation and the Origins of a Political Culture, 1775–1790	1
2. Warfare and the Creation of a Jeffersonian Identity, 1790–1796	19
3. Militias, Factions, and Public Opinion in a Shifting Political Culture, 1796–1810	41
4. Economy, Demography, and Diversification, 1796–1815	57
5. Ideological Division and American Nationalism in an Expanding Political Culture, 1796–1815	93
6. The Emergence of a Jacksonian Philosophy: Expansion, Banks, and Panic, 1815–1825	117
Epilogue: Slavery and the Transition to Jacksonian Politics	141
Notes	153
Bibliography	207
Index	227

Maps

The State of Tennessee, 1817   vii

Following Page 85

A Map of the Tennessee Government, Formerly Part of North
   Carolina, 1795
Tennessee's Counties in 1800: Total Population
Tennessee's Counties in 1800: Free Whites
Tennessee's Counties in 1800: All Other Free Persons
Tennessee's Counties in 1800: Slaves
Tennessee's Counties in 1810: Total Population
Tennessee's Counties in 1810: Free Whites
Tennessee's Counties in 1810: All Other Free Persons
Tennessee's Counties in 1810: Slaves
Tennessee's Counties in 1820: Total Population
Tennessee's Counties in 1820: Free Whites
Tennessee's Counties in 1820: Free Blacks
Tennessee's Counties in 1820: Slaves

Acknowledgments

Acknowledgments can be tricky, if for no other reason than there are so many people who have been so influential. Even so, a few folks particularly stand out. Appropriately, the list must start in Tennessee. I first want to thank Marcus Cooke for one incredible round of golf in Knoxville, circa 1997. Nothing of what has followed would have happened had he not challenged me to get off my lazy butt. Thanks also to Brad Austin, a fellow golfer and confidant from my days in Knoxville, who encouraged me at every point to continue along the path to North Carolina. A very special thank you to Wayne Cutler. Although he won't agree with all of this book's conclusions, his influence on my scholarly development has been profound. Thanks for being my friend, and for helping to provide a very timely entrance into the world of documentary editing.

In Chapel Hill, a big thanks to Steve Estes, Ed Slavishak, Ken Zogry, Paul Quigley, Andrew Dyke, Spencie Love, and Beth Millwood, all of whom graciously put up with my neuroses, read and commented upon various elements of this project, and never ceased to offer their support. Or in Steve's and Andrew's case, much needed non-scholarly diversions. Although I didn't know him in North Carolina, I would be remiss if I didn't say thank you to Michael Powell for giving me my first opportunity to teach. We may not agree on the causes of the Civil War, but Michael was more than generous with his time and his friendship.

As to the project itself, thanks to Mark Wetherington and Jim Holmberg for helping me gain access to the incredible wealth of material at the Filson Historical Society in Louisville, Kentucky. Carroll Van West, Christopher Phillips, Wayne Durrill, Stephen Aron, James Sharp, and Sally Hadden all read parts of the manuscript, and their criticism honed important elements of the larger project. Scot Danforth, John R. Finger, and Craig Thompson Friend all deserve medals for patiently reading through the entire manuscript and offering thought-provoking assessments. They have saved me from numerous historiographical and factual gaffes. Thanks for that. Sue Perdue, Andrew O'Shaughnessy, Mary Anne Andrei, Deborah Beckel, Leigh Sellers, and Doug Bradburn went above and beyond the call of duty by listening to me blather on about the project, providing well-timed criticism to keep it on track, and by offering their friendship during my time as an editor at the *Papers of Thomas Jefferson: Retirement Series* at Monticello.

Two particularly old friends deserve mention. Steve Bray was kind enough to put up with me, first in Waco and then when I arrived in Nashville to research this manuscript. I really appreciate having been able to use his (and Mojo's) couch, as well as his willingness to discuss topics far afield from internal medicine. George Clements is a native Nashvillian who got my historical fires burning over many a pint at The Albert in London. Since then he has offered me the use of his house, listened patiently as I laid out various ideas, and read and commented upon several drafts of the first few chapters. Hopefully this book addresses some of the issues he thinks are critical for all Tennesseans to understand.

This project would never have gotten off the ground if not for the careful reading provided by Peter Coclanis, Theda Perdue, and Donald Mathews. Thanks for saving me from critical errors of fact, bad writing, and for pushing me to tease out more of the story than I initially had done.

I'll conclude with the three people whose contributions are sine qua nons for my success. First, Bill Barney. His willingness to let me take his seminar on Jacksonian America has made all the difference in my academic career. He has since read almost every draft of this book, given me the chance to work on the magnificent Documenting the American South project, offered both encouragement and correctives when the manuscript went astray, and engaged in great discussions of college football and

Acknowledgments

major league baseball. Second, Harry Watson. Like Bill, Harry gave me a chance when he had absolutely no reason to do so. It was Harry who suggested the topic that eventually became this book, and it was Harry who patiently and methodically shepherded it to completion. Along the way he provided much-needed research support, career advice, reality checks, optimism, and good cheer. And since graduation he has gone above and beyond the call of duty by assessing the quality of journal articles, showing up to listen to conference panels, and making a last pass through this manuscript to make sure all was in order. Advisor, mentor, friend. That about sums it up.

Finally, Brandi Brown. From time to time I've told her that I don't know what I would have done without her. Perhaps not, but I am aware of what I would *not* have done. I would not have completed this book without her. I would not have grown into a responsible human being without her. And I would never have been able to meet Vivian and Blythe, the other two most important women in my life. Thanks for everything, and thanks in advance for continuing to put up with my myriad historical peregrinations.

Introduction

Political evolution in the region now known as Middle Tennessee was complex and contested in the early national period. During its territorial phase (1775–96), a small clique of surveyors and speculators controlled government institutions. They used land accumulation to establish themselves and ruled without consistent challenge because there was no mechanism by which ordinary settlers could question their authority. At the turn of the nineteenth century, however, a burst of militia elections gave Tennesseans access to positions of community importance. They also established a firm precedent for political opposition. Soon the elite had to construct broad constituencies in an increasingly vibrant popular democracy.

This shifting political culture coincided with unprecedented economic and demographic development. Between 1796 and 1801 the population grew 200 percent, and by 1815 there were 292,590 residents committed to cotton and tobacco cultivation. Commercial agriculture in turn created a mercantile class that integrated Middle Tennessee into a global economy. Yet competition associated with this economy created unforeseen popular divisions. Even as planting and merchant interests looked to the government to expedite commercial growth, ordinary farmers believed that limited land accessibility and excessive debt threatened their stability. They therefore used the political sphere to contest more expansive definitions of progress.

This book examines the intersection of a changing political culture with an emerging economy. It underscores that popular democracy developed through militia electioneering and demographic growth, and that divisions over the meaning of economic progress were in place before the Jacksonian era. It also shows that rapid development undermined Indian cultural prerogatives and gradually restricted Tennessee's slave and free black population. Studying the intersection of political culture and economy in early Middle Tennessee, in other words, clarifies the ways in which a broad southern community defined and came to grips with the question of "progress."

***

White immigrants settled in the Cumberland River basin in the 1770s, at a time when Americans were reevaluating traditional political assumptions. Colonial southern politics had revolved around the notion that society was regimented but interdependent, with each segment contributing to an organic whole. Institutionalized inequality of power was a function of larger British levels of dependency, which were controlled and ascribed by tradition, statute, and common law.[1] In such an environment the gentry held most offices of significance, and they expected ordinary folk to leave them to do their work as disinterested gentlemen.[2]

The land surveyors looking to control Middle Tennessee's territorial institutions emerged out of this political tradition. Taking advantage of connections to elite speculators and politicians in Virginia and North Carolina (Tennessee's mother state), they established defensive stations, organized militias, and acquired positions of political power. They also hoped to employ traditional political assumptions as a safeguard against the excesses of democracy. Virginia-based speculator Arthur Campbell, for example, noted that although "a real republican system is a delightful object for me to contemplate; I am not so deficient in the knowledge of mankind, as not to doubt the wisdom and virtue of a people that are yet far from being enlightened."[3]

The realities of early settlement ensured that ordinary Tennesseans would not move beyond abstract notions of popular democracy. Between 1775 and 1796 the settlement process was violent, unpredictable, and generally consumed by conflict between white settlers and the Chickasaw,

Cherokee, Chickamauga, and Creek Indian nations. Moreover, the small population had only minimal contact with institutional vehicles such as a press or consistent electoral opportunities outside of the militia.

Lack of institutionalization meant that ordinary immigrants did not have avenues through which to channel antiauthoritarian behavior. Thus they could not significantly alter the deliberative process. Particularly, they could do little to counterbalance the fact that seven out of their eight legislators to the North Carolina General Assembly, and eighteen of twenty-four county court judges, were either speculators or employed by them. After 1790, the restrictive nature of territorial government tightened surveyor/speculator control. In that year North Carolina ceded its western lands to the United States. Having done so before the passage of the Southwest Ordinance of 1791, state leaders insisted on the application of the only working model for territorial settlement: the Northwest Ordinance of 1787 (minus the Article 6 prohibition of slavery).[4] And the ordinance gave the territorial governor nearly unlimited power by authorizing him to convene legislatures and appoint "the necessary officers of Goverment, that is Justices, Sheriffs, Constables, Clerks, Registers, and Militia officers of every grade below a General."[5]

In short, violence, a small population, the lack of institutional vehicles, and the limiting nature of territorial government meant that common Middle Tennesseans found it difficult to make significant democratic inroads. In any case, most had little inclination to pursue change. For most of the territorial period the region was so engulfed in war with Cherokees, Creeks, and Chickamaugas that politicians and settlers in unison demanded national intervention. After 1790, the Federalist-dominated central government's decision not to step in alienated the frontier population and left the region with a seemingly united political will. Unlike other regions in the new American nation, where a Federalist interest ensured party competition, the end result was a limited "Jeffersonian" political culture with the territorial elite firmly in control of governing institutions.[6]

This elite looked to expand their political power at statehood in 1796 by attempting to control the militia. They saw that virtually all of the state's electorate belonged to militia companies. Hoping to create and extend networks in support of personal objectives, they electioneered to place themselves and their allies in key positions of martial leadership. In so doing, they unwittingly destroyed traditional political understandings on the

Tennessee frontier. At the turn of the nineteenth century, thousands of common white immigrants—who eventually fashioned themselves the region's merchants, artisans, farmers, and entrepreneurs—used these elections to obtain offices and positions of community importance. Through them they fully realized they were a legitimate source of authority, and their involvement fed a nascent political sphere that established a firm precedent for opposition.[7] Soon the elite had to emphasize the construction of broad constituencies in an increasingly contested popular democracy.

Demographic flux also sparked an unprecedented economic boom that altered regional society and culture. Profit-minded Middle Tennesseans increasingly committed themselves to cotton and tobacco planting, which in turn helped solidify a mercantile class whose national and international connections integrated Middle Tennessee into a global economy. By 1820, commerce and planting had become so profitable that entrepreneurially inclined residents stood at the forefront of the southern movement for internal improvement and economic innovation.

Yet the highly visible and increasingly unavoidable competition associated with a dynamic economy had divisive side effects. Even as planting and merchant interests looked to local, state, and federal governments to expedite commercial growth, many ordinary Tennesseans were coming to believe that unabated economic dynamism threatened land titles and placed upon them insurmountable levels of debt. They therefore used their political voice to demand protection from the excesses of the new market-economy. Initially tied to court reform and debtor relief, this more restrained notion of progress would transform into a key political position after the Panic of 1819.

Yet there was more to the region's transformation. The debate over progress took place against a backdrop of militant nationalism that brought Tennessee into the national political community. Whereas the region once had flirted with secession, this surge of American nationalism helped residents connect local issues with interregional and national coalitions.[8] When combined with the emergent split over the nature and meaning of progress, this nationalism solidified the foundation for a permanent party structure in Tennessee.

Introduction

What exactly is meant by progress and popular democracy? According to the *Oxford English Dictionary*, progress means "going on to a further stage, or to further or higher stages successively; growth or development; usually in good sense, advance to better and better conditions."[9] During the initial phase of settlement, most in Middle Tennessee would have found such a definition adequate, as an anonymous writer in the *Knoxville Gazette* perfectly encapsulated. In his comparison of "The Savage and the Civilized Man," the author wrote that the savage was "disengaged from the chace [sic], or war, [and] leads a life of stupid insensibility—there can scarcely be said to be any progress, or succession of events, in his existence—'tis one perpetual *now*." By contrast, "the civilized Man lives in himself—in his children—in the public;—and as he participates in the labours, he enjoys the happiness of his country and mankind."[10] Progress, in other words, meant the unfettered ability to work on behalf of family and community, which would end with a level of economic and social stability that could only improve man and country. All that was needed was security against those stuck in the "perpetual now."

With the frontier nominally secured after 1796, white notions of progress began to take two forms: (1) the desire on the part of certain entrepreneurially minded people to seek out new economic activities, including government funding for internal improvements, the embrace of technological innovation, and a push for urban development (with concomitant commitments to refinement and reform); and (2) the desire among others for greater control over an economy that was threatening to pass them by. This was not a view of the world imbued with nostalgia for a lost, idyllic age. To the contrary, it embraced economic development and accepted the idea of individual pursuit of gain—as long as debt was kept from spiraling out of control. It was around these ideas of economic progress that political institutionalization evolved.

By democracy, Americans typically think of governments in which power is vested in the people. Other historians have defined the historical process of democratization as simply "the expansion of voter participation within an increasingly open and free electoral process."[11] But popular democracy entails more than just the right to vote. As historian Sean Wilentz recently has put it, it is "a historical fact, rooted in a vast array of events and experiences, that comes into being out of changing human relations between governors and the governed."[12] It was during the Revolutionary era that Americans fully began to define this "historical fact." As elsewhere, in Middle Tennessee it meant that citizens performed an increasing number of public rituals to support or reject various political perspectives, usually in the form of patriotic society formation, toasting, "town hall" gatherings, stumping, parades, and effigy burnings.[13] In other words, politics on the southwestern frontier encouraged a broad and popular flair as ordinary white Tennesseans influenced activity in ways beyond the vote.

Can such vibrant and complex political institutionalization emerge within a slave society? After all, slavery was a critical part of life in the early Southwest, and its defense became a defining characteristic of Jacksonian democracy. It also eventually united Middle Tennessee with the South rather than the West or the northern Ohio Valley, with which it had much in common.[14] Nevertheless, slavery's political influence was ambiguous in the early national period.

Slaves arrived with the first white settlers in the 1760s and 1770s. Although few in number, they played an important role in the violent early days of settlement, when threat of Indian attack was constant. The tiny white population needed as much help as they could muster, which meant that slaves maintained complex relationships with their masters that allowed access to firearms and independent agricultural production.[15] That, combined with Revolutionary misgivings about the institution, left many locals with a sense of unease. In 1790, for example, Knoxvillian David Grant divulged to his friend John Owen his increasing concern for the plight of the slave population in the Territory South of the River Ohio. Although he refused to consider emancipation, Grant believed that slaves "or their fore fathers were born as free as myself & they are held in bondage by compulsion only & nothing but custom & the laws of an interested people, could by any means reconcile it to any ones concience, & when I consider that they are human creatures indeed with immortal souls capable of everlasting happiness or liable to everlasting misery as well as our selves, & to think that they are considered in the eye of the law & many times by owners no more than dumb beasts. It fills my mind with horror & detestation."[16]

Introduction

This is not to say that slave life on the Tennessee frontier was easy. During the 1780s and 1790s they routinely were given tasks that placed them in close proximity to Indian war parties, which captured them both to minimize white encroachment and to further their own economic agenda.[17] Slave families, moreover, lost loved ones in auctions from the earliest moments of Tennessee's settlement.[18] White Tennesseans also used slaves during this period as a form of cash and collateral, an activity that would continue well into the nineteenth century. At times, they even served as prizes in lotteries.[19]

The free black population found itself in a similarly ambiguous position. Although minuscule in number, free blacks arrived in Middle Tennessee almost simultaneously with white settlers. Initially they were able to mingle with the white community, and they particularly benefited from a loophole in the 1796 Constitution which stipulated that any male freeholder could exercise the vote and participate in militia musters. Since race was not taken into consideration, many black Tennesseans were able to play a role in regional affairs. Jetro Locklier was merely one such individual. Having arrived in Middle Tennessee in the late eighteenth century, by 1809 he had obtained his free papers and during the War of 1812 served under Gen. Andrew Jackson at New Orleans.[20] As late as 1825 white militiamen from Rutherford County asked the state to intervene because of their belief that free blacks had excessive influence over company elections.[21]

As the Rutherford petition indicates, white Middle Tennesseans ultimately came to fear the black population. In response to slave rebellions in other states, rumors of rebellion at home, and the emergence of antislavery movements in Tennessee and elsewhere, Middle Tennesseans by the mid-1820s looked to restrict living conditions for both slaves and free blacks. Proslavery advocates thus used the state legislature to tighten slave codes and limit free black autonomy. By 1834 this subordination was complete: in that year a constitutional convention took away the free black right to vote and participate in militia activity, and implicitly endorsed their removal altogether.[22]

By the 1830s, in other words, the society in which black residents lived was far different than the one they understood only thirty years before.

But if Middle Tennessee's social and cultural parameters were always defined by slavery, its early economic and political development does not render a stereotypically southern picture. Between 1775 and 1820 slavery and entrepreneurial activity were not in opposition to each other. To the contrary, the former tended to serve as a catalyst for the latter. Indeed, the cotton and tobacco trades, for which slavery was critical, provided a boost to those maintaining a more expansive definition of progress because sellers wanted easier passage to commercial markets. When high land values further increased planters' desires for internal improvements (to attain even easier access to markets), entrepreneurs found that plantation agriculture helped place them on an irrevocable path toward dynamic economic expansion.

In short, although slavery exerted enormous influence over early Middle Tennessee's social and geographic identity, it did not initially inhibit notions of progress and did not directly inject itself into the debate over its meaning.[23] It therefore only gradually played a role in the region's evolving political institutions. Looming larger at the turn of the nineteenth century were other questions: How and why did a small but influential group of privileged speculators and surveyors use a limited Jeffersonian Republican structure to accede to popular democratic impulses? How did they interpret the meaning of republicanism vis-à-vis the general population? How did American Indian tribes respond to pressure from white settlement, and how did those responses affect Tennessee's evolving economic and social institutions? How did the realities of early-nineteenth-century life (i.e., widespread militia campaigning, a burgeoning political sphere, high levels of demographic and economic flux, an emerging nationalism, and interest in Indian land) help transform Tennessee's political sphere? How were competing notions of progress expressed publicly? Finally, how and why did Tennesseans divide over the key issue of bank proliferation?

Examination of Middle Tennessee's evolving political-economic structure allows us to explore the issues, values, and visions around which politics coalesced, as well as how and why a more open (white male) democracy emerged in the early American Southwest. In so doing, it shows that the popular democratic political culture that emerged during these years established a foundation for the explosion in voting and contested ideological perspectives that defined life in Jacksonian Tennessee. This vibrant

Introduction

and contested civic sphere allowed a two-party system eventually to formalize around competing notions of progress. When combined with the region's social and economic diversity, this political division helps explain why an upper South state such as Tennessee kept a two-party system long after its collapse in the Cotton Belt South.[24]

***

A brief geographical note is in order. Although Tennessee is traditionally broken into East, Middle, and West, in the late eighteenth century white Americans went no farther west than the Cumberland (middle) region. During the earliest period of settlement, a fifty-mile-wide plateau served as a barrier for people hoping to move into the lush land there. For several generations the easiest point of access was either the Cumberland Gap—the point where Tennessee, Kentucky, and Virginia meet—or a more roundabout way down the Tennessee River to the Mississippi and then up the Cumberland.[25]

The presence of powerful Indian nations further complicated white settlement. Although no nation specifically lived on this land, the Cherokees, Creeks, and Chickasaws all used it for a variety of tribal and economic activities. In looking to assert their cultural and economic autonomy, they proved more than willing to use white settlers and their livestock and slaves to create and enhance capital. When combined with geographic obstacles, their presence would make late-eighteenth-century travel and land speculation difficult for anyone choosing to move into the Cumberland River basin.

Nevertheless, even the earliest white explorers made note of the region's remarkable potential. First and foremost was the large supply of game animals, springs, streams, and timber. Very quickly it also became clear that the grasslands of the Cumberland basin covered highly fertile soil, which made commercial agriculture a lucrative enterprise. The Cumberland River abetted development by serving as a route for regional commodities to reach markets via the Mississippi and Ohio rivers.[26] The possibilities were such that white speculators and settlers made little pretense about their desire to exploit the seemingly endless supply of natural resources. By the early nineteenth century they had succeeded.

Middle Tennessee's economic possibilities contrasted sharply with East Tennessee, which was bounded by the Appalachian Mountains in the east and Cumberland Plateau in the west, and whose soil was generally too poor for significant commercial farming. Geographic isolation further diminished entrepreneurial innovation: the mountain chains on either side made travel into and out of the region difficult, while the Muscle Shoals area of the Tennessee River made it all but impossible to reach the Mississippi. The other rivers in the region drained into the Atlantic rather than the Mississippi watershed, meaning that there were few avenues for riparian-based commerce. Farms in East Tennessee tended to be isolated and the region itself more self-contained. By the early nineteenth century both eastern and western leaders were aware of the Cumberland's unlimited potential relative to the east, and by the antebellum period they often would vote in sectional blocks regarding issues of economic and cultural development.

This intrastate rivalry was far from clear at the outset of Middle Tennessee's settlement, however. Our story begins in the 1770s, when geographic isolation and physical confrontation with Indians limited both economic and political development. Speculators and surveyors were able to take control of this volatile environment, and from this position they began both to tap into the region's economic potential and to establish the structure upon which the political system would grow. Chapter 2 explores the reasons behind the emergence of Jeffersonian Republicanism on the Tennessee frontier. In chapter 3 we will see how rapid demographic change altered elite political control. No longer able to maintain traditional networks, elites decided to engage the population through the militia system. In so doing, they established a solid conduit for popular democratic expansion. Chapter 4 will examine the ways in which the Middle Tennessee economy exploded onto a national and international stage, even as it became increasingly "southern." Chapter 5 will explore two ways Tennesseans came to deal with these changes, as well as an emerging commitment to American nationalism. Combined, these three issues would establish the foundations for a viable party structure based on competing views of progress. Chapter 6 examines the post–War of 1812 economy, the emergence

Introduction

	MIDDLE TENNESSEE COUNTIES
1790	Davidson, Tennessee, Sumner
1800	Davidson, Montgomery, Robertson, Williamson, Wilson, Smith, Sumner
1810	Davidson, Bedford, Dickson, Franklin, Giles, Hickman, Humphreys, Jackson, Lincoln, Maury, Montgomery, Overton, Robertson, Rutherford, Smith, Sumner, Stewart, Warren, White, Williamson, Wilson
1820	Davidson, Bedford, Dickson, Franklin, Grainger, Giles, Hickman, Humphreys, Jackson, Lawrence, Lincoln, Maury, Montgomery, Perry, Wayne, Overton, Robertson, Rutherford, Smith, Sumner, Stewart, Warren, White, Williamson, Wilson

of banks, the Panic of 1819, and the transformation of the more restrained economic perspective into a "Jacksonian" philosophy. The story will conclude with an exploration of slavery and its gradual impact on Tennessee's political culture. If it was not a major factor in the age of Jefferson, it would become a defining characteristic of the state's Jacksonian world view.

Chapter 1

LAND SPECULATION AND THE ORIGINS OF A POLITICAL CULTURE, 1775–1790

Notions of progress and popular democracy in eighteenth-century Tennessee were deeply embedded in the interconnected issues of land speculation and Indian relations. Because Revolutionary-era speculators' agents surveyed an immense volume of acreage, the stations they established led local Indians to believe "what was told some years ago by the Kings people i.e. if our elder brothers here overcome them, they would at last take all our hunting grounds and bring us to nothing."[1] For Cherokees, perhaps the most conspicuous Indians in the area, such intense interest in land, and the stream of migration it caused, threatened traditional channels of status and authority. Like other tribal nations in the Southwest, they increasingly saw that maintaining an independent culture might require a greater level of social and economic freedom from whites.[2] This conviction led many to abandon established patterns of interaction with Euro-American traders and led others to capture slaves, horses, livestock, and, occasionally, white settlers.

The Spanish government further complicated Euro-American efforts at improvement. As early as 1783, Spain received reports of armed Cumberland-to–Mississippi River expeditions and became convinced that western settlers "manifest an inordinate ambition and vast projects for conquering all the countries on the eastern shore of the Mississippi."[3] Hoping to establish a buffer zone between themselves and this American threat, Spanish ministers closed river navigation and promised the Cherokee and Creek Nations "ample supplies of arms and ammunition, to defend their Country from the encroachments of the Americans."[4]

The surveyors who were sent by eastern speculators to establish stations in the Cumberland region thus were confronted with significant issues in the 1770s and 1780s: how to protect land, establish the foundations for political institutionalization, gain access to New Orleans, and deal with Indian nations seemingly determined to go on the offensive. They created short-term modes of stabilization in the form of extralegal local government, but they also understood that meaningful economic and social progress required a strong, lasting political presence. When appeals for help to North Carolina and the Confederation government fell on deaf ears, the aspiring frontier elite looked for alternate sources of centralized authority.[5] Their efforts fell into two categories. First, as noted surveyor and frontier leader James Robertson made clear, there was always the possibility of looking abroad: "In all probability we cannot long remain in our present state, and if the British or any commercial nation who may be in possession of the mouth of the Mississippi would furnish us with trade, and receive our produce there cannot be a doubt but that the people on the west side [of] the Apalachian [sic] mountains will open their eyes to their real interest."[6] After 1788, however, leading frontiersmen found that the American government established by the 1787 Constitution could provide the authority to both secure their political interests and establish a foundation for economic and social progress. Given that several maintained ties to (or were in their own right) influential Federalists, these men easily transferred their support to the new government.

An important side effect of this volatile political situation was that it limited democratic institutionalization on the Tennessee frontier. The small number of surveyors who set up stations to assess contested lands for eastern speculators also took control of local positions of authority (such as justices of the peace, sheriffs, etc.) to legitimize their power. They used ongoing intimidation by Cherokees, Chickamaugas, Creeks, and Spain to dominate local militias, a critical source of political decision making on the frontier.[7] In effect, by 1790 this group of surveyor/speculators had created a less-than-democratic political structure that was acceptable because everyone had the same interests: security against the region's Indians, access to New Orleans, and an unencumbered labor force to purchase land and connect the region with the American and international economy.

Land Speculation and Indian Autonomy

Prior to the 1760s, Tennessee was part of a wider transatlantic market that brought nations such as the Chickasaws in the West and Cherokees in the East together with white traders in such a way that they interacted with European empires without falling under their influence.[8] This "middle ground" gradually created an Indian dependence upon European goods and eventually forced the Indians south of the Ohio River to confront economic and political change. For Cherokees, the nation with perhaps the greatest presence in Tennessee, their traditional notions of economy, manhood, and order were embedded in rites of hunting and thus to the large range of land that made up North Carolina's Western District. They also disdained the individual accumulation of wealth and understood the right to this land in terms of usufruct. That is to say, they owned the product of the land rather than the land itself, with various people having different yet legitimate claims to hunt and fish in defined places.[9]

Cherokees also had a tradition of self-governance that emphasized persuasion rather than coercion and relied upon the notion of reciprocity when treating with other groups. Their treaties reflected a belief that they were the "Principle People" and that all others were strangers. To treat effectively with the "other" required a fictive kinship connection. In this way, other Indian nations became grandfathers, while Europeans became fathers or brothers.[10] Over the course of the eighteenth century, the growing importance of war and access to treaty goods altered and enhanced the power of chiefs, but these older traditions did not disappear.[11]

Cherokees (and other southwestern Indians) particularly redefined autonomy, power, and economy when American explorers and long hunters appeared during and after the Seven Years' War. Personalities such as Daniel Boone eventually captured the popular imagination with their exploits, but Boone's and his colleagues' activities went beyond the mere harvesting of game animals. John Campbell, for example, "a very early pioneer of Southwestern Virginia," managed to explore "the valley of the

Holston as early as 1764, and purchase an ancient survey, where he and his father and his family afterwards settled."[12] Euro-American activity in the 1750s and 1760s foreshadowed much greater levels of land interest. Specifically, the 1768 Treaty of Fort Stanwix gave Americans access to land well beyond the 1763 Royal Proclamation line—down the Ohio River to the Tennessee River. The Treaties of Hard Labor (1768) and Lochaber (1770), meanwhile, gave speculators access to vast ranges extending from the Allegheny Ridge to the Kentucky River.[13]

The coming of the Revolution only made the situation more troubling to Cherokees (to say nothing of other southwestern Indians). One critical aspect of the Revolutionary movement was that whatever remained of royal restraint on westward migration collapsed. Britain had been constrained by the need to accommodate Indians on the frontier, which meant land could not be acquired in a rapid manner. In fighting the Revolution, Americans threw off this restraint.[14] The subsequent lack of authority in the Ohio Valley allowed some men to claim and sell land regardless of title or Indian approval, to sell land with overlapping claims, and to take advantage of French and Indian War veterans by swindling them out of their patents in backcountry Pennsylvania, Ohio, Kentucky, and Tennessee.[15]

The case of Richard Henderson is particularly instructive. Henderson was a native of Virginia who by the 1770s was heavily involved in land speculation both there and in North Carolina. One of his larger endeavors became known as the Transylvania Company. In 1775 the company purchased twenty-seven-thousand square miles in central Kentucky and Tennessee from Cherokee elders.[16] Although no Indians specifically lived on this land, the white settlement that resulted threatened to devastate available game by allowing free ranging livestock to reduce canebreaks and grasses that indigenous animals used for shelter.[17] There also was the Indian assertion that the land sale was fraudulent. Cherokee chief Old Tassel told federal commissioners in 1785 that Henderson was a "liar" and had forged names on the deeds.[18] When combined with the steady stream of white settlers, and the collapse of British authority on the frontier, Henderson's "purchase" provided too serious a threat to Cherokee autonomy and economy.

In the face of American encroachment, Cherokees began to alter political and economic assumptions. Justice, and the restoration of reciprocity, required that they control the land in question. Moreover, there was the issue of "stilling crying blood," or avenging deaths attributed to white encroachment and aggression.[19] All of this required more offensive military tactics. Meanwhile, a greater level of economic independence was required so that (1) tribal leaders could maintain authority in a network of political exchange increasingly hinging upon economic prowess, and (2) they would not be reliant upon Americans for vital goods and services.[20] Hunting remained at the center of their economy, but many also began to supplement their economic endeavors through the theft of slaves, horses, and livestock from white settlements. By the late 1770s and early 1780s, the Chickamaugas, a dissident group comprised of disgruntled Cherokees, runaway slaves, and white traders, and the main band of the Cherokees began to take active measures to stave off further encroachment.[21]

Land Speculation and the Creation of a Frontier Leadership

White settlers understood that procuring land posed a threat to their Indian neighbors. Surveyor/speculator John Sevier made this point clear in a 1785 letter to Alexander Martin, governor of North Carolina. "You cannot be insensible," he wrote,

> that North Carolina in opening her land Office tolerated all the lands on the North side of the Tennessee as far up as the mouth of Holston's river to be entered. Have you been informed that within this limit there is several Indian Towns, and the greater part of all the corn plantations belonging to the Chickamoggy lie on the north side of the Tennessee, together with all the principal part of their hunting ground? If not, I can assure your Excellency it is the case, and this alone I have sufficient reason to believe is the principal reason why the Indians commit hostilities.[22]

As Sevier intimated, North Carolina's Revolutionary-era land statutes reinforced tribal decisions to go on the offensive. Although the "Old North State" officially frowned upon Henderson's Transylvania Purchase, a solid faction of its political elite nevertheless provided golden opportunities for land speculation. Using the original patent of the colonial lords proprietors, the North Carolina General Assembly in 1777 created western boundaries covering the entire area of modern Tennessee.[23] At that time only approximately two thousand white immigrants were settled along a few eastern rivers.[24] In 1782, the assembly, in response to British threats, created a military district surrounding the Cumberland River and offered residents a minimum of 640 acres for service in the Continental army.[25] The act also provided preemption rights for people who had settled in the area prior to 1780 and opened a land office, called Fort Nashborough, in the newly created Davidson County.

The 1782 military district act created a situation that particularly benefited North Carolina speculators. Even if he could (and wanted to) hold on to war certificates, the average veteran could only secure a warrant after a potential tract had had its boundaries located and marked. The tedious process worked as follows. After a veteran received a warrant in North Carolina, he sent it to Col. Martin Armstrong, the primary surveyor in Nashborough. Armstrong would then send out surveyors to have it marked using metes, bounds, and natural features. Once denoted, he would return the warrant to the secretary of state of North Carolina, who would record it and issue a grant.[26]

At this point, however, grantees did not own any land. Before the grant was official, the individual had to register it in the appropriate county office in Tennessee. Without the means of getting to the military district, or paying for the surveys, most veterans found that their certificates were meaningless. Faced with this reality, and with a need for real money in the postwar economic recession, many veterans sold their claims to speculators for bargain prices. Those who kept them often were swindled. By 1790, 2.8 million acres had gone to people holding 3,723 military warrants, of which 60 percent had been acquired by land speculators.[27]

But they were not finished. In 1783 the North Carolina General Assembly established a new office at Hillsborough for the sale of all land in Tennessee save the military district and an eastern Cherokee reservation. They justified this action by pointing out that North Carolina needed to repay war debts and that Cherokees had forfeited their claims by allying with the British (a position in line with the "conquest" policy promulgated by the Confederation Congress).[28] Thenceforth, speculators seemed to operate with the understanding that the land they surveyed was owned by North Carolina, not Indian nations.

The procedure for establishing a claim was similar to that for the military district, with the obvious exception that the claimant had to come up with the purchase price. In 1783 it stood at ten pounds per hundred acres. But there was a catch: Largely useless Continental bills and specie certificates counted as receivable money. They had so depreciated by 1783 that land was really going for far less than the ten-pound minimum—at approximately five Continentals per hundred acres.[29] Leading speculators took advantage of the loophole to pad the land already obtained from war veterans. All told, speculators were able to obtain another four million acres through purchase.[30] And this does not even begin to describe the bribery that took place between men of relative means. North Carolinian Thomas Polk, for example, noted that he had to pay as much as 2,250 pounds merely for the *opportunity* to purchase sixty thousand acres in the military district, "because no certain entries can be made otherwise."[31]

However they received their certificates, once in possession, speculators would employ agents to go to the Cumberland District and carry out the necessary surveys. Men such as James Robertson, John Donelson, Isaac Bledsoe, and Kasper Mansker set up stations to defend the small white community, assess contested lands, gather claims of their own, and use padded surveys to increase their acreage.[32] This group would use their eastern connections, their access to and control over tens of thousands of acres, and their position at the head of local militia companies to become the frontier elite in the 1770s and 1780s.

Isaac Bledsoe provides a great example. Born in Culpeper County, Virginia, Bledsoe initially settled in East Tennessee. While hunting and exploring the Cumberland River in 1772, he "discovered" what became known as Bledsoe's Lick and Bledsoe's Creek. In 1779, while helping to survey the Virginia–North Carolina state line, he selected a site for a fort near the lick. His knowledge of western lands and his connection to North Carolina speculators soon made him a member of the Court of Triers of the Cumberland Association, and he thereafter became a justice of the peace in the first Davidson County Quarterly Court. He also served as first major of the county militia and as a guard for the surveyors of the North Carolina Military Reservation. In 1786 Sumner County split off from Davidson County, and Bledsoe served in that county's first quarterly court. He also was first major of the county militia and became a lieutenant colonel in April 1788.³³ Recent archeological evidence at Bledsoe's Station further confirms his social status, as remains of fine china and accouterments have been found there that would have been available only to people of relative wealth.³⁴

As Bledsoe's experience makes clear, the hopeful frontier elite enhanced their power through local militia offices. Although eastern militias mostly were becoming dining and toasting devices used to organize local political movements within a national framework, on the frontier they served as both a serious military option and an outlet for the isolated community.³⁵ In addition to overseeing government functions such as census enumeration, they provided the most meaningful exchanges and contested elections in which ordinary men were involved prior to statehood in 1796.³⁶

The combination of geographic isolation and threat of Indian attack made organized military mobilization and extended command difficult at best. As such, most militias created structures that both recognized traditional lines of authority and ensured that capability and resolve under fire would make rank irrelevant to militia (and thus community) leadership.³⁷ Invariably, the best Indian fighters seemed to be the surveyors who opened settlement stations. Bledsoe was a great example of this, as was Kasper Mansker. Mansker was a surveyor of North Carolina's military reservation in whose station boarded (at various times) Isaac Bledsoe, Andrew Jackson, and John Overton. French botanist André Michaux also seemed to have paid the station a visit. In 1787 Mansker parlayed his prominence into the position of major in the Sumner County Militia and was able further to extend his reach through service on the first Sumner County grand jury.³⁸

Bledsoe's and Mansker's experiences show that controlling stations and militia offices gave surveyors an opportunity to establish themselves as the military and political leaders of the Tennessee frontier. Given their isolation vis-à-vis the state and Confederation governments, this leadership was able to establish local governing institutions of varying effectiveness.³⁹ In 1772, for example, a small group of settlers in East Tennessee created the Watauga Association. Using Virginia law as its foundation, the association created a court of five elected magistrates to conduct executive, legislative, diplomatic, militia, and judicial business.⁴⁰ In 1780, station communities in the Cumberland District authorized the Cumberland Compact. They elected representatives to form a twelve-man "Tribunal of Notables" which "dispensed justice, received and dispersed funds, settled claims, and regulated the land office."[41]

Perhaps the most interesting local endeavor came in the form of the State of Franklin. Having grown concerned that both the North Carolina General Assembly and the Confederation Congress had abandoned them to the Cherokees, opportunistic Watauga settlers used a proposed land cession from North Carolina to the United States as a pretext to create Franklin. Although wary of the fallout, the newly elected governor, John Sevier, justified the logic behind the secession when he wrote to Richard Caswell that "a real necessity, to prevent anarchy, promote our happiness, and to provide against the common Enemy—that always infest this part of the World, induced and compelled the people here to act as they have done innocently thinking at the same time, your acts tolerated them to the separation."[42] In other words, Franklin was put in motion to secure a foundation for progress.

Prominent North Carolina assemblymen feared that an independent land-granting power in the territory would limit their claims and potentially massive future profits.[43] Thus they rescinded the 1784 cession and simultaneously struck out at the reputations of leading Franklinites by equating their movement with anarchism and unadulterated greed. The situation worsened when North Carolina loyalists raised militias and established political institutions of their own. This in effect created the confusing situation of having two governments that taxed, held court, issued land grants, and demanded the loyalty of the scattered white settlements. The division became heated, as one Anthony Bledsoe made clear: "Politics in this part of the country run high. You hear in almost every collection of people frequent declarations, whorah for North Carolina! And others in the manner for the State of Franklin. I have seen it in much warmth."[44]

In 1788 the situation finally exploded. In February Sevier became enraged when North Carolina sheriff Jonathan Pugh executed a judgment against him by seizing some of his slaves. The governor quickly called out the Franklin militia, which he personally led to retrieve his unlawfully confiscated property. After a two-day siege he was beaten, forced to retreat, made into a fugitive from North Carolina justice, and faced with the rapid loss of nearly all pro-Franklin sentiment in the Eastern District.[45] The experiment had failed and ceased to operate after 1788.[46]

Indians, Spain, and the Quest for Centralized Power

If they provided local governance, settlers primarily used these extralegal institutions "to get out to the land."[47] This relentless push had significant repercussions, as Arthur Campbell, a resident of Virginia with extensive connections in Tennessee, made clear. In 1784 he noted, "Numerous parties of men, were excited last Fall, and Winter, to range through the heart of Indian country, [and] to locate lands, which drove out parties of the Indians from their hunting grounds, and naturally enough, caused a general alarm."[48] This general alarm soon resulted in open warfare. After all, were not the emerging white settlements threats to the Creeks,' Cherokees,' and Chickamaugas' political, economic, and cultural identities? If so, what better response than to attack them?[49] Between 1783 and 1789 these three groups conducted enough raids throughout North Carolina's Military District that they destabilized the region for white settlers.

Their activities particularly helped them acquire valuable capital. At times they even eschewed military necessity in order to secure livestock and tools. In 1785, for example, white settlers in East Tennessee routed Cherokee warriors because the latter were too taken by the idea of stealing horses.[50] Only three years later, an army of two thousand Cherokees and one thousand Creeks stopped an assault upon Gillespie's Station in East Tennessee after seizing more plunder than they knew what to do with.[51] Horse theft was especially profitable. By 1789 so many raids on Cumberland horses had taken place that residents complained to the new George Washington administration that losses were "considerable."[52]

Amid this volatile situation emerged a threat from Spanish Louisiana. Although ostensibly an ally in the Revolution, Spain had been a problem since 1783. In the treaty ending the war, both countries agreed that the Mississippi would remain open to Americans, but the reality was that Spain controlled New Orleans, the west bank, and thus the length of the river. This control presented a significant problem for the infant Republic—it could, many feared, limit westward migration and economic growth. North Carolinian Richard Spaight noted that no issue in front of Congress bore "so serious and alarming an aspect as the dispute between Spain and the United States respecting the navigation of the Mississippi, and their taking possession of part of the western frontiers of the southern States."[53] The

Land Speculation and the Origins of a Political Culture, 1775–1790

situation only became worse when Spain made overtures to closing the Mississippi entirely and to creating alliances with southwestern Indians as a means of putting a buffer zone between themselves and the new American Republic.

Ultimately, the Spanish threat of closing the Mississippi, in combination with the desire to open Iberian ports to American shipping, led the Confederation government to send Revolutionary leader John Jay to Spain to negotiate a compromise. In the meantime, frontier leaders understood that they needed to control Indian opposition and develop the region for white settlement. Thus they moved beyond local political devices and appealed to North Carolina and the Confederation government for assistance.[54] They were quickly disappointed. For North Carolina, the issue was simple. Although it provided more than generous land laws and allowed for the seating of western representatives, the limited availability of funds and manpower meant that the assembly could not offer anything more than token military and economic aid. Perhaps Arthur Campbell's lamentation made this point most clear. From his station in southwestern Virginia, he wrote that it was "peculiarly mortifying we are without Magazines for Arms and Ammunition, and hardly the appearance of government, especially in the Counties lately ceded by No. Carolina."[55]

Pending word from Jay, the Confederation government seemed equally unable to help, despite repeated memorials "to explain to Congress our political circumstances and the views and interest of the people settled in this part of the Western Country."[56] The 1785 Treaty of Hopewell provided the quintessential example. It not only bypassed state and local authority by dealing directly with the Cherokees and Chickamaugas but also left white settlers on the "wrong" side of new boundaries for the Watauga District and provided that the Cherokees could punish trespassers as they saw fit.[57] Such an affront to their legitimacy led frontiersmen and speculators alike to believe that the government represented "an inhuman lack of concern for the plight of white settlers on the frontier."[58]

This "lack of concern" seemed only to get worse in 1786, when word came from Spain that Jay had proposed that the United States agree to a twenty-five- to thirty-year closure of the Mississippi. To those with frontier interests this was absolute betrayal. Losing the river trade would not only minimize economic opportunities for the few settlers already on the

Cumberland frontier but also severely limit immigration and thus future growth.[59] As surveyor and future territorial secretary Daniel Smith made clear, Mississippi navigation simply was "as the light of the sun, a birth-right that cannot be alienated." Although Congress rejected Jay's proposal and his negotiations with Spain collapsed, his efforts left Tennesseans with a feeling of distrust toward the Confederation government.[60]

The response from frontier leaders and their eastern allies to North Carolina's and the Confederation's limited assistance was twofold. First, they negated the limiting nature of the Treaty of Hopewell by opening "the land office once more [to] Grant all the Western Country and leave Congress no further hopes of obtaining it from us to whom it justly belongs."[61] Second, following the example of James Wilkinson in Kentucky, some aspiring elites, such as Superintendent of Indian Affairs James White, offered their services to the Spanish government and "assured [them] that the western country would surely secede from the United States and unite with Spain and England in order to obtain access to the entire length of the Mississippi River."[62] A young Andrew Jackson later remarked that allying with the Spanish also seemed like "the only immediate way to obtain a peace with the savage."[63]

But there were more to these overtures. Reopening the land office, or allying with His Catholic Majesty, were not the primary issues. Centralized power was. A stronger presence was necessary to facilitate migration, protect land investment, and see to it that the Indian threat was kept in check—all of the ingredients necessary for the region to stabilize and improve economic and social conditions. A Spanish alliance, in short, offered a real avenue to stability and the foundation for progressive improvement.

In 1788 it became clear that the new Constitution did as well. That a stronger U.S. government could provide the proper authority led most surveyors and speculators to support ratification.[64] The problem was to convince the rest of North Carolina that the new government would provide palpable short and long-term benefits—no small task given that anti-Federalist forces had already mobilized so effectively as to undermine ratification by North Carolina.

In 1788 their advantage proved too strong for Federalist partisans, but after New York and Virginia accepted the new government, most North Carolinians reconsidered lest they become isolated.[65] At approximately the same time, the North Carolina General Assembly decided to cede its western territory to the new government. Simply put, assemblymen had grown tired of dealing with the constant struggle between Cherokees, Chickamaugas, and white settlers, and of having to confront Franklinites and Spanish intrigue. Three days after approving the Constitution, the assembly thus gave to the United States the entire Western District. It did present stipulations: The federal government had to guarantee all old land titles, protect the institution of slavery, and ensure that North Carolina could continue to grant land to war veterans. Otherwise, settlement had to follow the procedure established by the Northwest Ordinance of 1787. In other words, the region would remain under federal authority until it reached a population of sixty-six thousand, at which point it could vote to become one or more states. Thus in 1790 the federal government created the Territory of the United States South of the River Ohio.[66]

Political Power on the Tennessee Frontier

In 1893 historian Frederick Jackson Turner theorized that frontier settlement represented a unique and inherently democratic process of self-governance. His assessment was extremely ethnocentric and has largely been modified over the last one hundred years, but it continues to resonate for the simple reason that political development did in fact appear to be different on the frontier.[67] Obviously this development was limited to white males, but for the moment let us put aside the gender and racial limitations of Turner's formulation. Was the process a clean and positive parade of American democratic progress even for white men?

Tennesseans would have offered a mixed response to this question. No one doubted that the Revolution brought with it an accession to abstract notions of popular sovereignty, and that the frontier exacerbated significant, locally oriented democratic outbursts. In effect, life on the frontier was such that hereditary status meant little—particularly when confronted with the brutal reality of daily life. Common people conferred (conditional) power upon male leaders known for their physical courage and military prowess, as well as for their ability to create and enhance capital.[68]

Moreover, in the early 1790s East Tennessee would become a hotbed of localized democratic activity. In 1791 Thomas Paine's *Rights of Man* found a prominent position on the front page of the new *Knoxville Gazette*, and between then and 1796 citizens engaged in an increasingly lively print culture. They also sent numerous petitions to Congress and rebuked the territorial government when they believed it necessary. As we shall see, they particularly expected the Washington administration to alleviate their problems with the Cherokees, Creeks, and Chickamaugas. Easterners also vociferously opposed Governor William Blount's attempt to siphon county fees and fines into the territorial treasury. At other times county courts would ignore Blount's directives, and on occasion they even rebuked him for activities unbecoming a servant of the people.[69] Greater population density (in 1790 white settlements totaled 28,649 residents in the East and 7,049 in the Cumberland) combined with this basic institutionalization to allow for the development of a nascent public sphere in East Tennessee.

There were limitations to this emerging political culture, however. Easterners could do little about the fact that all major offices in the new territorial government were appointed by a governor and thus not subject to electoral oversight. This allowed Governor Blount to consolidate power in a handful of well-placed surveyor/speculators. One of a trio of powerful North Carolina brothers, Blount had served in the North Carolina legislature, as a delegate to the Confederation Congress, and had acted as a delegate to the Federal Convention in 1787. His political experience and connections, combined with his vast holdings in Tennessee, virtually ensured that President George Washington would appoint him to the post of territorial governor.[70] Blount recognized the position's potential. "The appointment is truly important to me," he wrote John Steele, "more so in my opinion than any other in the Gift of the President could have been, the Salary is handsome, and my Western lands had become so great an object to me that I should go to the Western Country to secure them and perhaps my presence might have enhanced their value."[71] Moreover, given his longstanding position that "it is a principle with me never to . . . stand between a friend and a benefit," Blount's formal appointment meant that major land speculators and their operatives would come to represent the overwhelming majority of the new territorial government.[72]

For example, Stockley Donelson, an eastern resident who claimed hundreds of thousands of acres in the Cumberland region, became a legislative councilor. Another easterner, Daniel Smith—who claimed several thousand acres—became territorial secretary. Well-known surveyors and early Tennessee leaders James Robertson and John Sevier were appointed militia generals, and Sevier also served as a legislative counselor. On and on it went. James Winchester and James Ford, both of whom held title to thousands of acres, became militia colonels, and Winchester was appointed legislative counselor. David Campbell, whose family included prolific speculators throughout the Southwest, became a territorial judge.[73]

Blount's first act as governor cemented a network of support that further constrained democratic outbursts. Upon his arrival in the Southwest Territory, the new governor visited all of the major settlements, familiarizing himself with local concerns and legitimizing the power of local authorities. He also accepted nominations by militia companies for the positions he was soon to appoint. His efforts in this routine activity created a group of loyal lower-level lieutenants who remained part of his "machine" throughout the territorial period. When Governor Blount called a legislature in 1794, for example, twelve of the thirteen members were part of his larger network.[74] Loyalty to Blount in turn helped several aspiring young lawyers—including John McNairy, Archibald Roane, Andrew Jackson, and John Overton—establish themselves as the next generation of leadership in Tennessee.

Surveyors and speculators, in short, were the arbiters of political power prior to 1796. Since there were few broadly held avenues to challenge political leadership, and since local leaders were incorporated into Blount's network, the widely dispersed population of ordinary white settlers did not have a strong impact on territorial policy.[75]

Middle Tennessee, the subject of this study, better encapsulates the complexity of democratic development on the Tennessee frontier. As we have seen, surveyor/speculators controlled the region's political positions from the beginning: In the 1780s seven of eight representatives to the North Carolina legislature maintained sizable land claims. Even local governing institutions were less democratic than they appeared. In every case western compacts made land protection and survey the highest priority. They also were intended only to be interim measures until a more centralized authority could step in. The Clarksville Compact of 1785, for example, made clear that local leaders intended to attach to the Confederation Congress at the earliest convenient moment.[76] As the first resolution put it,

"Whereas the Hon'ble the Congress of the united States have not as yet adopted any mode or plan for the Regulation & Government of this our infant Settlement, it is become necessary to form certain Regulations for the better security of our Lives and Property . . . which may not be incompatible with the Constitution of the united States or the Resolutions of Congress."[77]

The issue here was not local control but the maintenance of constitutionally feasible laws until Clarksville could acquire greater oversight. On this the Cumberland Compact of 1780 was in full agreement, noting that a local court was necessary for the adjudication of damage and debt "until we can be relieved by government from the many evils and inconveniences arising therefrom." The signers of the compact also made clear that *"we find ourselves* constrained from necessity to adopt this *temporary* method" (emphasis added).[78]

Surveyor/speculator control would continue into the 1790s. The nineteen justices of the peace appointed in Davidson County between 1790 and 1795, for example, held an average of 7,170 acres, with four holding more than 20,000 acres each.[79] Democracy in Middle Tennessee was further hampered by a miniscule population and a lack of a print culture such as the one growing in Knoxville.

In short, violence, a small population, and a powerful group of men at the top restrained popular democratic reform throughout the Territory South of the River Ohio, particularly in the Cumberland District. While one may grant that public perception played a role in molding the course of government, the accession by leading men to revolutionary notions of popular sovereignty was less than it appeared. Whatever the elite had in common with settlers stemmed from the fact that the two groups had similar goals—to reduce Indian assaults, assure land titles, protect land value, enhance economic growth, and foster immigration.

Governor Blount's administration came to power believing that the federal government would create an atmosphere conducive to speculation, immigration, and commerce. Thus they were initially friendly toward the new Washington administration. But this good working relationship was undermined by white Tennesseans' unceasing quest for land, which put Indian nations on the defensive and made for a bloody decade in the 1790s.[80] Frontier war came at a moment when the new Republic's political institutions generally were in a state of flux—newspapers were proliferating, public political rituals were becoming more vociferous and meaningful, and, perhaps most important, two distinct political "parties" were emerging in the form of Federalists and Jeffersonian Republicans. Both of these coalitions were interested in western development, and both looked to obtain the approval of the small white population on the trans-Appalachian frontier. And since by 1793 the Federalist philosophy held sway over many members of the Washington administration as well as over Congress, Federalists had first crack at establishing political loyalty. Their reticence in the face of unceasing land speculation complicated territorial commitments to centralized authority, hampered progressive economic development and helped define political life in Tennessee well into the nineteenth century.

Chapter 2

Warfare and the Creation of a Jeffersonian Identity, 1790–1796

Washington administration agent I. H. Williamson was optimistic in the summer of 1789. Relieved that the American government had stabilized under the new Constitution, Williamson informed James Robertson that Cumberland District problems were about to dissipate. The new Indian commissioner, Gen. Benjamin Lincoln, he wrote, "will impress the Southern Indians with an idea that trifling is at an end, and that they must seriously treat and faithfully abide by what they promise. It is possible that the troops will be left as a barrier on the frontier to see that neither parties [sic] break the treaty. This I believe is the beginning of general Peace and security against the Indians."[1] He added, "If you have seen any News Papers you may have observed that Congress Have established a Post on the Ohio, not with much hope as you must be assured, of collecting many Duties on Goods brought up the Mississippi, but to part fair and let Spain see that the new Government is resolved to maintain its Claim to the Navigation of that River."[2]

The new government's resolution to maintain its western claims was a powerful assertion of centralized authority. And as we have seen, many in the new Territory South of the River Ohio believed that that was exactly what was needed. As such, settlers generally offered little opposition to the transfer of authority to the new federal government. They may have grumbled about the ineffectual nature of the Confederation, but most cautiously envisioned a new, positive relationship with the Washington administration. As President Washington himself recorded in a memorandum, Tennesseans "look to the Genl government [for support] & hope not to look in vain."[3]

The period just after the ratification of the Constitution provided a rare opportunity to establish meaningful relations between the new government, white settlers, and southwestern Indians. In 1789, Cherokees called for a peace based on the end of white encroachment and murder. Chickamaugas, meanwhile, flirted with the notion of peace as they began to achieve a level of economic prosperity. And then there was the Washington administration. Having asserted the idea of greater authority, it looked to the frontier for organized settlement and increased revenue. Governor William Blount's administration thus came to power on a wave of good tidings that portended the possibility for stability and security—the building blocks for meaningful economic and social progress.

Land speculation closed this window of opportunity. By 1790 the area that would become Tennessee was a haven for land jobbing. A slippery term because everyone was involved to some degree, major speculators were distinguishable by their claims to tens of thousands, and in some cases, millions, of acres. Friendly relations between the Washington administration and the territory deteriorated early in the 1790s, when the former realized that aggressive speculation was costing the government millions of dollars in revenue. They became more tenuous when the federal government decided not to intervene in an emerging frontier war. Land speculation was causing a frightful escalation in settler-Indian tensions by pushing white Americans onto contested land in the Cumberland basin. When Creeks, Cherokees, and Chickamaugas went on the offensive to protect their interests, and when the Spanish facilitated their posturing, Tennessee settlers of all stripes demanded federal protection.

After careful consideration, the Washington administration decided not to help. They came to feel that southwestern conflicts grew out of a land-grab impulse that left Cherokees and Chickamaugas more in need of protection than white settlers. Seeing that better opportunities for a federal presence lay in the land rich-Northwest, they refused to impose any meaningful central control over the region. Their decision had tremendous political and social ramifications in Tennessee. Socially, it meant that federal officers lacked the means either to restrain settler attacks on Cherokee, Chickamauga, and Creek settlements or to stop excessive land speculation.[4] Politically, it alienated frontier leaders and settlers looking for stability and government-sanctioned improvement. It left many wary of federal authority and the region without the means to establish an effective party structure. Unlike other trans-Appalachian regions, where a Federalist interest—however small—ensured party competition, the end result was a limited "Jeffersonian" political culture that would not falter until well into the nineteenth century.[5]

The seeds of confrontation were planted in 1789, when, despite specific orders from the administration to minimize confrontation with Creeks and Cherokees, southwestern speculators pressed Georgia to sell its western (or "Yazoo") lands. William Blount (as well as John Sevier) became part of the Tennessee Yazoo Company, which looked to purchase the land surrounding the Muscle Shoals area in the great bend of the Tennessee River.[6] Unsuccessful in this endeavor, the new governor in 1790 generously construed directions from Secretary of War Henry Knox that he reaffirm or revise the eastern Cherokee boundaries that had been in relative limbo since the 1785 Treaty of Hopewell. His suggested boundaries were so generous that the Washington administration grew concerned: As Knox noted to the president, Blount's interpretation of Hopewell's boundaries was "materially different from the one suggested in his instructions." He feared that it, "combined with the attempts of the Georgia [Yazoo] companies, would have pernicious effects" on settler-Indian relations. Knox believed that the "Cherokees would complain, and with justice, that all assurances given by the new government . . . were deceptions, and calculated to ensnare them."[7]

A new treaty would help clarify these boundaries and perhaps limit land speculation, so Washington called for a new round of negotiations. Cherokees and Chickamaugas agreed. They looked to undo what they felt were unfair claims dating to the 1770s and certainly did not look to lose more land. Cherokees subsequently also asserted their autonomy by recasting whites in the child role in their fictive kinship diplomacy and by linking their position as the white's fathers to their title as original possessors of the land.[8]

Blount expressed his willingness to both oblige Cherokees and serve as a representative of federal power, albeit in such a way as to maximize the potential for land jobbing.[9] In the resulting Treaty of Holston, Cherokees ceded a vast swath of land east of the Clinch River and "north of a line running eastward from near the mouth of the Clinch along the divide between the Little River and the Little Tennessee River to North Carolina."[10] Why they signed the treaty is unclear, but tribal leaders nevertheless feared that Blount had managed to procure too much land.[11] They also were concerned that no federal authority was attempting to remove white trespassers. Thus they sent ambassadors to Philadelphia to remonstrate against the Treaty of Holston. Washington was sympathetic but endorsed the treaty to maintain cordial ties to Blount's government. Even as the Senate ratified the treaty, however, the administration quietly provided a deputy agent and fifteen hundred dollars in gifts to placate Cherokee leaders.[12]

It soon became clear that the administration would not stop the settlers, surveyors, and speculators who, in expectation of eventual cession to the federal government, continued their encroachment. As Cherokee leader Bloody Fellow lamented to Blount, "The talks we had [with the administration] was that we should not war with one another, and that [settlers] should not encroach on our land. But in place of that they are daily encroaching and building on our land; this is not what [we] had agreed upon."[13] More candidly, he told his own people that Blount, President Washington, and Congress all were "liars."[14]

Moving onto contested land increased an already palpable regional tension. Despite the peace overtures of the late 1780s, Cherokees and Chickamaugas were ready aggressively to pursue their economic and political autonomy. After the failure of the Treaty of Holston, they went into action. On the one hand, attacking the frontier destabilized white settlement and made it more difficult for them to continue land speculation. On the other hand, property theft offered a way to undermine white stability and enhance capital.[15] Americans would have to pay to reacquire stolen livestock, slaves, and kidnapped whites. Spain would transfer these "commodities" into more welcomed forms of capital, trading contraband for guns, ammunition, and vital goods. Certainly local observers saw the impact of this dual approach. As James White noted to James Monroe, not only were "creeks & cherokees" spilling "american blood with impunity," they also had become "too long accustomed to the allurements of plunder, to be restrained by treaty."[16]

By the fall of 1791 younger Cherokees and their Chickamauga counterparts thus rejected the advice of tribal elders and began to apply more forceful means of protecting what remained of their territory. The dual objective behind their attacks became clear in an early raid on Middle Tennessee. In 1792 an army of Cherokees moved into the region and split into two groups: one that successfully attacked Ziegler's Station and one that was supposed to go to Nashville to steal horses. The Ziegler's Station attack killed four and wounded four others, but equally important, thirteen white settlers were made prisoners. Blount noted to Secretary Knox that of these thirteen, nine were subsequently "regained by purchase." Given that three of the remaining four were African American, it seems reasonable to think that Cherokees were holding out for a better price.[17]

Ziegler's Station shows that slaves and horses were particular targets. As early as 1774 Cherokees and Creeks were on the record as having stolen slaves in Tennessee. While often used for labor, slaves also generated the possibility for significant revenue because they were a major commodity and form of capital on the frontier.[18] Tennesseans also were greatly concerned about horses—so much so that in Article 10 of the 1791 Treaty of Holston they made clear that "if any Cherokee Indian, or Indians, or person residing among them, or who shall take refuge in their nation shall steal a horse from, or commit robbery or murder or other capital crime on any citizen of the United States—the Cherokee Nation shall be bound to deliver him or them up to be punished according to the laws of the United States."[19] That same year Cumberland residents noted that over fifty horses had been stolen and requested that the Washington administration do something about it.[20] In 1792 James White complained that Creeks "took from me the remains of a large stock of horses, into which I had turned much of my property. The rest they had plundered before."[21] It became so lucrative that in 1794 Blount decried the horse trade at "Swannano, North Carolina, Ocunnee Mountain, South Carolina, and Tugelo Georgia" and demanded that the government "divide a company of Fœderal Troops into three parts & station [them] at well chosen spots upon the Indian boundary near each of those places."[22]

Problems with the Creeks and Spanish made the situation more precarious for white settlers. Indeed, the Yazoo intrigue of 1789 and the Treaty of Holston's expansive boundaries put Creek lands within the easy grasp of a growing number of Americans. Creeks had already attacked settlements in Georgia because of white encroachment. It seems reasonable to assume that the survey expeditions resulting from these developments were enough to make them fear Tennesseans might follow a similar path.[23] Creek leaders made their position clear to British agents: "The Americans have distressed us for some time past to a great degree, we are at length determined to extricate ourselves and maintain our lands, or die in the attempt."[24] They soon proved more than willing to attack the Cumberland settlements from which many survey expeditions originated.

Creek offensives reflected the nature of their alliance with Spain. The Spanish, as Henry Knox warned President Washington in 1789, had long objected to the onslaught of American immigration. "The jealousy [Spain] entertains of the extension of the United States," he wrote, "would lead them into considerable expense to build up, if possible, an impassable barrier."[25] By 1793, as Indian agent John Speed wrote to Kentucky Governor Isaac Shelby, they had become even more "jealous of Americans."[26] Seeking Indian support, the Spanish government reminded southern Indians (most specifically the Creeks but also Cherokees and Chickamaugas) that they were "not like Americans—first take your land, then treat with you, and give you little or nothing for them."[27]

In all, by February 1792 settlers in the Cumberland District had made it clear that "they have much to dread from the Indians as the Spring Season approaches; the recent Murders and Ravages committed by them too evidently proves their intentions on this quarter."[28] Six months later they were proven correct. In August, Henry Knox wrote to Creek leader Alexander McGillivray that it had been firmly "ascertained, that parties of Creeks go to the Tennessee, under pretence of hunting, but in reality, to murder and rob."[29] That same month James White made it clear that the Middle District had become "the most easy prey & the most out of protection."[30] In September, Governor Blount relayed to James Robertson and Secretary Knox that the Creeks had attacked settlements along the Cumberland frontier.[31] He also feared a Cherokee attack on Middle Tennessee and noted that "the settlements of the district are very extensive, and the guards for the protection thereof in no ways equal to the weight of an unexpected attack."³²

Even so, the territorial government initially was not overly concerned. The only thing that was needed to maintain stability, after all, was a "vigorous national war . . . [to] bring the Indians to act as they ought."³³ Such an action, Blount told his political allies, would surely occur. "Congress, who alone have the right to declare war," he wrote James Robertson, "or in other words to order offensive operations are to meet on the 5th Instant, November and no doubt is to be entertained, but they will do what the dignity of the government requires and redress the sufferings of their frontier citizens."³⁴

A few months later, after escalating assaults led settlers to demand military retaliation, Blount made clear to Robertson that he should not "despair of the protection of Government. Congress ended their session the 4th, Instant and no doubt have left power in the hands of the President to manage Indian affairs as he shall judge proper and in that case there is the greatest certainty that he will cause perfect justice to be done."³⁵ Perhaps the governor most explicitly expressed his commitment to the Washington administration in 1793. In that year French diplomat Edmond Genet conspired to remove the West from American jurisdiction. Blount rejected the idea and argued that "all attempting to injure our happy Government, the best yet discovered, serve to strengthen and to call more fully into view its worth."³⁶ This even as Thomas Jefferson privately endorsed Genet's efforts and provided letters of introduction for André Michaux in his secret trip to garner support in Kentucky.³⁷

Yet by autumn of 1793 the continued federal hesitancy to offer any substantive monetary or military assistance put Blount in the unenviable position of having to relay to the Cumberland District that because "the most rigid economy is enjoined on me by the federal government, I cannot enlarge my [militia] order . . . more than to allow in the whole a company of mounted Infantry on duty at any one time."³⁸ Initially, Blount placed blame on an unsympathetic Congress, commenting to James Robertson that "it is to be lamented that Congress with which the power of peace & war rests have not hitherto understood it as well as everybody else seems to have done, and it is equally to be lamented that foolish uninformed people have done the cause of the suffering frontier people so much injury in the eyes of the people of the Atlantic states. It is to be hoped that the next Congress will be more enlightened."[39]

He soon became aware, however, that the problem was worse than he had thought: The entire Federalist coalition, not just its congressional wing, was explicitly retreating from any appearance of support for the territory. The reason, it seemed, was that high levels of speculation limited their ability to use the land for federal sales. Although the Territory South of the River Ohio belonged to the federal government, North Carolina's 1789 cession guaranteed old land claims and protected their right to continue to issue military warrants. This in effect took away from the government almost all of the prime land in the region. What was left tended to go both to speculators who had padded legal claims in expectation of gaining access to unavailable land and to squatters who invoked their preemption rights to much of the remainder. Secretary of State Jefferson's 1791 report brings the land situation clearly into focus: In that year he showed that the government had only three hundred thousand acres available to it.[40]

Anecdotal reports from the territory only made Federalists more cynical. As agent James Seagrove pointed out, "I find the Creeks have been killing some white people on their Western frontiers. In my talks with the Indians, I am led to believe that the people killed, belong to a settlement South of the Cumberland river, and on lands that never have been sold, or ceded by the Indians; that those people have repeatedly been ordered off by the Indians, but will not go."[41]

Other evidence indicates that Seagrove's anecdotes were accurate. By early 1793 land speculation had become so brisk that reports from the Cumberland District often blurred the distinction between surveying and Indian attack. Resident John Nichols provides a key example. While requesting that North Carolina land broker William Lytle purchase for him one hundred acres in the Cumberland District, he delivered the news that "your old friend Col Isaac Bledsoe was unfortunately killed and scalped about the middle of last month."[42]

Amid this bloody situation, large-scale land grabs continued unabated. William Lytle was typical of lesser-known speculators. A Revolutionary War captain from Orange County, North Carolina, Lytle had managed by 1796 to obtain 8,010 acres of prime Davidson County real estate. By 1810 he personally held title to approximately 22,000 acres in Middle Tennessee.⁴³ In 1794, moreover, land office manager Martin Armstrong and legislative counselor Stockley Donelson wrote to North Carolina secretary of state James Glasgow of an opportunity that eventually would embroil all of them in scandal. "We are ever Sensible of your Friendship," they wrote to him in Raleigh, "and it would be ingratitude at This Period to Secret The lucrative views That now presents to us more capital in the Western Territory Than any yet discovered. Our communications are good. We wish you to be connected in the benefits That may after wards acrue [sic] and without ceremony We are desirous to purchase all the Military and State Land warrants That may be had on reasonable terms to cover a tract of Sixty Thousand Acres."⁴⁴

Governor William Blount's ambitions were similarly large. Looking to complement his already substantive holdings with good Cumberland land, he admitted to James Robertson that he would not purchase "unless I would possess myself of a large body laying together near the settlements say from sixty thousand to hundred thousand acres."⁴⁵

Taking so much land violated instructions not to encroach upon Indian country and minimized the potential for federal control.⁴⁶ The Washington administration and its allies thus decided to distance themselves from the territorial government. As early as 1792, Secretary Knox relayed to Blount that offensive measures against Cherokees and Chickamaugas were "a very great and . . . insupportable evil. Everything indeed depends upon your exertions to avert the event of a war, that will be reluctantly entered into and at best but illy supported."⁴⁷ Only a year later Knox—ironically, himself a speculator of the first order in Massachusetts's District of Maine—better encapsulated the emerging Federalist consensus when he wrote Blount that "it is not to be supposed that [the United States] will support the expences of a war brought on the frontiers by the wanton blood thirsty disposition of our own people."⁴⁸ Perhaps the *Knoxville Gazette* best summarized the administration's position when it lamented that the government was "not disposed to believe that the necessity of justice really exists, and if it does, that it is the Indians that should be protected and not the whites."⁴⁹

This move away from the Southwest Territory came at a time of increasing raids by Indians. Although they did not engage in many large-scale attacks, they were consistent in causing economic and property damage. William Blount, for example, estimated that five hundred horses were stolen from white settlers in 1792 alone. When necessary, Indians were careful also to inflict casualties. Although most of their attacks took the form of uncoordinated raids, a significant battle did occur when four hundred Creeks and Chickamaugas attacked Buchanan's (Cumberland District) Station in September 1792.[50] Blount subsequently reported that only twelve hundred men were over sixteen and eligible to protect the vast Cumberland frontier from future attacks of this kind.[51]

The Washington administration's decision therefore hamstrung a territorial government that was obligated to carry out federal orders and left many settlers (particularly in the Cumberland) wondering, "What are the blessings of Government to us? Are we to hope for protection? If so, when?"[52] By 1793 tensions had reached the boiling point—so much so that territorial secretary Daniel Smith wrote of a palpable "spirit for war against Indians [that] pervades people of all Ranks so far that no order of Government can stop them."[53] Unofficial raids became particularly prevalent and were deemed a serious threat to territorial interests. Thus Smith authorized an "exploratory expedition" through which Gen. John Sevier's militia could show settlers that the government was doing something to "pursue and chastize the enemy."[54] Sevier's militia burned several lower Cherokee and Creek villages before returning to Knoxville in October 1793.[55]

The militia campaign showed that the federal government's unwillingness to impose meaningful central controls minimized their ability to restrain the territory from attacks on Cherokees, Chickamaugas, and Creeks. And it was this lack of central authority that had led the region to ally with the federal government in the first place. With land values stagnating and immigration to the Cumberland slowing to a trickle, the Washington administration seemed to settlers to have shirked the only duty required of it: To stabilize the region and facilitate efforts at economic and social progress.

The situation worsened in 1794, to the point that some observers feared "the Cumberland settlements cannot get ridd of [the] savage's barbarity."[56] As Cherokees, Creeks, and Chickamaugas again lashed out at the Middle District, Governor Blount appealed to the federal government for help. When no significant aid was forthcoming, many in the region reevaluated their position vis-à-vis the federal government. As Cumberland District attorney Andrew Jackson wrote, "This country is Declining very fast, and unless Congress lends us a more ample protection this Country will have at length to break or seek protection from some other Source than the present."[57] An editorial in the *Knoxville Gazette* was equally blunt: "It is to be hoped that the members of Congress, in whom the power of declaring war is solely vested, will individually apply [our] case to their own families and feelings, and act accordingly. It is a fact not to be denied, that the most extreme frontier family, in their poverty, are as much entitled to protection as the most wealthy member of Congress in his ease and luxury."[58]

A large number of Cumberland settlers went a step further: Whereas Jackson and the *Gazette* (publicly) searched for a political solution, many settlers by the spring and summer of 1794 were defying federal orders and once again turning to individual acts of revenge. Davidson County resident James Taylor's account provides merely one example. In a letter to William Lytle he pointed out that "the Indians are very troublesome on the frontier of Cumberland" and that when Indians killed "5 persons in my neighborhood, about 100 men followed them, came up with them on the head of the Elk river, killed them and took 2 squaws which composed the whole party."[59] Moreover, militia captains successfully recruited Kentucky troops to enter Cumberland and go on the attack.[60]

Militia endeavors had both implicit and explicit support from territorial leaders. Even as Governor Blount moved toward the creation of a legislature to address public concerns, he allowed indiscriminate attacks on nearby Indian settlements. In August 1794, Blount looked the other way while the Cumberland militia, under Gen. James Robertson, destroyed the Chickamauga towns of Nickajack and Running Water.[61] This expedition, in conjunction with Sevier's late 1793 campaign, proved to be a turning point in the Indian war. Particularly after Robertson's campaign, Cherokee leaders began to rethink their commitment to attacking the frontier.

These militia raids infuriated the Federalist coalition in Philadelphia.[62] President Washington certainly grew wary of John Sevier and was loath to bequeath upon him any military or political favor.[63] By 1795 the government generally had become so hostile that no amount of Indian depredation could justify to them the need for an offensive counterattack. To congressmen such as William Vans Murray of Maryland, southwestern land was held by Indians, who used it legitimately for purposes of hunting.

And in said use, he argued, they were the more civilized inhabitants of the territory.[64] Newly appointed Secretary of War Timothy Pickering agreed. Responding to Blount's request for federal troops he stated, "Upon the whole, sir, I cannot refrain from saying that the complexion of some of the transactions in the south-western territory appears unfavorable to the public interests." As such, he made clear, "all ideas of offensive operations are to be laid aside and all possible harmony cultivated with the Indian tribes."[65] Pickering also proclaimed that Blount should cease complaining about Indian depredations, noting, "Tranquility on the frontiers is not to be expected while we permit our Citizens to encroach on Indian lands. One species of robbery affords as just grounds of hostility as the other."[66] The secretary's hostile review was by no means a lone voice, either. Territorial congressional delegate James White consistently had to defend settlers against federal charges of being "bloodthirsty and semi-savage."[67]

Blount by this point seemingly was stuck between a territory dangerously close to mutiny and a federal government that had decisively rejected requests for aid.[68] As Cherokee leader Bloody Fellow pondered, "For many years they have been killing the People of this Country; is it that this country is not under the Protection of the U.S., or is it that the President is uninformed of the many murders and Thefts committed by the Creeks?"[69] With this question ringing in his ears, Blount considered any means by which to extricate the territory from its quagmire.

Privately, he remained open to outside sources of support, which in 1796 would lead to not-so-quiet feelers to the British for assistance in placing part of the Southwest under the crown.[70] In public, however, he made clear that "the wished for period [of peace] will never arrive until this Territory becomes a State and is represented in Congress."[71] He was aware that such a step would lessen his near hegemonic authority, but Blount nevertheless believed that Congress could not ignore the needs of a new state.[72] After two-plus years of violent confrontation, the territorial population agreed. As John Sevier pointed out in 1795, "The great body of our constituents are sensible of many grave defects of our present mode of government and of the great and permanent advantages to be derived from a change and speedy representation in Congress."[73] With the public clearly behind him, and with a subsequent enumeration that showed 77,262 residents, Blount moved forward with a constitutional convention for January

1796.[74] Within four weeks, the convention unanimously approved a document that was submitted to Philadelphia for approval.

It was typical of other state constitutions of the period, with one exception: The eleventh article was a declaration of rights that included free navigation of the Mississippi. Despite the ostensible separation of the three branches of government, the legislature was the dominant political force. Both the executive and the judiciary were firmly under its control, and all appointments throughout the state—down to justices of the peace—were made by legislators. In terms of democratic practices, it gave all freemen over twenty-one the right to vote, regardless of property ownership; provided for a written ballot; and apportioned representation based on taxable inhabitants. Although acknowledged by contemporaries and historians alike as rather democratic, the document was created by an elite convention and never offered to the people for approval.[75] Moreover, it carefully protected those men who seemed to have the greatest economic stake in Tennessee. Because all land except town lots were taxed at the same rate, regardless of value, speculators were able to minimize their duties to the state.

Becoming Jeffersonian

Over this same period Blount and his political machine openly aligned with the Jeffersonian Republican coalition, a move that significantly displeased Federalists. Given the rancorous debate between the two "parties," the territorial leadership's movement into the Jeffersonian camp meant that statehood "would have the most serious effects [because it would provide] one twig of the electioneering cabal for Mr. Jefferson."[76] Since 1796 was a presidential election year, Federalist Party leaders chose to fight Tennessee's petition.

First, they questioned the validity of the territorial census, arguing that only Congress had the power to perform such an act and that Blount conveniently scheduled the census for the time of year when, as South Carolina congressman William Loughton Smith pointed out, there was "the greatest emigration through the territory of Kentucky and Cumberland." Moreover, Smith argued that no territory could "claim an admission into the Federal Councils until formed into one or two states," which Congress—not the territory itself—had the power to do. Finally, Federalists noted that the Tennessee constitution was faulty and "in several parts repugnant to the Ordinance of 1787, and to the Constitution of the United States." Specifically, they feared that the legislature had no checks on its power, disliked the provision that land would be taxed at the same rate regardless of quality, felt the article regarding Mississippi navigation was unnecessary, and questioned the stark religious requirements for office holding.[77] The Jeffersonian-dominated House of Representatives managed to quiet the opposition and throw its collective support behind Tennessee's request. But it would take a sympathetic conference committee finally to force the entire Congress into approving statehood, only two days before the end of the session.

The unsurprising result of this contentious debate was that Federalism fell even further in the estimation of both the territorial administration and most settlers. As newly appointed Senator William Cocke soon made clear, the "people of this state, of every description, express a wish that [Thomas Jefferson] should be the next President of the United States."[78] Many within the political elite even made voting against Federalist candidate John Adams a sort of vendetta. Newly appointed Senator Blount, for example, noted, "Truth is that I have taken a great agency in this election and have been induced to do so by the part the adverse party took against the admission of the State of Tennessee."[79]

Perhaps more important, the new state's early political culture was entirely devoid of a Federalist interest, meaning that there was no opposition through which a party system could come into existence. Unlike other regions of the new United States, early national Tennessee had only one party through which to voice its political views. Although economic and ideological differences emerged, this one-party political system would last well into the nineteenth century.[80]

Amid the statehood debate, frontier settlers managed to obtain a modicum of peace with Indians. A critical element in this détente was Spain's withdrawal from southwestern intrigue. By 1794 the Spanish government had become convinced that France's revolutionary crusade in Europe threatened its sovereignty. As it focused on achieving peace with Paris, the Spanish government negotiated the Treaty of San Lorenzo with the

United States. Once ratified, it opened the Mississippi River, ended Spain's informal support of Indian hostilities, dismissed their remaining land claims in Tennessee, and established a U.S.-Spanish boundary well to the south of white settlements. Although they would sporadically interfere in the Southwest until Napoleon sold Louisiana, Spanish withdrawal nevertheless left the Cherokees and Creeks without a powerful ally.

This development came at the same time that Gen. Anthony Wayne emerged victorious over a pan-Indian alliance in the Northwest Territory. In 1794 Wayne's army of three thousand faced approximately thirteen hundred Delawares, Shawnees, Wyandots, Miamis, and Ottawas, as well as a rear guard of British militia at Fallen Timbers. The entire action lasted about three hours. Americans lost forty and had another eighty-nine wounded. The Indian army lost between forty and fifty, with an unknown number of wounded, but they also lost villages, supplies, cornfields, and storehouses in the vicinity. The victory was an American success on several levels. First, it ended British hopes for an Indian preserve north of the Ohio River and reduced the possibility for future alliances. Second, it showed the British, Spanish, and Indians, in both the North and South, that the United States had the manpower and will to succeed on the frontier. Cherokees further feared that it might free federal troops for duty in the Southwest.[81]

Spain's withdrawal and Wayne's victory thus strengthened Cherokee elders' desire to reestablish contact with the Blount administration and put a halt to Cherokee assaults upon white settlements (while doing little to stop the stealing of horses and livestock). Although the Creeks resisted a bit longer, losing Spanish and Cherokee support, in conjunction with a potential war with the Chickasaws, led them to pursue peace in 1796. Some Native American resistance would continue into the nineteenth century, but the cessation of hostilities in 1795 and 1796 removed some of the last major obstacles for white settlement in East and Middle Tennessee. This in turn led to a flood of immigration, which gave speculators the opportunity eventually to restart the cycle of exploitation in West Tennessee.[82]

The seeming inexorability of Indian marginalization drew from the fact that southwestern Indian nations did not fit into white conceptions of economic and social progress. As early as 1792 the *Knoxville Gazette* had argued that "the Savage" led a rudderless existence. "There can scarcely be said to be any progress," noted the paper, "or succession of events, in his existence—'tis one perpetual *now*." Civilized Tennesseans, by contrast, continually looked to improve, and in so doing were able to enjoy "the happiness of his country and mankind."[83]

This perception fits what would become the hallmark of Jeffersonian sentiment regarding progress and southwestern Indians. Indians were both civilized and useful to the new American nation, as Jefferson himself put it in 1812, so long as they have "good Cabins, inclosed fields, large herds of cattle & hogs, spin & weave their own clothes of cotton, have smiths & other of the most necessary tradesmen, write & read, are on the increase in numbers." As he wrote he noted that a "branch of the Cherokees" was even "instituting a regular representative government." His great fear, however, was that, due to contact with the British, "the backward will yeild, & be thrown further back. these will relapse into barbarism & misery, lose numbers by war & want, and we shall be obliged to drive them, with the beasts of the forest into the Stony mountains."[84] This theme of backsliding from the virtues of progress, and thus of the basic necessity of jettisoning those Indians who had done so, as historian Peter Onuf has reminded us, was prevalent throughout Jefferson's epistolary and public record.[85]

It also was firmly entrenched as early as 1800 in Middle Tennessee, and it put Cherokees, Creeks, and increasingly the Chickasaws in West Tennessee permanently on the outside of regional development. Civilizing Indians may have been an abstract option for Jefferson and a real possibility for Federalists, but removal ultimately made the most sense to white Tennesseans.[86] Judge David Campbell put it best in an 1804 letter to Jefferson. He feared that Cherokees would be incapable of assimilating into white society:

> The Cherokee Nation of Indians will not, in my opinion, exchange the Country they now occupy for any other directly, but time and perhaps not very remote will accomplish every object necessary for the good of the Citizens of the U. States and of the Cherokee Nation. I will yet call them a Nation, though they are not all together independent in reality, but so in form. They will willingly relinquish all the lands North of the Tennessee for an equivalent on the Waters of the Mississippi for hunting grounds. This relinquishment will make the State of Tennessee compact, and a respectable territory.[87]

Campbell's argument makes Jeffersonian Tennesseans' position clear: The region would not achieve a measure of respectability as long as Indians remained. For their sake as well as that of white settlers, moving them farther west was the only option. As we shall see, the early nineteenth century brought with it repeated efforts to implement just such a policy.

At any rate, by statehood most Federalists agreed with Timothy Pickering's 1795 assessment that southwestern settlers were "the least worthy subjects of the United States."[88] Subsequent scandals only reinforced their view. William Blount's efforts while a U.S. senator to acquire Louisiana for the British, for example, convinced Federalists that the former governor had operated in a manner unbecoming an officer of the federal government. In 1795 Blount, whose potential fortune seemed to be slipping away in a stagnant economy, began to look for outside sources of support for the Southwest Territory.

In 1796 it led him into a secret negotiation with the British. Blount promised the government in London that he could deliver large swaths of western territory should the British provide the funding and support. In return, he expected a prominent role in whatever new state emerged. The British never appeared more than mildly interested, and Blount had the misfortune of leaving a damning letter in the hands of James Carey, who was supposed to read and burn it. That it ended up in Federalist hands in 1796 led to an awkward situation: Here was a sitting senator of the United States conspiring to remove territory from within its borders. Even after Blount resigned and hastened back to Knoxville, Federalists charged him with treason and commenced impeachment proceedings.[89]

In 1797 the new Adams administration angered the region with its decision to redefine Tennessee's still vague southeastern Indian boundary. To do so, President Adams sent in the federal army to "remove off the Cherokee Lands any citizen or citizens who may remain there in violation of the laws of the United States."[90] Such seemingly blatant affronts led some Tennesseans to call for open resistance. The situation became dangerous for federal troops, as Col. Benjamin Howard angrily noted. In a letter to U.S. Army captain William Preston in Knoxville, he wrote, "I am sorry to find you and your Brother officers rendered unhappy between the daring demagogues of faction and the unfortunate misled; instead of being considered the protectors of your Country [you] are viewed as the

Engines of oppression and your toils rewarded only by the suspicions and insults of those around you."[91] Ultimately, only Governor Sevier's political savvy kept the state from plunging into armed chaos. By alternately appealing to the local populace, remonstrating to Philadelphia, allowing for the implementation of federal policy, and serving as a treaty commissioner to the Cherokees, Sevier kept the peace and got the Adams administration eventually to purchase confiscated squatter land.[92]

Amid the boundary controversy emerged another scandal that confirmed to Federalists that their longstanding fear of the region was well warranted. In early 1798 newly appointed Senator Andrew Jackson "was informed by a Mr. Charles of the rascality carried on at Nashville" in the land office and deemed it worrisome enough that it was "sufficient inducement to make it known to the Governor of North Carolina" of potentially fraudulent activity.[93] When North Carolina governor Samuel Ashe initiated a formal inquiry he received word of a large "number and variety of frauds, perjuries and forgeries, [which] the gentlemen of the board [of inquiry] have strong grounds to presume have been committed, with procuring military warrants and grants, in all stages of business both on this, and the other side of the mountains."[94]

Judge H. O. Tatum of Tennessee soon described the framework through which the frauds occurred: "Many locations originally made by A and recorded, now appear to be the property of B and this by erasing the name of A and the number of the warrant, and inserting the name of B and the number of his warrant, and this can be proved by comparing the file, with the book of Record." Moreover, there was the problem of filing blank locations and filling them in years later. "Should it so happen," wrote Tatum "as it often will, that some other person has made a fair entry subsequent to the [aforementioned] blank one, the filling of this blank renders the honest locators right doubtful, it not appearing on the books at what time the warrant & name was annexed to the blank location."[95] Many speculators were even bolder: Ashe's investigating commission ultimately reported that officials issued military warrants to individuals who had not served in the Continental line or who were dead. It also presented evidence that speculators had assigned themselves as attorneys for veterans or their heirs and subsequently issued warrants under their own name.[96]

Public disclosure of widespread fraud, which eventually became known as the Glasgow conspiracy, sent shockwaves through unknown and prominent speculators alike. Most embarrassed were men such as Sevier, William Blount, Stockley Donelson, and North Carolina secretary of state James Glasgow, all of whom were connected to millions of acres in fraudulent claims. Concern over extensive public exposure was so great that Governor Sevier refused to allow Governor Ashe access to the warrants in question. Several other conspirators met at Blount's home in Knoxville to destroy the most dubious claims. In North Carolina, William Tyrrell and James Glasgow even hatched a plan to burn down the statehouse in Raleigh, lest the illegal warrants end up in Governor Ashe's possession.

To Federalists, the Glasgow conspiracy justified their decision to employ a restrained policy on the southwestern frontier. Federalist leaders firmly advocated western settlement, to be sure, but also insisted that it follow "an orderly process . . . closely supervised by the government, with a major role for the United States Army."[97] That they were more successful on the northwestern frontier—and much more willing to engage in said policy—did not diminish their abstract desire for the same in the South.

The problem was that southwestern leaders had a different idea of the means by which a centralized authority should facilitate regional progress. Whereas the Washington and Adams administrations wanted an organized process that would maximize land sales for federal coffers, the territorial elite felt the government should merely sanction and develop their activities by providing military and financial support. When Federalists saw the extent to which this policy undermined their own notion of development, and the extent to which speculation had already minimized available land, they had little reason actively to alleviate territorial problems with Indians.

Jeffersonian Republicanism, with its friendlier conception of immigration, empire, and nation building, thus became the lens through which Tennesseans fulfilled the envisioned social, commercial, and political promise of their region.[98] As nineteenth-century Tennessee gradually took on the characteristics of a more settled state, "federalism" became a derogatory label placed upon political enemies.[99] Even if, that is, the gentlemen in the region still hoped to maintain social and political authority over the unrefined masses.

But did this anti–Federalist Party sentiment mean that Tennesseans rejected more centralized power in favor of local determinism? The answer is complicated. Regarding Indian issues, it certainly did. The six-year Indian war led an otherwise nationally oriented territorial government to endorse local sovereignty by sending the militia to do what Federalists would not. Tennesseans generally disliked that the federal government restricted their ability to treat with Indians and lamented that (from their perspective) Indian nations showed no compunction about ignoring the parameters of federally sponsored treaties. They also disliked that the government was willing to "engross the Indian trade" by building and maintaining trading factories in East Tennessee.[100] As such, they believed that the power to treat and deal with Indian nations should remain at the local level.[101] This position is a manifestation of a "doctrine of limited federalism," or the idea that Tennesseans had the right to formulate local Indian, self-defense, and property-protection policies.[102] Said doctrine carried over into the early nineteenth century and remained a point of contingency between the state and the Jefferson administration.

Even so, many Tennesseans were willing to entertain federal oversight on other military issues, as well as on issues of economy and identity. For example, entrepreneurs and their allies believed that federal oversight was needed in order to fund internal improvement schemes and facilitate intraregional economic growth. Moreover, white Tennesseans longed to create a stronger American community in the Southwest, as was made clear in their plan for Indian removal, in Fourth of July celebrations, and, as we shall see, in connecting the region with a mythical Revolutionary past. They also demanded a stronger American presence in the lead-up to the War of 1812 and longed to act on behalf of the country once the war did break out.

Perhaps congressional candidate James Lyon best encapsulated Middle Tennessee's emerging nationalism. In 1807 he considered running for state representative, but finally decided his talents would be better utilized in Washington. He thus wrote to his potential constituents that, having "reflected on the political advantages which might result from a bold, active, perservering attitude in our national policy; and animated with an ardent zeal for the welfare of my Country, I have felt an ambition to become an actor on that stage."[103] As we shall see, this interest in federal policy and the nationalism it engendered would become critical components in the region's political institutionalization.

By 1796 Middle Tennessee had undergone transformations that I. H. Williamson could not have foreseen when he wrote to James Robertson of the burgeoning relationship between the region and the federal government. In ten years the region had gone from a contested zone of interaction between Spanish, Indians, and the small but increasing population of slaves and white settlers to a speculator-controlled political and economic system about to undergo transformation. Although the Cumberland District had barely more than 11,500 residents when John Adams was elected president, over the next twenty-five years it would mushroom into a white and slave population of 287,501 that was increasingly committed to plantation agriculture and land speculation.[104] Because of this growth, the Cumberland River would become a highway for trade goods, which, in turn, would create a mercantile class that relied upon the produce of local cotton and tobacco farmers to perpetuate the increasingly vibrant economy.

Such economic and demographic change placed those who inherited the territorial government in a political quandary. Statehood ensured that the political elite would have to appeal to a rapidly expanding population in order to maintain their positions of power. What initially emerged was a system that lacked the symbolic expression necessary to create a permanent party structure and thus revolved around temporary factions and attempts to build broad popular constituencies. This new culture created particularly visible personality clashes between Andrew Jackson in Middle Tennessee and John Sevier in the East. Illuminating its development is critical to understanding the evolution of political institutionalization in early national Tennessee.

Chapter 3

MILITIAS, FACTIONS, AND PUBLIC OPINION IN A SHIFTING POLITICAL CULTURE, 1796–1810

The rancorous relationship between Federalists and frontier leaders virtually guaranteed that all of Tennessee's electoral votes would go to the Thomas Jefferson "ticket" in the election of 1800.[1] And with the presidential question settled by late February 1801, the *Tennessee Gazette* happily reported that the "tide of political controversy [was] on the ebb." Now, the paper noted, the region was "left at liberty to pursue such other subjects as may appertain to our honor or interest."[2]

Such a proclamation implied that Tennesseans lacked internal political divisions, and at first glance that seemed plausible. Anger over the Federalist-dominated central government's decision not to step in during the Indian wars had left them with a seemingly united political will. The result was a limited "Jeffersonian" political culture with the territorial elite firmly in control of governing institutions.[3]

This elite would not have had it any other way. Even as they espoused the "democratic" rhetoric of the Republican Party, they clearly differentiated between republican notions of the rule of the people and the practical application of popular democracy. As to the former, they understood the legacy of the Revolution and plainly endorsed the principle that free men had earned the right to political participation.[4] Even if they acceded to abstract notions of popular sovereignty, however, these men nevertheless carried into statehood their belief in the key features of colonial and

Revolutionary-era southern political culture, including honor, deference, and personal networks.

Simply put, the elite believed that "the people" needed only to provide their votes for the appropriate gentleman and then leave them to maintain a virtuous form of government. Speculator Arthur Campbell sheds significant light on the elite mindset: "Under the Constitution of the United States," he wrote,

> every honest station of life is honorable, since they are all part of the great social body. Between the Chief Magistrate and the People, the great and the mean, the rich and the poor, the acute and the dull, the learned and the ignorant There is no difference as to the rights of citizenship, but in possession of different powers, and in the discharge of different offices peculiar to each capacity and useful to all; and if one of them have a just demand for submission and obedience, for honor and respect, for convenience and ease; the other have as just a claim for protection and defence, for the administration of justice and the preservation of equal liberty, for the supply of their wants and the relief of their distresses, for *instruction* and *good example*.[5]

Perhaps an early July 4 toast—a ritual which helped reinforce notions of status and power within the community—best illuminates their understanding of "the people": "To the freemen of Tennessee—may they exercise the right of suffrage with judgment, and remember that the welfare of themselves and posterity, requires that men of patriotism, talents and integrity should alone be preferred to office."[6]

The elite saw no reason to alter this position at statehood. Rather than appealing directly to the small but expanding population, they attempted to create personal networks through the Tennessee militia. As we have seen, the militia had served as an outlet for political activity since earliest settlement, and in 1796 virtually all of the state's electorate belonged to various companies. Corralling this group of potential voters, particularly the officer corps, could provide the elite with the means to create and extend traditional networks. Thus they electioneered to place themselves and their allies in key positions of martial leadership.

It soon became clear that a network of officers would not ensure political success. An eruption of contested militia elections stimulated a nascent public sphere that gave ordinary Tennesseans a firm precedent for political opposition. Soon a structure emerged wherein the elite minimized their emphasis on patronage and attempted to construct broad constituencies in an increasingly contested, popular democratic culture.[7]

Yet this new culture remained one of transition. Tennessee's universal Republicanism meant that no meaningful opposition could emerge through which to create a viable party system. Lack of institutionalization led politicians to create temporary, personality-driven factions in order to attract broad popular support.[8] This blend of tradition and democracy served as a transitional phase for politics in Tennessee, a point between the elite controlled world of the territorial period and an era where ideological divisions based on competing notions of progress provided a foundation around which party interests could coalesce.

In 1796 Middle Tennessee's political sphere began to emerge from twenty-plus years of control by land speculators. Prior to that point few people outside of this small clique had provided substantive input on questions of territorial and federal institutional growth. The combination of the Northwest Ordinance, a virtually nonexistent print culture, a small population, and a legislature that only met for the last two years of the territorial period ensured that ordinary Tennesseans would lack the tools to bring consistent pressure to bear on territorial leaders.[9]

After 1796 things began to change. With statehood, the general public began to realize their role as arbiters of power in an emerging democratic state. This realization meant that the elite would have to commit to more concrete notions of popular sovereignty. Looking for a way to appeal to the people without losing their grip on the state's political institutions, the elite noticed a curious happenstance: more Middle Tennesseans showed up to vote for militia officers than were taking part in recent civil democratic exercises. In Davidson County alone as many as 725 men had voted in the militia elections of 1796—112 more than had appeared during the 1795 statehood vote.[10]

Upon reflection, the elite probably should not have been surprised. Given that the territorial government allowed so little input from ordinary settlers, organizing and electioneering within militia companies had been the most visible avenue for advancing "views on local, state, national and international issues." It also helped them maintain a presence through legislative petitioning, tax collection, and oversight of census enumeration.[11] Militias, in short, gave ordinary folk a tangible link to frontier authority.[12] And since lower-level officers generally maintained solid reputations within the local community, elites assumed that controlling the officer corps might provide them a way both to appeal to the growing population and to establish more traditional personal networks.

A particularly visible early attempt to control militia companies came in the 1796 officer election and its aftermath. In that year Governor John Sevier looked to enhance his tenuous popularity and weak political network in Middle Tennessee. The best means of doing so was to have an ally elected as the Cumberland's brigadier general. The task seemed simple enough, and a quirk in voting procedure ensured that the possibility existed to turn the situation explicitly in Sevier's favor. According to Tennessee militia law, field officers in each district determined their brigadier. Newly elected officers were unable to take command, however, until they received a formal commission from the governor. And in 1796, Middle Tennessee cavalry elections happened to coincide with brigadier voting. In other words, because of the delay in the delivery of commissions, the older territorial cavalry would be the only official officer corps. Controlling their vote meant control of the district's general.

Unfortunately for Sevier, it was more difficult to manipulate this group than he had reasoned. The 1796 campaign for brigadier boiled down to two individuals, James Winchester and James Ford. Sevier favored Ford, but Andrew Jackson, at the time Tennessee's representative in Congress, had other ideas. Eyeing the possibility that Winchester's election might catapult him to the prestigious position of major general, Jackson turned all of his political capital into achieving that result.[13] His and his allies subsequent electioneering was so strong that Montgomery County resident Robert Prince feared the governor's aspirations for a western political network soon would be "d—d and trod under foot by their opponents."[14]

Sevier and his other supporters agreed, and the election became a public battle for supremacy between two temporary "factions." Robertson County resident Thomas Johnson, for example, wrote to Sevier that "at present there appear a great Anxiety amongst the Citizens, in the

Respect to the Appointment of Brig General. The Chief of our elections were Intirely Conducted by parties, & those parties had nothing else in View but the Appointment of a Brig Gen."[15] Johnson suggested that "as it was by no Means the Intention of the Legislature, that the Old Territorial Officers should elect the Genl. I hope your Excellency will send blank Commissions on to some person on whom you can depend, to fill up immediately to those Elected."[16] Although perhaps legally questionable—and from the Jackson camp's perspective, utterly corrupt—Sevier agreed and sent James Robertson blank commissions a few weeks before election day.

Jackson and his allies immediately opposed what they saw as a blatantly political maneuver and warned the public that it was an insidious tool for the creation of a permanent "party." More pointedly, Jackson declared that he was "sorry, that I was compelled to Expose the ignorance of the governor, in his attempting to communicate to another, those duties, that by the Constitution was confined to him alone."[17] Ultimately the district militia agreed, and they demanded that the blank commissions remain out of the fray. "As party runs uncommonly big in the Election of Brigadier General," Robertson wrote to Sevier shortly after election day, "I did not think myself at liberty to fill such Commissions[.] It is beleaved your Excellency intended by sending and otherising [sic] me to fill them to give general satisfaction to the District."[18] Not using the commissions meant that Winchester—and Jackson—had won.

The confrontational nature of early national politics ensured that what one person saw as legitimate activity another viewed as thoroughly corrupt.[19] After the outcome of the campaign was assured, Sevier thus made known his offense at Jackson's machinations and public proclamations. Already unsure of Tennessee's congressional representative because of his relationship with former Franklin enemy John Tipton,[20] the governor subsequently used his influence to deny Jackson the position of major general.[21] Sevier also made it known that Tennessee's representative was little more than a "scurrilous . . . poor pitifull petty fogging Lawyer [to be treated with] Contempt."[22] A showdown seemed imminent when Jackson demanded an explanation.

The still-influential Senator William Blount understood how dangerous the situation was, however, and quickly sent James Robertson to intervene.

He proved persuasive enough that Governor Sevier subsequently saw "the matter in a different point of view" and greatly softened his contempt.[23] Mutual ally Senator William Cocke went a step further than Blount by personally interceding. He rejected Jackson's request to deliver a controversial letter by stating,

> I met [Governor Sevier] at Mr. Haneses and had not Spoak [sic] three words to him before he inquired after you in the most effectionate manner and declared highest approbation of your conduct as the representative of the state of Tennessee as well as his personal esteem for you the friendly trust you have been pleased to repose in me and the great reguard I had for discharging that trust in the best Possable manner induced me to decline delivering the letter as I knew you never desired to make any man an enemy who wished to be your friend.[24]

Such powerful intermediaries, in addition to the passage of enough time, were enough to cool the offended parties. As Sevier subsequently noted to Jackson, "Although (in my opinion) your Attack on my public Character was unmerited, I was not authorised to view you as a private enemy."[25] The two men agreed to a personal meeting to sort out any remaining difficulties. Although the meeting never took place, the matter seemingly ended there. After all, Sevier wanted to maintain the governor's chair and could not afford an open feud with one of the more powerful western leaders, and Jackson simply did not have the necessary capital to break with the universally popular governor.

In the next few months Congressman Jackson worked so tirelessly on federal compensation for Sevier's 1793 militia expedition that he not only restored professional (if not altogether friendly) ties with Sevier but also "heightened the esteem of the people for the General Government and secured [for himself] a permanent interest."[26] In response to his endeavors, Sevier supported Jackson's appointment to the Tennessee Superior Court, even though he was fully cognizant it would provide a boon to Jackson's social standing and political future.[27] Without a meaningful foundation upon which to create permanent party structures, factional divisions could disappear as quickly as they arose. Thereafter Tennessee's leadership returned to business as usual—geographically contested at times, wary of the militia officer corps, and generally cooperative as regards issues of serious political importance.

They soon found that gaining control of the militias was not a reliable foundation upon which to build a political system, however. Population growth stood at the heart of the dilemma: The number of militia companies grew so rapidly that keeping new officers within a neat political network was impossible. In January 1796, for example, there were four Cumberland regiments under the control of government appointed officers. Within fifteen years there were thirty-four, all of them under a popularly elected leadership.[28] People who previously might have held little political clout suddenly found militia command well within their grasp. And increasingly they acted on their own initiative rather than at the behest of their "superiors."

The 1796 campaign, in short, helped release the democratic genie from its bottle. Having endured a flurry of official protests regarding "tainted" votes, the political elite over the next few months and years watched as aggrieved candidates from an exploding population contested militia election after election.[29] Upon losing the 1796 Davidson County race for second major, for example, a disgruntled William Nash wrote to Sevier that "one William Walker a Resident of the County of Sumner and therefore not authorized or entitled to Vote in the County of Davidson, voted at the said Election in behalf of [my opponent] which [otherwise] would have [left] a Majority of Legal votes in favor of your Memorialist."[30] So questionable was the outcome that Sevier associate William Lewis soon wrote to the governor of a high level of "dissatisfaction among the Citizens." Continuing, he made clear "that the Officer fairly elected was Mr. William Nash, and that very unlawful means were made use of to carry the Officer that it is Pretended is Elected."[31]

Ultimately Nash did not obtain his office, but his failure did not stop other men from pleading their cases. Only a few months after Nash's complaint, candidate George Blackmore called for the nullification of a Sumner County election that had been "held by three private Citizens unqualified" to hand out commissions rather than by the sheriff as county law had mandated. His ally Leeroy Taylor even provided a list of illegal voters, along with their respective places of residence.[32]

The problems continued well into 1797. In January of that year Sevier supporter Thomas Johnson wrote to the governor in reference to a Cumberland District cavalry vote, "I have been informed that some of the Counties do not like the [results of the] Election & intend to send to you their protest against it."³³ The following September, James McQuestion of Davidson County noted still more corruption of Cumberland voting procedures. "After [our] Company was laid off," he wrote to Sevier, "an election was advertised by the Col and on the day of the said election I was elected by a respectable majority. Upon which the Col being opposed to my election, told the managers they could not give a certificate as the election was disputed. Upon which a new election was ordered to be held in much less than the legal time."³⁴ James Nichols added to McQuestion's remonstrance the fact that in the second election, "some voters which was Eight in number moved in the District for the purpose of [electing another]."³⁵

As the population grew the protests only became more widespread and organized. In many cases entire militia companies met to discuss issues and present petitions to the government. In 1809, for example, a Dickson County company demanded an emergency legislative session to address the question of debtor relief. That same year the Davidson and Smith County Militias called meetings at their respective courthouses to debate President Jefferson's embargo and its effect on local residents. They also suggested the propriety of circulating petitions at militia parades to gain the maximum number of signatures.³⁶

Just as often, however, political action took the form of petitions such as one from John Hanes. In 1798 Hanes relinquished his militia command and asked the governor for both a new election and a new company, arguing that "the people wish a division, as it will be much more convenient" given the growing population.³⁷ Only a few years later, a similar petition from Montgomery County argued that the "limits of this County are much greater at present than by the law they ought to be and the inconvenience of attending Genl. Musters and Elections to the Inhabitants [is] considerable." The petitioners therefore called for a reduction in the size of the county and asked that those citizens outside the new lines "who are almost but not altogether sufficient to form a County, shall until such time as a new County can be formed, be considered as a appendage of this County, but be allowed separate Genl. Musters and Election Districts."³⁸ Other important petitions covered issues as diverse as religious favoritism in the militias, requests for changes in militia laws, and the need for election procedural reform.

By far the most numerous requests came in the form of demands to create new counties. And new counties did pop up. In the 1800 census there were only seven in Middle Tennessee; by 1810, there were twenty-one.[39] The number grew so rapidly that the legislature created two new political and judicial districts out of the older Cumberland District: Robertson and Winchester.[40] All told, a minimum of three hundred petitions with at least eighteen thousand separate signatures went to the legislature between 1799 and 1810, to say nothing of the dozens that passed across the governors' desks.[41]

As local institutions grew, residents would request even more extensive reform, usually by calling for a "clean up" of corrupt militia campaigns or requesting specific guidelines for more systematic, fair, and popular democratic civil elections. Isaac Roberts was one of several who called for such measures. In 1799 he worried that a recent election for "Sinnators to Represent Davidson County was not conducted agreeable to law, either through corruption contempt of the law neglect or ignorance."[42] The solution, he felt, was for the legislature to reconsider the vote and call a new election. Similarly, in 1809 Sampson Williams announced that a legislative race in which he participated was tainted and he hoped "to be able to prove that he is entitled to the Seat, notwithstanding a certain Thomas Harris got a certificate of his election . . . because there was a greater number of illegal votes given said Harris than he got of a Majority."[43] He provided with his ultimately unsuccessful petition almost a dozen affidavits of support from various voters in his legislative district.[44]

Middle Tennesseans during this period also performed an increasing number of public political rituals, usually in the form of patriotic society formation, toasting, "town hall" gatherings, stumping, parades, and effigy burnings.[45] One of the most prominent early examples of public ritual came in the form of a "procession in condolence of the death of General Washington," which included cannon fire and both a civil and military parade.[46] And throughout the first decade of the nineteenth century, public toasting and their textual reproductions served as centerpieces for Fourth of July celebrations.[47]

Clearly, the state leadership's attempts to create orderly political networks had failed. Perhaps "Slim" best described the situation. In a satirical essay designed to belittle "Federalists," Slim proclaimed that "the electioneering system ought to undergo a complete reform. Is it not a bare faced absurdity to see every man who pays taxes, or a militia man, together with emigrants not more than two or three years in the country, walk into the courthouse and pass a vote! I call that the *mad Jefferson plan!*"[48] Absurdity or not, Tennessee's elite found they would have to adjust their politics to reflect the realities of this new civic world.[49] In effect, a culture emerged wherein they minimized their emphasis on networking and engaged the new and contested democratic culture to win broad popular constituencies.

Yet there was more to this new political atmosphere. At statehood, Tennessee had nothing resembling a lasting party structure; universally Republican, its "imagined community" was singular rather than plural.[50] The absence of parties meant that civic occasions such as Fourth of July celebrations would become rituals of unity rather than division. Thus public contests for office between members of the elite continued to create transient factions among the voters. This culture proved to be a transitional phase between the elite controlled world of the territorial period and the popular democratic world of the nineteenth century.

The high point of this transitional phase was the 1801 gubernatorial race, an innocuous campaign in which Sevier was constitutionally obligated to retire because he had served three consecutive terms. His removal from political affairs lit a spark under Andrew Jackson, who believed he could strengthen his own statewide network by consolidating his eastern and western supporters behind a popular replacement. Thus he pulled together disparate former protégés of William Blount—including John Overton in West Tennessee and Blount's half brother Willie, Joseph McMinn, and Hugh Lawson White in the East. As a block they threw their political capital behind Archibald Roane. Roane, an eastern figure with strong ties to the Western District, also received Sevier's blessing, which again points to the elusive and short-lived nature of early political coalitions in Tennessee. He ran unopposed and received the entire 8,438 votes cast.[51] With such firm support both from the West and East, and with Jackson and Sevier maintaining a solid professional relationship, it seemed that the 1801 *Tennessee Gazette* announcement of a profound reduction in "the tide of political controversy" was a harbinger of a new level of regional cooperation.[52]

Jackson would soon alter the dynamics, however, and provide a fresh opportunity for the state's leaders to divide into temporary, personality-driven factions. In 1802 Jackson felt that his service to Blount and Sevier, combined with his commitment to Roane, had firmly established him as a substantial leader in Tennessee. He thus made himself available for the highly esteemed and recently vacated position of major general of the militia.[53] This move pitted him against Sevier, who felt he was the natural military leader of the state by virtue of his Revolutionary War and territorial service and by 1802 was so popular that his election seemed like a fait accompli. Surprisingly, however, the race ended in a tie, which meant that Governor Roane was constitutionally bound to cast the deciding vote. With little hesitation he gave the post to his friend and ally, Judge Jackson. To Sevier and his supporters such an outcome smacked of corruption, and they immediately began to lay the groundwork for the "Nolichucky Warrior" to restore the integrity of Tennessee's political institutions by running him once again for the governorship.

What they did not realize was that Jackson and Roane anticipated this move and had dredged up incriminating letters, falsified land books, and suspect North Carolina land grants that connected Sevier to the old Glasgow conspiracy.[54] Just as Sevier's coalition began to work toward the 1803 gubernatorial race, the new major general "presented" these materials to Governor Roane. Then he publicly proclaimed his incredulity at such scandalous behavior. "Is it possible," Jackson wrote the editor of the *Tennessee Gazette,* "that any man can believe John Sevier so ignorant as not to know that altering a grant agreeably to his request, so as to make it speak a lye, was a crime of the highest nature? No honest man, attached to private character and honest to the interest and respectability of this country, who is informed of the charges against Gen. Sevier will vote for him."[55] Jackson/Roane supporter John Carter went further by publicly declaring his desire to "prevent a character, charged with crimes of a deep dye, from ascending to the executive chair; an event which would wound the character of the State and reflect disgrace upon every good citizen in it."[56]

Shocked that their opponents had resorted to the old land conspiracy, Sevier's supporters responded by labeling the disclosure the quintessential example of political dishonesty. "Mr. Roane," it was declared, "published the falsehoods against General Sevier, with an intention to destroy his character, prevent his election, and to build his own greatness on the ruin and downfall of his rival."[57]

What is clear from such rhetoric is that evidence either of a tainted militia election or of land fraud was not as important as the public perception that one's opposition lacked integrity, a potentially damning charge in a culture where one's claim to power hinged upon the successful public defense of honor and political acceptability.[58] And in this case, as Jackson ally Arthur Campbell noted, the "exertions of the opposition party" in East Tennessee were so extensive that Jackson's and Roane's machinations were overcome. In the first hotly contested election in Tennessee's history, the number of votes spiked and the more populous Eastern District banded together to elect Sevier by a count of 7,733 to 5,219.[59] His vindication was strong enough that when Jackson men subsequently sent the Glasgow material to the Tennessee legislature, there were enough pro-Sevier legislators to ensure exoneration. As a block, they then retaliated by bringing an impeachment charge against Jackson associate Judge David Campbell—a vehicle through which both to keep Jackson's and his allies' questionable character in the public realm and to deliver a warning to Jackson's men to end their anti-Sevier crusade.

Amid this confrontational atmosphere both Jackson and Sevier grew convinced that the other was engaged in a dishonorable vendetta. Their convictions nearly culminated in a trip to the dueling ground. Fortunately, the affair petered out before anyone was physically wounded. After several letter exchanges the two men simply could not agree to an acceptable place for the duel (Jackson wanted a spot near Knoxville, Sevier preferred going out of state), and Sevier decided that he had had enough.[60] Having pointed out to Jackson that "the whole tenor of your great readiness is intended for nothing more than a cowardly evasion," he made it clear that he would accept no additional communications.[61] Short of formal notification of a date and acceptable dueling ground, the matter was finished for Sevier, although Jackson tried one last time to induce a confrontation by assaulting Sevier on October 16, 1803, on a road outside Knoxville. During the attack the governor hid behind a tree while the judge drew his pistol. Cooler-headed intermediaries finally managed to broker a tenuous cease-fire.[62] No other exchange of letters took place, and neither man attempted to reinitiate the code duello.

Perhaps no other event so effectively shows the nature of partisanship and political contests in early national Tennessee. Drawing initially from a struggle over the position of major general, the 1803 Sevier-Jackson dispute quickly devolved into a circus wherein "factional" leaders publicly promoted themselves and their allies at the expense of their enemies.[63] And it soon became clear that Jackson stood as the loser in the battle for public absolution. Having been humiliated by the combination of the dismissal of the Glasgow conspiracy, Roane's electoral defeat, and the impeachment of his friend David Campbell, the judge simply could not maintain the public esteem he once had claimed. Perhaps an anonymous writer to the *Knoxville Gazette* best illuminated Jackson's public predicament when he noted that "the citizens of Tennessee . . . by their free suffrage have chosen to invest power in hands they like much better; and such is the reason for all this great noise and bussle, and is the only cause the public tranquility is so much agitated and disturbed."[64]

Sevier made the loss of power even worse. To add salt to what must have been already painful wounds, he divided the militia into two districts, thereby watering down Jackson's position of major general. No doubt remembering how military victory over the Cherokees had restored his own political standing after the Franklin fiasco,[65] he shortly thereafter rebuffed Jackson by giving mostly East Tennessee militia companies the honor of supporting the United States during the transfer of Louisiana from France and Spain—despite the shorter distance between that territory and Middle Tennessee and the obvious fact that Jackson was first in line to serve.[66] Once Sevier achieved the upper hand in the quest for public vindication, Jackson could do little to maintain his position as a viable statewide figure.[67]

The Sevier-Jackson political feuds show that the *Tennessee Gazette* had been a bit hasty in its 1801 encomium to harmony.[68] But once these affairs concluded the lines demarcating factions and feuds became blurry at best.[69] After Jackson retired from the scene they even seemed to disappear. Sevier offered no resistance to pro-Jackson Willie Blount's succession to the governor's chair, for example, despite his role in the Glasgow conspiracy campaign of 1803.[70] Moreover, the former governor and his supporters maintained continual and friendly relations with some of Jackson's closest allies, up to and including his in-laws the Donelsons.[71] Sevier even had John Overton, one of Jackson's closest confidantes and a replacement as head of the "faction," on legal retainer.[72]

A more solid case for divisions based on geography rests on the fact that day-to-day political questions revolved around an East-versus-West dialectic as early as 1795, when forward-looking Middle District leaders looked to form a state of their own. Thenceforth both eastern and western leaders were cognizant of Middle Tennessee's unlimited potential and often would vote in sectional blocks regarding issues of economic and cultural development. But in the early years of statehood even these divisions were more fluid than the geographical rhetoric sometimes indicated. Both Cumberland and eastern leaders maintained carefully groomed connections in the other region so as to provide the extra support necessary to ensure victory in any given contest. They also shared access to state and federal political institutions.[73]

Throughout these years, in short, there was little to demarcate clear factions within the leadership, whether considered geographically or along the Jackson-Sevier fault line. Until ideological divisions could establish competing wings within Jefferson's coalition, "parties" and "factions" rose according to personality clashes and disappeared as quickly as they came.[74]

By the early nineteenth century white Tennesseans fully accepted that they were the arbiters of power. Although they remained at the top of the political culture, the elite now had to negotiate their authority through the rituals of the public sphere.[75] In an 1807 letter to the *Impartial Review and Cumberland Repository*, "A Farmer" best reflected this new reality when he urged Tennesseans "not to circumscribe the field of choice by illiberal attachments to your town, or to your local or professional interests or opinions; you will, with true republican ingeniousness, cast your eyes over our widely extended district, and honor that candidate who [possesses] most of the essential qualities."[76] Only two years later, in a letter to the *Carthage Gazette*, "A Friend of the People" went even further. Concerned with the consequences of the embargo upon the debtor class, he wrote, "People of Tennessee! now is the trying time to look to your candidates for future elections; now is the time to probe their principles to the bottom; if you see them stemming the torrent of overbearing aristocracy and foul avarice, if you see them boldly defending your rights in public meetings, if you see them animating the weak and resisting the strong—then my friends remember them on the day of the election."[77]

Tennesseans increasingly followed this advice, requesting that candidates make clear the issues to which they would devote their attention. In 1809, for example, citizens of Smith County demanded that candidates for

Congress address their views on the embargo, non-intercourse, reformation of the military establishment, and disposal of public lands.[78] Two years later, "A Citizen of the 3d Circuit" published a request that "those who have, or may hereafter declare themselves candidates [for the legislature] declare their sentiments and publish them in the *Carthage Gazette*."[79]

Politicians saw the propriety of heeding these demands for greater openness. When in 1807 Robert Foster announced his bid for reelection to Congress, he did so with a declaration of his intent to oppose federal land laws and alter the tax structure on warrants.[80] In 1809 Smith County candidate Thomas Harris specifically published a platform that revolved around his support for reforming the judiciary to make it less oppressive for ordinary folk.[81] Later that year, newly elected Representative Harris noted that although he had intended to vote against a debtor relief bill, such a large "number of communications by letter, from different parts of the district" had come to his office that he felt "constrained to conform agreeably to the will, of what I conceived to be a large majority of the people whom I had the honor of representing."[82] When politicians failed to heed their constituents' concerns, or when they failed to make the public aware of their positions, they were accordingly castigated. "Pray, Mr. Printer, ought our representatives to represent themselves or their constituents," wrote "A Free Citizen of Smith County" in 1811? "If their constituents, surely they ought to be acquainted with their political sentiments, and what medium so convenient as a free press?"[83]

Embedded within these lively exchanges were critical demographic and economic issues that only recently had exploded onto the stage. Because of this explosion, the brief period of temporary, personality-driven factions gave way to more substantive issues-based electioneering. Nowhere was this more apparent than in Middle Tennessee, which grew from 11,500 residents when John Adams was elected president to over 32,000 by Jefferson's inauguration. Over the next fifteen years the Cumberland District would experience remarkable growth, and as more people entered the region, the once limited territorial economy evolved into one that included cotton and tobacco planting and a turn toward the more systematic use of credit networks.[84] Because of this growth the Cumberland River became a highway for trade goods, which in turn created a mercantile class that relied upon the produce of local cotton and tobacco farmers to perpetuate the increasingly vibrant economy.

The new political culture became entrenched around this stunning economic and demographic growth. Indeed, the ordinary folk who had found a new political niche faced a new economic situation: Expansive growth meant that landownership was more precarious and that "more people could fail owing greater sums of money to larger numbers of creditors than had been possible" in the insular economy of the territorial period.[85] Land loss and high levels of debt were particularly troublesome when the economy contracted, as it would in 1808 and 1819, and led many people to want more control in the commercial revolution.

The market, in short, may have been liberating for everyone who chose to get involved in it, but its reliance on extensive credit networks potentially put everyone in the region in a bind. The end result was that Middle Tennessee's economic dynamism divided the people and moved the political realm into subtle but identifiable divisions over the meaning of progress. Tennesseans once had stood unified in their desire to achieve stability and security. Now they faced an increasingly significant debate over the future of the regional economy.

Chapter 4

Economy, Demography, and Diversification, 1796–1815

In February 1801, in a letter to the *Tennessee Gazette,* "A" wrote that "of all the objects worthy of [Middle Tennessee's] attention, none more forcibly present themselves, than the present state of our commerce and agriculture. Those ought to be considered as primary objects of civil polity."[1] Only a year later French traveler François André Michaux reinforced this opinion. He noted that the region was so inaccessible that merchants to the north

> have still to make a passage [down the Ohio River] of two hundred and nineteen miles to reach the mouth of the river Cumberland, and a hundred and eighty miles to arrive at Nashevhille [sic], which, in the whole, comprises a space of one thousand five hundred and twenty-one miles from Philadelphia, of which twelve hundred are by water. Some merchants get their goods also from New Orleans, whence the boats go up the Mississippi, the Ohio, and the Cumberland. This last distance is about twelve hundred and forty three miles.[2]

The implication was clear: Middle Tennessee's isolation and recent Indian troubles had left the region economically stagnant and in need of improvement.

Yet such a backward image of the Cumberland basin was in the process of receding. Although in 1800 Middle Tennessee stood at the fringe of white civilization, by 1812 it had embraced a complex market economy that revolved around land speculation and the production of short-staple cotton and tobacco.[3] These activities made the Cumberland River a highway for trade goods, which in turn helped establish a mercantile class that used local farmers' produce to connect with national and international markets.

In conjunction with unprecedented demographic growth, this boom effectively transformed Middle Tennessee. Where once the region held small numbers of yeomen settlers, squatters, and land speculators, now there was a diverse economic population that included merchants, planters, and intraregional commercial interests.[4] These latter groups tended to coalesce around an expansive interpretation of progress, and together they began the process of refinement that they hoped would transform what was still a frontier.

Ordinary folk would find as much concern as promise in such an economic environment. Scholars have been clear in their contention that southwestern settlers pursued markets for cash crops—far more so, in fact, than their counterparts in the northwest.[5] Yet if most early Tennesseans embraced the market, debt stemming from farm start-up costs, land payments and taxes, and merchant credit also left them concerned about the effects of market contraction.[6]

In effect, white Tennesseans in the early nineteenth century divided over how best to define economic "progress." On the one hand, certain entrepreneurially minded people began to seek out new economic trends, including government funding for internal improvements, the embrace of technological innovation, and a push for urban development (with concomitant commitments to refinement and reform). On the other hand, many began to see that the economy needed tighter control. This was not a view of the world imbued with nostalgia for a lost, idyllic age. To the contrary, it embraced economic development and accepted the idea of individual pursuit of gain—as long as land could be secured and debt could be kept from spiraling out of control.

This increasingly complex debate took place amid the expansion of the institution of slavery. It was during this period that slavery became an essential part of Middle Tennessee's social and cultural fabric. Understanding its role, as well as the ambiguous nature of life for Tennessee's free black population, is critical to understanding economic development in the Volunteer State.

Perhaps the most curious aspect of slavery in early national Middle Tennessee is that it did not inhibit planters' and merchants' commitment to entrepreneurial innovation. To the contrary, the cotton and tobacco trades provided a boost to those maintaining more expansive definitions of progress. When dramatically higher land values increased planters' desires for internal improvements (to attain easier access to markets), entrepreneurs found that plantation agriculture helped place them on an irrevocable path toward dynamic economic expansion. Until faced with political crises such as the Missouri question of 1819 or the emergence of a homegrown antislavery movement, Tennesseans did not see that slavery inhibited progress. Thus it did not directly inject itself into the emerging debate over its definition.[7]

In short, in only eighteen years a vibrant commercial (albeit slave) society took shape on the Tennessee frontier. In the process the white population laid the foundations for an ideological division over the meaning of progress. This debate would define the parameters of Middle Tennessee's economic, political, and social transformation from frontier to southern community.

Land and Demographic Change

Isolation and the constant threat of Indian assault ensured that prior to 1796 the Cumberland economy would remain largely self-contained. The land certainly offered a wealth of possibility, but the shortage of labor, a lack of equipment sufficient to maximize efficiency, and the distance from markets made life for settlers in the Mero District (what eventually would become Middle Tennessee) difficult at best.[8] Even the acquisition of basic supplies was complicated. Overland routes from Knoxville were dangerous because there were no suitable roads for the transport of large quantities of goods. Using the Tennessee River also presented extreme danger because of the threat of Indian assault and because of the difficulties of navigation near present-day Chattanooga and the Muscle Shoals. Slightly easier but rather expensive was the Ohio–to–Cumberland River route, which took supplies to Nashville from Louisville, Kentucky, and Pittsburgh, Pennsylvania.[9]

A critical lack of population further inhibited meaningful market growth. Between 1790 and 1796 the Territory South of the River Ohio's population grew by 116.5 percent, while the population per square mile doubled from .9 to 1.8.[10] Differentiating between East and West, however, reveals a startling contrast. Even though the territory grew from approximately 33,000 to 77,262, Middle Tennessee rose from 7,000 to only 11,000.[11] The utter lack of a trading currency made things worse and meant that whatever market structures existed tended toward barter and store credit. In effect, local merchants such as Lardner Clark and young David Allison acted as both bank and trader for lead, gunpowder, farm equipment, and other essential commodities.[12]

Statehood and the end of the Indian wars provided the opening through which Middle Tennessee could begin to grow.[13] Almost overnight the population rose dramatically. Between 1796 and 1800 the Cumberland District grew from 11,000 to 32,183, an increase of approximately 300 percent.[14] Ten years later the population stood at 160,360, 500 percent larger than the 1800 level. By 1820 the region would grow to 292,590.[15]

To those already in Middle Tennessee, the population explosion was immediately apparent. As early as 1799, for example, Judge David Campbell petitioned the legislature to lengthen court sessions and reduce the seemingly "insurmountable delays" caused by a flood of new cases.[16] A letter from Joseph Young to his grandfather in North Carolina brought immigration further into focus. From Sumner County he lamented that an 1802 "wet spring" had limited his corn and tobacco yield, while worms had decimated his cotton. He was worried that he would not have enough money to buy corn on the market and hoped it would not "be such a price this year as it was last, tho the reason was that so many new cummers [sic] came in last fall and spring that it made Corn a Dollar a Bushell and not to be had at that."[17] In 1805 Rutherford County up-and-comer Hugh Robison pointed out, "Our Country is settling fast, and Reducing the Cane Breakes, into fruitful fields—and the howling wilderness is become a populous Country." Continuing, he noted, "When we Came to Overall's fork of Stones River we had but one Neighbour nearer than five or six miles; And now there is twenty two famileys living in the Distance of two miles from our house, some of them on land of their own and some on Leace."[18]

Robison's observation indicated that land was critically important. Its availability for migrating up-and-comers such as he instilled an enormous sense of possibility.[19] Virginian Arthur Lee Campbell, for example, noted that when he "crost Cumberland the scene was a large and rich level and beatiful country."[20] James Norman Smith recalled a similar landscape upon his arrival from North Carolina. When he, his family, and a sizable number of slaves "crossed the Cumberland River—near the mouth of the Caney Fork," he noted, they "got into very rich lands, well cultivated and many farms on the road."[21] Hugh Robison sheds more light on this sense of promise as well as an emerging impulse toward upward mobility. In 1802 he wrote to his uncle in North Carolina, "The land here is exceedingly good and appairs [sic] promising to the Industrious farmar."[22] Thomas Jefferson would have agreed. In 1796 he wrote John Garland Jefferson that "Tanissee is a good field for a man of industry, integrity and talents: and it is a good country to lay out advantageously the profits of business."[23] For those willing to get ahead, in other words, the region's rich land and business opportunities offered the promise of a new, financially secure life.

Yet people like Robison were lucky. Already a landowner in 1802, he had explicitly chosen not to buy more land because he was "not satisfied what part of this Extensive Country to live in—nor I have not yet met with a suitable opportunity of purchasing to my satisfaction."[24] The vast majority of migrants found land harder to come by, however. And for every Hugh Robison who could afford to wait for the right purchase, there were hundreds of poorer immigrants who were forced into tenancy or squatting.[25]

A land system that often undercut legitimate claims lay at the heart of the problem. When combined with formidable farming start-up costs, it forced large levels of debt upon many immigrants. The overwhelming majority of land problems drew from twenty-plus years of turmoil regarding fraudulent purchases, military claims, and speculation. As early as the "Land Grab" of 1783, surveyors had blurred boundaries, overlapped claims, and "padded" legitimate ones so that more land was given than appeared in the records.[26] As in Kentucky, overlapping grants posed the most common dilemma, as they led to endless lawsuits and caused underfunded litigants to sell or face expulsion.[27] Having not received clear title to 150 acres in Davidson County, for example, surveyor Frederick Stump in 1792 requested that his former employer, John Overton, help him clear up the mess. "I have risqued my life in doing the business I engaged for you," wrote Stump. He demanded action because "others are now Laying warrants on the Land from a presumption I shall not obtain a right."[28]

The warrants themselves made things worse, as North Carolinian Daniel Dunham's case made clear. Issued in 1788, Dunham's claim pointed to land "on the North fork of Thompsons Creek about two miles from the Head. Beginning about half a mile from Spring, Turning from thence down the Creek on both sides and to include the Spring at the Tree."[29] Overlaps and counterclaims were the natural result of such confusing descriptions. Deforestation and other ecological changes that altered boundary markers only enhanced the problems.[30]

Land issues continued well into the nineteenth century. In 1806 Tennessee, North Carolina, and the federal government settled a longstanding feud over Revolutionary-era warrants, state prerogatives, and Indian boundaries. Although North Carolina veterans maintained the right to make claims in the old military district, thenceforth they could only do so through the Tennessee land office. The final part of the compromise gave the federal government control over the western portion of the state, including those lands still within the Chickasaw boundaries. A few North Carolina warrants aside, this land became known as the congressional reservation, and would remain in federal hands until Tennessee speculators again demanded freedom to purchase.[31]

This settlement minimized the remaining Cherokee presence in Middle Tennessee and opened large areas of land to sale. Speculators quickly went to work. Nashville commissioner William Anderson, for example, wrote to surveyor John Coffee, "People prepared as we are will be the only persons who can locate. We will have command of all the warrants that we wish for and must get rich."[32] In 1807 Tennessee congressman George Washington Campbell sent to Treasury Secretary Albert Gallatin two warrants worth a thousand acres each and requested Gallatin's help in settling a Richland Creek tract belonging to him and William Polk of North Carolina "as soon as possible." He also let Gallatin in on his plan to "remove" warrants—or to relocate an already marked warrant to a different piece of land. In so doing, they removed others who might have had more recent claims, and they were quick to demand payment from squatters. Since "direct authority by act of assembly to remove them, does not seem to exist," it was only logical to Campbell that they undertake the exercise.[33]

No wonder so many land-hungry immigrants saw speculators as "avaricious, who like the vulture of Prometheus are gnawing at the vitals of their country."³⁴ For "Manlius" the issue was simple. Speculators, he wrote, "endeavor to make as many dependent on their favor as possible, by which means their influence becomes the more irresistible and dangerous."³⁵ Even wealthier settlers found themselves swindled. Upon their 1807 arrival from North Carolina, James Norman Smith recalled that some of his father's land had "the Title contested by a Gentleman who lived in the Neighborhood of Nashville."³⁶ A few years later they learned that "it was lost in a lawsuit" to what he termed the "clever" gentleman.³⁷ In 1807 Robert Thompson pointed to a 2,360-acre tract recently "entered in the name of John Ford" and remarked that he had a "warranted deed this seventeen or eighteen years for one thousand acres out of the tract." He also warned, "In order that future trouble may be prevented, I take this method to forwarn all sheriffs from selling the above named thousand acres, and all persons from buying the same."³⁸

Perhaps "A" hit the nail most squarely on the head. Although speaking of the Natchez District in a period when out-migration threatened to undermine Middle Tennessee's economic promise, "A" nevertheless spoke a universal truth concerning land in his part of the country. The issue, he pointed out, was that "multiplied litigations pervade the mass of land titles, owing to the various changes and revolutions the country has undergone, whether by cession or by conquest. Those comprehend Indian, French, English, Spanish and American proprietors, all producing nothing but a scene of controversial claims that must take a series of years to render even the successful ones permanent."³⁹

Squatters made the situation even more confusing. In 1787 approximately 87 percent of the population either squatted or were tenants.⁴⁰ By the early nineteenth century it had become particularly prevalent, when the flood of immigration ensured that poor farmers would need land to engage in the increasingly fast-paced economy. Although tolerated in an era when warm bodies were needed to protect against Indian assault, by the early nineteenth century squatters were coming under fire. An 1806 petition from Montgomery and Robertson Counties made this point clear. Thirty-one landowners that year appealed to the legislature for a law to "authorize any Person that have become a purchaser or may hereafter become a purchaser to be at full liberty to remove [squatters], whether the oldest or youngest."⁴¹ More powerful owners, such as Congressman

George Washington Campbell, meanwhile, spent years attempting to remove them through the avenue of the U.S. circuit courts.[42] And in 1809 Governor Willie Blount actively campaigned to regularize payments on state lands to keep squatters from undermining state support for colleges and academies.[43]

Squatters would combat moves such as these by making noticeable improvements on the land and by pointing to longstanding preemption laws.[44] In an 1806 petition, for example, fifty-two signatories asked for relief from speculators because of "the great uncertainty hitherto Existing relative to obtaining Titles to Land many Citizens have purchased and Settled under Spurious Tittles and more have Settled and made Considerable Improvements on land where no Title have Existed."[45] Those who were unsuccessful in protecting their preemption rights either purchased land on credit or were removed by local government institutions.[46] Faced with such an intimidating situation, most squatters became tenants, moved into remaining Indian territory (which the state encouraged), or went farther west.

Those who stayed behind did so because they could procure land and engage the emerging market economy. Although they kept a system of noncommercial exchange between households, most Tennesseans made farming a "lucrative enterprise" through which to obtain the money to pay taxes, settle debt stemming from land, and purchase an increasing array of market commodities.[47] Given the massive in- and out-migration of the period, those who were interested in subsistence lifestyles probably went west rather than settling in Middle Tennessee.[48]

Cotton and Tobacco

If settled Tennesseans embraced market activity, many also grew concerned that debt stemming from land purchase and market interaction might give creditors control over local economic behavior.[49] Indeed, by the early nineteenth century Middle Tennessee had created and enlarged upon such a pattern of debt that some scholars have found it "hard to believe that the proportion of indebtedness was as high in the whole of the young United States as in the small world of the Cumberland."[50]

North Carolina native William Coghlan's experience is a brilliant example of what could happen to common settlers in early national Middle Tennessee. In 1811 he wrote former president Jefferson that he had arrived in Columbia "about Eighteen months ago together with another man with the following property between us, Viz. two Stills a wagon & four indifferent horses a Military land warrant for 640 acres of land, & no money." Neither man could get the warrant located because of securities required for surveyors to initiate their work, and after some time they were "compelled to sell it for two Shillings [per] acre." Thereafter Coghlan's colleague returned to North Carolina. Coghlan could not, "on account of some debts I contracted for provisions a few cows &C: to support my Family & am now indebted about $120 which I am unable to pay & am at the eve of loosing every little thing I possess & seeing my poor family perrish if not relieved." Continuing, he noted:

> If I could sell what little I have at near its Value I could pay without troubling your Excellency or selling my still the only support of my poor family money is so scarce here that nothing will sell for money & nothing will satisfie my creditors but money, I offered them property it wont do, I offered to pledge as security for $100 for one year six cows & calves two horses forty hogs two beds & some little articles of household furniture all worth at least $200 & twenty [per] Cent. intrest but could not obtain a loan unless I gave thirty [per] Ct.[51]

Land uncertainty is at the heart of Coghlan's tale of woe, as it was for hundreds of others during this period. But another, interrelated commodity was an equally important part of a widespread debt problem: short-staple cotton. Increasingly, local farmers relied upon specialized merchants in Nashville, who in turn looked to national and international markets in order to value crop yields. This widened market brought with it an expansive economic phenomenon: the assignability of debt, which made promissory notes to local merchants part of a wider circulation. Assignability allowed Nashville's exporters to pay distant creditors with local farmers' promissory notes. These creditors in turn used the notes eventually to demand payment from local farmers, a process that made the economy both more efficient and more impersonal. The new market meant that many republican yeomen would espouse the ideal of independence long after it had lost its economic meaning.

Cumberland settlers had grown modest amounts of cotton since their arrival in 1780, and more than one observer had noted the possibility for a prosperous commodity. In 1789, for example, Barthelemi Tardiveau wrote from Kentucky, "Our climate is not favorable to [cotton growth]; and we shall always be obliged to get it from Cumberland; the expense of transporting it overland on horseback is at the present time only twopence a pound: in the future it will be less; and still less by water."[52] Three years later there was enough cropped that John Hague advertised in the *Knoxville Gazette* his desire to open a "Cotton Manufactory in Cumberland."[53] By 1799 Michaux was reporting that the frontier was "united by commercial interests, of which cotton is the basis, and the Ohio the tie of communication, the results of which give a high degree of prosperity to this part of Tennessee, and insure its inhabitants a signal advantage over those of the Ohio and Kentucky."[54]

By the early years of the nineteenth century the crop had become Middle Tennessee's major agricultural commodity. According to Hugh Robison, it was even "the principal article of Merchandize, and the only crop that the farmar can raise money from."[55] Its position as the "only" profitable crop was an exaggeration. Nevertheless, as Thomas Jefferson put it in 1810, Tennesseans truly benefited because "of the rich production of cotton for their staple."[56] Locals understood their advantage, too. As Michaux observed, new immigrants who could attain land almost invariably made it their primary crop by their third year in residence.[57]

Over the next few years national and international demand for cotton rose precipitously, and along with it grew Middle Tennessee's supply.[58] Whereas in 1796 there was little meaningful production, by the early nineteenth century farmers were producing over one million pounds in a single year.[59] By 1803 cotton held such potential that the legislature passed a law stating, "It is expedient that the State of Tennessee do purchase the patent right to the making, using and vending the said new invention of a machine for cleaning of cotton from the seeds, commonly called a saw gin." They also levied a tax of thirty-seven and a half cents on all extant gins to pay for the purchase.[60] Within another two years the yield was high enough that broker John Baird could successfully advertise a Baltimore commission to buy cotton in the amount of "10 or 15,000 dollars, say from 70 to 100,000 wt."⁶¹ Similarly, A. Foster announced in 1806 that he was authorized "by a respectable Mercantile House in New Orleans to purchase one thousand bales of cotton."⁶²

As Baird and Foster intimated, Middle Tennessee cotton received attention from every major market in the United States. Of these, location and high prices made New Orleans the most important. After the Treaty of San Lorenzo in 1795, and particularly after the Louisiana Purchase in 1803, the market in New Orleans became the gateway for expediting Tennessee produce "to New York and Philadelphia, [and] direct to Europe."⁶³ As early as 1800 New Orleans broker H. Denison urged Nashvillian John Hillsman immediately to ship his supply because cotton stood at "27 Dolls, [although] we very soon expect it to fall from that price."⁶⁴ Only a year later the editor of the *Tennessee Gazette* reported prices of $25.00 to $26½ per hundredweight and proclaimed his satisfaction that the "trade of the Western country is daily increasing."⁶⁵ Although prices over the next few years occasionally went much higher, by 1804 Tennessee cotton had stabilized at $15.00 to $17.00 per hundredweight.⁶⁶

Even volatility across the Atlantic could not significantly diminish production. Because international markets offered rates around "15½ to 15¼" per hundredweight, foreign political affairs and commodity prices also were subjects of significant interest.⁶⁷ And with the ongoing Napoleonic wars shifting into high gear, many feared grave effects upon local trade. Certainly the editor of the *Impartial Review* feared as much. In 1808 he wrote that European conflicts had destabilized the market, hastened President Jefferson's embargo, and generally threatened to undermine Middle Tennessee's growing economy.⁶⁸ Private brokers and consignment agents watched the scene equally closely. Gen. James Winchester, for example, had his Nashville and New Orleans contacts give him consistent updates on the cotton market as global events grew unstable.⁶⁹

Although international prices would drop off after 1808, domestic quotes for first-rate cotton remained in the fifteen-dollar range.⁷⁰ Even deliberate attempts to limit prices proved ineffective. In November 1807 "A Cotton Planter" protested that local merchants had attempted to "fix the price of Cotton at 12 dollars loose, and 14 baled," despite the fact that the previous August they had offered as much as eighteen dollars for a "superior quality" product.[71] Such negative publicity ended any deliberate collusion on the part of Nashville's brokers.[72] All told, by 1811 output rose to three million pounds.[73]

Middle Tennessee entrepreneurs found that more than raw cotton could turn a profit. Nashvillian Willoughby Williams remembered that in 1809 George Poyzer ran a successful spinning manufactory.[74] The 1810 census showed three other public cotton manufacturers that, combined with Poyzer's, made ninety-five hundred dollars. Even larger revenue awaited those willing to spin at home for profit. In 1810 Middle Tennesseans produced 1,790,514 yards of cotton cloth for sale, which census takers estimated at nine hundred thousand dollars in value.[75]

Tobacco stood alongside cotton as a significant commodity for the commercially inclined Middle Tennessee farmer. Tobacco in the 1780s had provided the Cumberland basin with its first real commercial crop.[76] And with the end of the Indian wars in 1796, Cumberland settlers began to grow the weed at an astonishing rate. So quickly, in fact, that within a year the legislature authorized Davidson County to build "public warehouses, appoint inspectors, regulate salaries and levy an annual tax on tobacco."[77] By 1799 the volume of trade had grown to the point that residents in upper Davidson County and lower Sumner County asked the legislature to build a more centrally located warehouse for storage.[78] They also helped establish the village of Clarksville as a regional market center.[79]

Even as cotton became the primary focus of economic growth, counties with inferior soil remained enmeshed in the tobacco trade. In 1806 Sumner County petitioners argued that they dealt with such volume that it "renders it highly necessary that Publick Scales and weights should be procured for the purpose of ascertaining with accuracy the weight of all Tobacco inspected [because] the inspectors being annually appointed cannot reasonably be expected [to] furnish scales and weights at their own private expense."[80] And although they never matched the profits attained by cotton planters, tobacco farmers nevertheless saw their income grow. Between 1801 and 1806, for example, the New Orleans market went as high as $5.50 per hundredweight, although prices generally stayed between $5.00 and $3.50.[81] Although the Napoleonic conflicts led the price briefly to drop to $2.00 in 1807, it quickly rebounded and remained at or above $3.00. As late as 1811 growers received quotes of "$3–4."[82] By that point, the trade had become so lucrative that sixty-four Sumner County residents petitioned the legislature for a reformed system of inspection—it was too clumsy and inefficient and thus was hindering their profits.[83] After the War of 1812 men like Smith County resident David Burford would amass wealth through businesses designed to expedite the shipments of tobacco to Nashville and ultimately to European markets.[84]

Planters and Slavery

The burgeoning cotton and tobacco markets of the early nineteenth century gave wealthier Tennesseans the opportunity to expand into plantation agriculture. The arrival of plantations in turn ensured that slaves would become "the most valuable property in this country."[85] In 1800, 13,584 slaves lived in Tennessee, of which the Middle District maintained 8,074, or approximately 60 percent of the total slave population and 25 percent of the regional population.[86] Reflecting the growing importance of cotton and tobacco, the number of slaves grew to 35,000 by 1810, or 79 percent of all slaves and 22 percent of all Middle Tennesseans. By 1820 it had risen to approximately 67,000, or 84 percent of all slaves and 23 percent of Cumberland residents.[87] And by 1830, 141,603 slaves comprised 21 percent of the total population. Of these 97,174, or 69 percent, lived in Middle Tennessee. Given that 379,644 people resided in the region, it meant 26 percent were bondsmen (see pages 86–91).[88]

The wealthiest Tennesseans in this period established their fortunes in land speculation but eventually divided their attention between that and agriculture. While consolidating his plantation interests, for example, William Dickson took the lead among a group of high-profile Tennessee planters who speculated in what would become northern Alabama. Included in his group were William Anderson and John Coffee (both close associates of Andrew Jackson), James Jackson (who would become known for his bitter opposition to Old Hickory), and Edward Ward, who ran unsuccessfully for governor in the 1821 campaign. As a group they purchased for resale thousands of acres in what is now Madison County, Alabama.[89] In 1808, moreover, Andrew Jackson published his intention to survey West Tennessee claims filed by Stockley Donelson twenty years before.[90]

And so it would continue; Middle Tennessee planters would remain in the business well into the nineteenth century. Nevertheless, the gradual reduction of land available for speculation in the Cumberland meant that planting and large numbers of slaves would become a defining characteristic of the upper class.

The slave population had maintained a complex relationship with the white community since the territorial period. Slaves had come to the Cumberland District as early as 1779, when John Donelson and James Robertson began their trek from the eastern settlements. Along with them came the North Carolina slave code of 1741.[91] Given slavery's relative importance to the mother state's identity, it was not a surprise that the 1789 land cession demanded federal protection for the institution. When Congress accepted this condition, North Carolina law became the bedrock upon which slavery in Tennessee stood.

The Indian wars ensured that slavery in Mero District would operate in a slightly different manner than was provided for by the 1741 code. Population and the lack of viable holding cells meant that runaways who had been caught tended not to go to the public jail. Nor were they hired out wearing a collar emblazoned with *PG* (public gaol). And because of the need for mutual protection, few frontiersmen paid attention to the statute that made it illegal to arm slaves "upon any Pretence whatsoever."[92]

Yet a more relaxed interpretation of the law did not diminish the brutal nature of life for the early national slave. Perhaps the most obvious issue was that, like other areas in the Southwest, slaves routinely were given missions and tasks that placed them in close proximity to Indians.[93] Slave families, moreover, lost loved ones in auctions from the earliest moments. Historian Anita Goodstein has shown that almost all sales in Tennessee between 1784 and 1803 were of single slaves.[94] Although few ordinary white settlers engaged in buying and selling, the territory's leadership used the institution to their financial advantage. In 1792, for example, Governor William Blount diverted federal funds to purchase slaves in Maryland and sell them in the Cumberland District.[95] White Tennesseans also used slaves during this period as a form of cash and collateral, an activity that would continue well into the nineteenth century. As late as 1814 James Moore King left his children "$5–600, to be paid in Cash or Negroes."[96] At times, slaves even served as prizes in lotteries.[97]

These last two examples reflect that many Tennesseans viewed slaves as a commercial advantage and an unusually flexible form of property.[98] Certainly planter John Trimble thought so. In 1803 he complained to slave dealer Robert Whyte that the latter had sold him a useless product. "I wish you to send me another Negrow by the first of next month a greable to our contract," wrote Trimble. "Easter is of very litil Sarvas to me and has ben for some time past—You know that you promised to me that if Easter proved with child you would put another in her pleas. I don't want a Negrow to [?] or worse. I want one to Coock the chickin."[99]

A particularly cruel example of slave as commodity made its way to the legislature in 1809. In that year the state executed one of Edmond Blackman's slaves, and he argued in a legislative petition that "a leading principle in Government [is] that no man's property should be taken from him without his consent—and as it was for the public good, the said slave had been executed, he hopes your honorable body will take this particular case into consideration and also decide whether some general provision should not be made for those who may be alike unfortunate."[100] Blackman's request not only reflects a slave-as-commodity mentality but also shows an emerging public detachment to the plight of the black community. Said detachment was facilitated by the media. In 1807, for example, the *Impartial Review* reported a tragedy that an anonymous author saw fit to end on a flippant note: "On the 16th [of February 1807] an unfortunate accident took place in Sumner County. The powder mill of Mr. Isaac Pierce, containing three hundredweight of powder and other articles, was blown up. A Negro man, who was at work in the house, was also blown up, which put an immediate end to his existence."[101]

If the slave community was increasingly viewed in terms of detached commoditization, their urban experience indicates that for a time many of them were able to maintain a level of autonomy.[102] To be sure, white governing officials did what they could to restrict slave life in Nashville. In 1802 merchants faced fifty-cent fines for trading with slaves without permits from their masters. Residents, meanwhile, were charged one dollar for allowing an assemblage of African Americans after dark, while the town sergeant had standing orders to disassemble "riotous collections of Negroes." Finally, "to prevent slaves from rambling about the town after 10 O' Clock at night, [the town sergeant could] give them any number not exceeding 15 lashes well laid on with some lawful implement of correction."¹⁰³ In 1807 the city commission got even stricter. On the Fourth of July, ironically enough, the *Impartial Review* published that they would appoint "four fit and proper persons as patrollers" to serve three-month terms. They simultaneously prohibited the sale of liquor to slaves—a means of getting at the tippling houses of which white residents had complained since 1799.¹⁰⁴

The town also restricted slaves from hiring themselves out. In 1802 the city commission decreed that "no Negro slave shall be permitted to hire him or herself to any citizen of the Town either with or without their master's or mistresses permission." If they did so, the town sergeant was authorized to take them and auction their services for one month to the highest bidder.¹⁰⁵ Commissioners even made it clear that slaves were not to hire their time from their own masters.

Former slaves' testimonies after the Civil War indicated that these restrictions were not difficult to get around, however.¹⁰⁶ Neither did they stop slaves from selling goods and produce at religious revivals or at the local market, which in effect was another way of hiring their own time.¹⁰⁷ Certainly concerned owners saw it that way and were willing to advertise against the practice. "Notice," William Goodall published in the *Carthage Gazette*, for example, "I do hereby forewarn all persons from trading with any of my NEGROES without an order from myself, for I am determined to put the law in force against them."¹⁰⁸

Moreover, restrictions did not stop *masters* from hiring out their chattel. In May 1806 R. Winn of Nashville posted a request in the *Impartial Review* to hire "a NEGRO WOMAN until the first Friday of January next."¹⁰⁹ A year later Thomas Overton advertised that he had "Negroes of several descriptions, to hire, among which are sawyers, a blacksmith, stone mason & a segar maker."¹¹⁰ William B. Wood wrote to President James Madison that, given that the season for making a crop had passed in June 1811, he felt "it best to hire out our negroes and rent a House [in Nashville]." His profits were so large that he was able to travel around the South and look into purchasing land farther west in Mississippi.¹¹¹ That same year John Tate offered twenty dollars as a reward for a runaway slave who was "the property of Colonel William Roberson, and hired to the subscriber for the interest of four hundred and twenty dollars."¹¹² Even government institutions got in on the act. In 1803 Davidson County offered to lease the time of seventeen slaves to help their owners pay tax debt, and the city of Nashville by the 1820s owned as many as twenty slaves for municipal use.[113]

The process of hiring out created a rather ambiguous category for urban slaves. On the one hand, they certainly had more autonomy than the average field worker. To be able to control one's own time, and perhaps even retain a measure of wages, was a level of independence that few outside of town could have dreamed possible. On the other hand, as Nashville's ordinances made clear, slaves found absolute freedom elusive. What little they had could be rescinded at any time, and as Middle Tennessee became more "civilized," slaves' relative autonomy faced increasing and public contestation.

The free black population found itself in a similarly ambiguous position. Although minuscule in number, free blacks arrived in Middle Tennessee almost simultaneously with white settlers. And although they lacked all of the freedoms enjoyed by their white yeoman counterparts, free blacks nevertheless mingled with the white community. Nashvillian Jane Thomas wrote of their strange identity. "John Thomas was a colored barber," she noted, "and was a very prominent Negro. His oldest daughter married Graham, a barber. She had a big wedding, and invited all the prominent white people in town, and they all went. He was a very respectable, upright, humble Negro. Gen. Andrew Jackson attended the wedding, and McNairy danced the reel with the bride."[114] Similarly, Willoughby Williams remembered that by 1806 Black Bobb's Tavern was a resting place consistently frequented by local whites. Also known as Robert Rentfro, he had opened his pub in 1794 and had made enough of a profit that he purchased his freedom in 1803.[115] Whites also petitioned the legislature to allow free blacks of good standing such as Sherwood Bryan and Jacob Stone to prove debts owed them by white residents and stave off bankruptcy.[116]

The free black community further benefited from a loophole in the 1796 Constitution, which stipulated that any male freeholder could exercise the vote and participate in militia musters. Since race was not taken into consideration, many black Tennesseans took the initiative and asserted a fairly prominent position in regional affairs. Jetro Locklier was merely one such individual. Having arrived in Middle Tennessee in the late eighteenth century, by 1809 he had obtained his free papers and during the War of 1812 served under General Jackson at New Orleans.[117] Locklier's militia service was by no means an isolated occurrence. As late as 1825 ninety-six white militiamen from Rutherford County complained that the free black population had excessive influence over the county's company elections.[118]

Both slaves and free blacks found a voice within the confines of the region's proliferating churches.[119] The Wilson Creek Baptist Church, for example, provided open forums through which any member of the church, white or black, could query, be tried, or be expelled.[120] Similarly, the white and black congregation of the Mount Olivet Baptist Church put the following into its bylaws: "All Matters not Respecting Fellowship shall be decided by a majority vote *of the entire membership;* fellowship matters need a ⅔ vote."[121] Mill Creek Church allowed its African American members to testify, exhort, and even preach. In 1806 its members resolved "that the Black Brethren at the time of the Church's Society Meeting have, and enjoy, the same liberty of exercising public gifts as white members do have or enjoy."[122] According to nineteenth-century historian John McFerrin, by 1828 African Americans would come to represent three-quarters of the membership of Methodist churches in the Nashville area.[123]

Amid this ambiguous racial atmosphere, many ordinary Middle Tennesseans came to believe that owning slaves would make them more economically successful. John Shofner was a typical example. A small-time operator from Bedford County, Shofner owned five or six slaves whom he used to help maintain the farm's crops for market production. By the 1830s he had become both highly successful and a devoted Whig and proponent of entrepreneurial growth.[124] Most slave owners in Tennessee were like him: 1816 Davidson County tax lists show that the average owner held approximately three to four slaves. Bedford County census data from 1820 show a similar average.[125]

Shofner's example underscores that between 1790 and the 1820s, slavery tended to serve as a catalyst for entrepreneurial activity. Indeed, the cotton and tobacco trades provided a boost to those maintaining a more expansive definition of progress because sellers wanted easier passage to commercial markets. Dramatically higher land values enhanced planter's desires for internal improvements. So in effect, entrepreneurs found that plantation agriculture facilitated dynamic economic expansion.

A New Economic Order

The small but growing town of Nashville particularly benefited from the early expansion of the market economy. Although tiny, dirty, and subject to the violent and unpredictable nature of in- and out-migration, Nashville had an advantage over other Middle Tennessee villages: It served as the primary port along the Cumberland River, which put it in a position to benefit from the region's agricultural potential.[126] When cotton emerged as a viable commodity, progressive planters, lawyers, and merchants became boosters of that crop and of the small town. As early as 1801 "Cato," in a letter to the *Tennessee Gazette*, made clear that if Middle Tennesseans wanted to increase their wealth they would have to "sow less grain, raise more sheep, and cultivate the Cotton plant."[127] That same year several prominent residents of Nashville and Davidson County petitioned the legislature to grant a bounty of five hundred dollars to help underwrite a cotton manufactory then under construction.[128]

Meanwhile, a coalition of fourteen separate brokers, "being desirous of encouraging the production of Cotton, as well as allowing the highest prices that Foreign or Home Markets will justify," announced that they would "give for Merchantable gined Cotton, delivered at such gins as will best suit the convenience of the Planter & Merchant, FIFTEEN dollars per hundred for loose Cotton, and SEVENTEEN if baled & delivered."[129] By 1805 cotton output was high enough that boosters announced in the *Tennessee Gazette*, "Our Brethren of the East are now invited to leave their worn out Farms, and come and participate with us in the peaceable possession of this truly desirable cotton country."[130]

As to local promotion, as early as 1799 Nashville's commercial sector made it clear that they were "ever anxious to promote the advantages of the public by indeavoring to remove every obstruction within their County, that might impede a free intercourse, [and to] erect such Bridges over Water Courses as may allow a perfect thoroughfare to the town of Nashville."[131] Only two years later, when the city was only "four brick buildings, one, the public market, and three other small, one-story houses . . . built of cedar logs," local merchants pushed for (and received) "a law appointing commissioners with full powers to prevent incroachments on and keep in repair the streets &c. and furthermore to do every thing which may be necessary for the promotion and prosperity of said Town."[132]

Prime location, a heritage of market activity, and consistent promotion helped make Nashville a commercial center unlike any other in Middle Tennessee. By 1806 local merchants had become so diversified that some, such as J. H. Smith, could offer in the *Impartial Review and Cumberland Repository* bar iron, plows, hoes, axes, trace chains, clover seed, writing paper, bottled porter, twilled bags, tow cloth, cider, and salt.[133] By 1811 as many as twenty general and specialized merchants operated in the growing town, to say nothing of the multiple weaving and dying factories catering to the increasingly immense cotton output.[134]

Promotion of Nashville and the burgeoning cotton trade led Middle Tennessee into larger entrepreneurial efforts. Throughout this early period boosters demanded some level of state and federal aid in their quest to expand the regional economy. One of the first projects to which they turned was river navigation. The Cumberland River, they felt—and through it the Mississippi and Ohio Rivers—was the sine qua non for economic growth. So much so that the 1796 convention wrote the right of passage into the constitution as one that could not be conceded.[135]

Many early-nineteenth-century entrepreneurs believed that Congress was well suited to carry out riparian improvements. As early as 1799, Mero District petitioners demanded that the legislature ask Congress to fund a canal across the state of Tennessee. That way, the petitioners felt, it would become possible to have "water transportation for the Districts of Washington, Hamilton and Mero & also the State of Kentucky & the Territory North of the River Ohio."[136] More pointedly, "A Citizen of Mero District" wrote in 1807 of his hope for federal funding on behalf of the Muscle Shoals area of the Tennessee River. This part of what would become Alabama had been under the hopeful gaze of speculators and boosters at least since the 1770s. Now was the time to make a move, felt "A Citizen," because although "the general government alone are competent to make such regulations as are likely to ensure the object in view, [they may] accede to any propositions made on the part of this state, if our legislature should think proper to clothe our representatives with powers to treat upon that subject." Unfortunately, he noted, nothing had yet "transpired to warrant a belief that any measures are yet adopted to promote this desirable end."[137]

Another means of improving regional access and thus enhancing the growing market was to request federal aid for turnpikes. Understanding Bishop Francis Asbury's charge that Tennessee roads were "equal to any in the United States for badness," many boosters felt turnpikes would both better connect the Cumberland hinterland with the port in Nashville and help facilitate the growing livestock trade in Middle Tennessee.[138]

Their efforts ultimately led to roads all over the South and Southeast. In 1804, for example, A. Parker published a "Road Bill" that listed fares for travel to dozens of places in Virginia, Tennessee, Kentucky, and Washington, D.C.[139] That same year the legislature authorized "the executive of this state to contract for cutting and marking a road to Georgia, the measure [being] productive of many beneficial advantages to the citizens of this part of the state."[140] Another important enterprise was the creation of the Columbian Highway from Natchez to Nashville. Better known as the Natchez Trace, this highway expedited travel between Middle Tennessee and New Orleans and significantly enhanced the already burgeoning trade between the two locations. Similarly, in 1805 local leaders sought federal aid to open a "military road" connecting the growing town of Franklin with what they hoped would become an important port in Mobile.[141]

Most regional boosters, however, firmly believed that federal actions needed concomitant state efforts. At statehood urban entrepreneurs and cotton brokers used their growing political influence to have the legislature confer upon regional streams "communal" status.[142] Local residents could not make any riparian alterations unless they specifically could show that their improvements benefited the public. Lackluster petitions invariably failed; the legislature tended to approve only those with widespread and compelling interests (i.e., grain and cotton mills) that either would not block passageways or would provide locks.[143] By 1799 Nashville's commercial leaders had petitioned the legislature to improve river access to Mobile Bay via the Tennessee and Tombigbee Rivers.[144] In 1807, meanwhile, "A Citizen" called for the improvement of the Cumberland River, to be funded partially by state money and partially by the proceeds of land sales south of the Holston and French Broad Rivers.[145]

State aid for improvements nevertheless came at a slow pace, which many Middle Tennesseans found embarrassing. In 1809 the *Carthage Gazette* made it clear that lack of progress was cause for serious concern: "How disgraceful is it to the State of Tennessee that two or three streams which are small, compared to the hundreds of others that are bridged in other States, either of which might it is believed be bridged for 150 dollars, should so often impede the mail, & interrupt the progress of travelers."[146]

Continuing, the editor noted that the "United States have expended large sums on the Wilderness road to Natchez, and we observe by the last papers that 5,000 dollars more are about to be appropriated by Congress for the same purpose—and the State of Tennessee either from private cupidity or Public neglect will not cause two or three trifling bridges to be erected, which might be of immense service to the State and the nation."[147] And when nothing had come from the legislature regarding the 1799 petition to connect Mobile Bay with the Tennessee and Tombigbee Rivers, exasperated Smith County boosters wrote to the legislature to request "the interposition of the general government in removing the difficulty and embarrassments which at present obstruct a free communication with the Ocean, by Way of the Tombigbee and the Mobile." A year later Governor Willie Blount agreed, and shortly thereafter Representative John Pope introduced the measure in Congress.[148]

Many entrepreneurs also looked into private forms of capital for expansion, and their quest eventually turned into the first bank in the state of Tennessee. Local boosters in March and again in October 1807 placed in the *Impartial Review* a notice for a gathering of all "citizens of Mero District who are disposed to promote a BANK in Nashville."[149] A few months later the legislature formally approved their proposal and granted a ten-year incorporation for the Bank of Nashville. Capital stock was two hundred thousand dollars in United States Bank notes, to be divided into shares of fifty dollars each. Subscribers had to pay an initial ten dollars on each share, in United States coin. They were then obligated to provide another five dollars per share within ninety days. The government had a vested interest in the bank as well, for the charter directed that three hundred shares of capital stock go to the state of Tennessee.[150]

The charter also laid out a nine-member board, which in turn was to elect a president for the new institution. Not coincidentally, the initial directors comprised the Board of Commissions for Nashville as well and generally were acknowledged to be some of the most prominent entrepreneurs in Middle Tennessee: George Deadrick, William Tait (combined these two were arguably the most powerful merchants in Middle Tennessee), Washington Jackson, John H. Smith, George Poyzer, Alexander Porter, Joseph Park, and William Wright. In order to maintain the appearance of propriety, they bound themselves to specific internal safeguards:

Discounts were legal only if authorized by the president and any three directors, and the bank's debts were not to exceed its capital.[151] They would lose sight of this latter provision after 1815, when a wildcat speculative market helped the Nashville Bank and its four subsequent branches open the floodgates of paper currency and credit. With debt climbing to exorbitant levels, their lack of concern for charter policy would provide a powerful impetus for the Panic of 1819.[152]

Clearly, Middle Tennessee was witnessing an explosion of economic boosterism. Thomas Yeatman provided perhaps the quintessential portrait of the most progressive of this emerging element. Taking advantage of his early commercial and banking connections, Yeatman by 1820 owned all or part of several steamboats that specialized in cotton and tobacco. He made his largest fortune while in Philadelphia in 1819. There Yeatman became aware that local brokers were about to offer heavy advances in cotton. Thus he returned to Nashville and "bought up all the cotton there at 12½ cents." His brother Preston Yeatman, living in Huntsville, bought all the cotton there. Cotton soon advanced to twenty-five cents a pound, and the Yeatmans made a fortune. Yeatman subsequently "retired from business and went into banking," noted Willoughby Williams, and "commenced building the Cumberland Ironworks." When he finally died of cholera, he left behind an estate estimated at five hundred thousand dollars.[153]

Entrepreneurs such as Thomas Yeatman helped change the way in which business was conducted in Middle Tennessee. This new ethic was particularly visible in Nashville. According to Willoughby Williams, the town by 1809 held two thousand people who were "none but professional men and merchants."[154] This untamed frontier city had grown respectable enough that aspiring entrepreneurs such as a young David Campbell "thought his capitol was two [sic] small to begin in Nashville [so he] concluded to go out to Franklin."[155] A local merchant's sales guidelines are particularly instructive. Upon opening his new store, John McFarlane provided employee Arthur Lee Campbell with specific instructions: "1) No credit to be given to any person whatever, but those on the List of persons to be credited 2) No credit to be given but for Cash payable in three months 3) The Books to be kept up to date 4) The Store to be kept open every week day, all day,& no card playing nor drinking to be allowed of, in the Store, nor any saunterers to be allowed to frequent it, nor countenanced in any shape to be near it, for such are the bane of Industry & a monstrous tax upon the time of people in business."[156] Gone were the territorial days, when Middle Tennessee's economy of necessity was largely self-contained. Entrepreneurial merchants and progressive planters had begun to use their far-flung economic ties to create and expand upon the cotton market, and in the process they asserted themselves as leaders of a new commercial world.

❧❀☙

In sum, Middle Tennessee underwent a remarkable transformation in a short amount of time. As late as 1801 Hugh Robison pointed out that the region seemed doomed to "the frontiers, in a great measure Destitute of society."[157] That same year "A" lamented, "This is not a country matured and grown opulent by the advantages of commerce. It is an infant district which never knew the plastic hand of refinement, nor the inestimable attainments of social perfection." He concluded with a charge to the local population: "Since it is our peculiar destiny to inhabit it, it is our own industry and perserverence [sic] that must produce an order of things that will reduce us from contempt."[158]

By 1810 the scene had changed dramatically. Boosters in Smith County marveled at the pace of development: "The annals of the world do not afford an instance of a country so swiftly advancing to wealth and importance, as the western part of America." "The time is easily recollected by thousands around us," continued the editor of the *Carthage Gazette* (in a highly exaggerated essay),

> when the sound of the axe was unheard in our forests, and savages and beasts of prey inhabited every part. The contrast is sublime as it is astonishing. The arts and sciences have already attained to a degree of perfection, which in many countries would have required the experience of centuries; and in no part of the continent has agriculture flourished to a greater extent. The world might in vain be searched for a country, where all the necessaries, and many of the luxuries of life, could be so easily obtained, as in this favored clime; Manufactories, also, recently have received considerable attention. At this day the western country exhibits a scene of prosperity, unrivalled by the examples of former years.[159]

The editor of the *Impartial Review* published a similar expression of elation. "We congratulate our fellow citizens on the flattering prospect of the increasing commerce of our infant country," he noted in 1807, "and trust that the time is not very distant when the Cumberland will be a source, through which vessels of considerable magnitude will convey the product of our rich and fertile soil to market."[160] By 1809 riparian commerce was so commonplace that George Richardson noted to Thomas Jefferson that small vessels "frequently come from Orleans to Nashville."[161]

And yet the emergence of this dynamic, entrepreneurial element did not lack for critics. As Nashville's commercial boosters became more enmeshed in the cotton trade, they moved well beyond local exchanges and ultimately dragged all of the region's residents into a faceless economic system. François André Michaux pointed out that merchants did so because "few cultivators take upon themselves to export the produce of their labour, consisting chiefly of cotton; The major part of them sell it to the tradespeople at Nasheville."[162] These "tradespeople" would ship the commodity to dealers in New Orleans, Lexington, Kentucky, or other regional outlets.[163] It would then move on to New York, Philadelphia, or Baltimore, where brokers would ship to Europe.[164] In return these men would send consumer goods to businessmen in Middle Tennessee on bills of exchange.[165]

Such a distant economic structure, reliant as it was upon extended lines of credit, placed local farmers at a disadvantage: with little specie (hard money) in the region, they found themselves taking on particularly large amounts of debt. And such extensive borrowing constrained other economic choices.[166] As Kentuckian "Aristedes" pointed out in 1803,

> At the end of the year [the farmer] finds the amount of his labor eaten up. His stock of cash is sunk to purchase merchandize, which has been altogether consumed within his family. His farming utensils are in some measure worn out; his land somewhat wasted by cultivation, and he finds upon calculation, that he is in a worse condition than at the beginning of the year. He has not been enriched one penny. He is put to his [shifts?] to raise another fund of money to purchase goods from the merchant, and with his eyes open pursues from year to year the same unwise policy, that at length gets him in debt, consumes his land without profit, and breaks his constitution by corporeal and mental embarrassments.

> In the meantime the merchant is reaping the benefit of the farmer's improvidence and folly. The very policy which impoverishes one, adds to the wealth of the other.[167]

Debt was not particularly dangerous during periods of economic prosperity. But since most transactions relied upon credit, and since what little specie was in the region generally went to distant suppliers to pay off bills of exchange, Middle Tennesseans found themselves unable to procure enough hard money to pay off debts when called upon. Recession or other economic changes could potentially cause severe contraction, which threatened to undermine the system in which these people had come to operate.

Thus the Napoleonic conflicts and American reactions to them wreaked havoc on debtors in Middle Tennessee. In 1806 Joshua Wilson wrote of his inability to pay off a four-hundred-dollar legal decision against him, noting to Joseph Hamilton, "I can assure you it is hard time, so much indeed that I should think myself writing improperly should I fix upon any time for you to expect the money I owe you."[168] Unable to pay a debt in early 1808, Robert Akin wrote to James Winchester, "I am sorry that we are in a Cuntry That Cash is so little in Sirculation. I made 10 Cottin gins last year and sold them all and have not recd but 100 dolers in Cash yit, the Season being so bad for Cottin."[169]

By 1810 it had become clear that economic contraction had placed a premium on obtaining specie, as Thomas Knox noted in a letter to his in-laws. Asking for a large advance, Knox wrote, "I would not urge so much, but necessity calls aloud, and for it."[170] Only a few months later he lamented that because of a "grate famin for the want of money in our country, Much property has been sacrificed, and much more will be sold far below the real value until our Country gets clear of Debt."[171] In an age when cotton production was becoming critical to personal and familial security, excessive amounts of debt meant that Middle Tennesseans could have a hard time in the evolving economic structure.

Thus many ordinary people began to look for ways politically to keep the new economy from spiraling beyond their control. This economic philosophy was not antiprogress, to be sure. The quest for land and the willingness to engage in the cotton economy was proof of that. In 1811 "L," in a letter to a local paper, remarked that "foreigners who have visited our country [have noted] that an inordinate desire for the accumulation of wealth, seems to pervade all ranks of citizens."[172]

Nevertheless, many in the region were uncertain about the implications of excessive debt. Their concern manifested itself most clearly in a wave of protest over the political issues of judicial reform and debtor relief from President Jefferson's embargo. Whereas entrepreneurs, merchants, and planters wanted government-sanctioned (and -funded) development, this more restrained definition of progress called for government-induced control over the economy. Through these debates would emerge the political divisions necessary eventually to establish a party structure in Middle Tennessee.

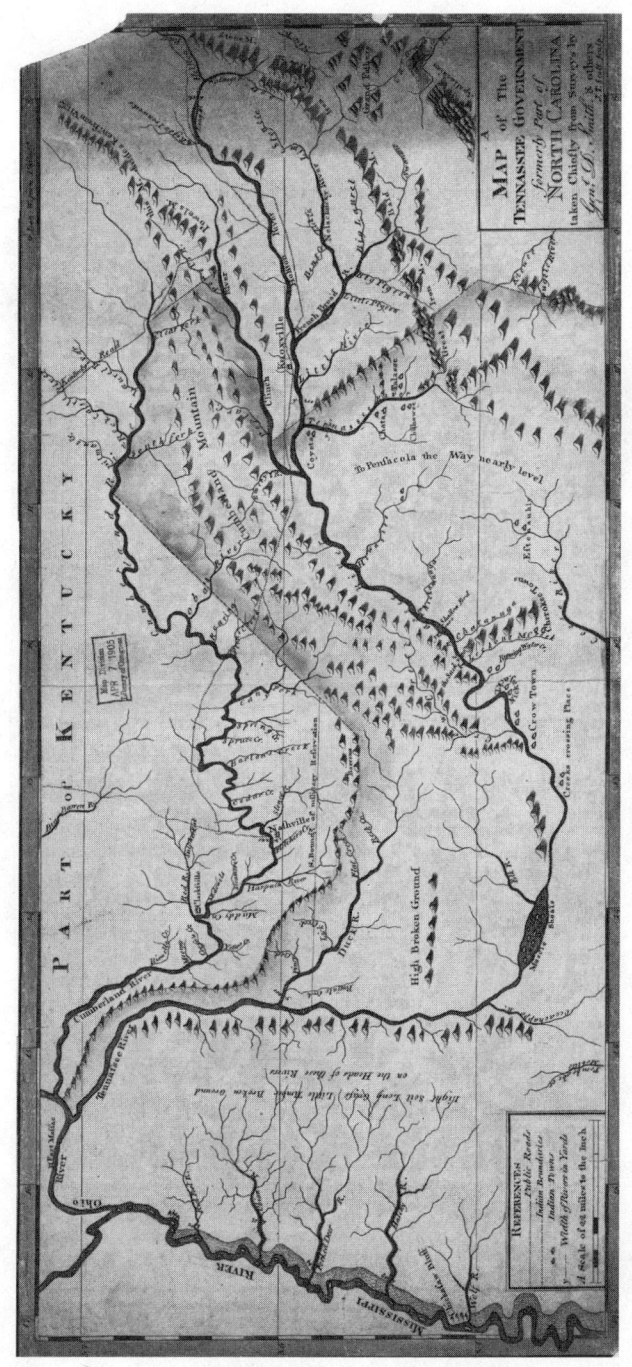

"A Map of the Tennessee Government, Formerly Part of North Carolina." From Mathew Carey's American Atlas, 1795. Library of Congress.

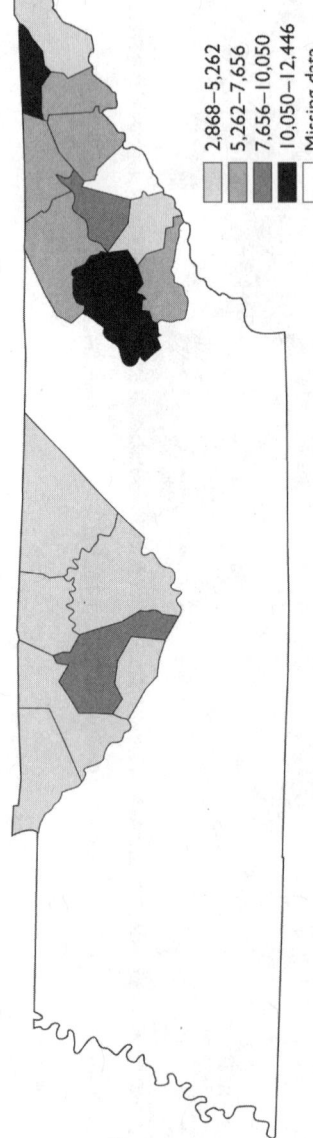

Tennessee counties in 1800, total population. Based on data from University of Virginia Library Historical Census Browser.

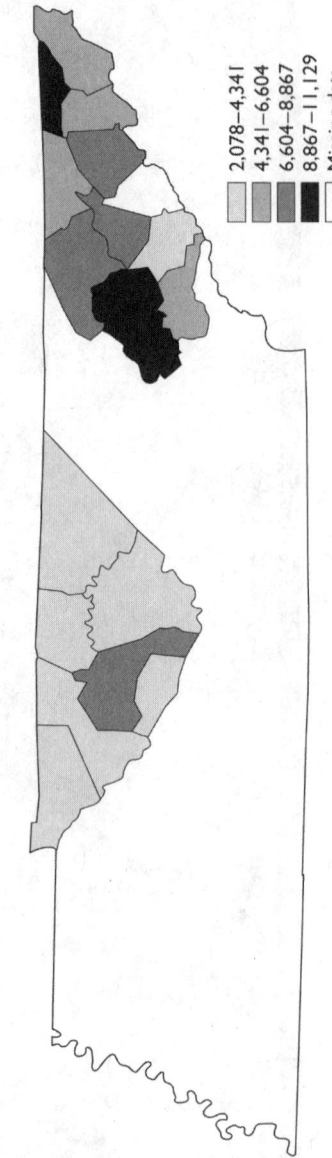

Tennessee counties in 1800, free whites. Based on data from University of Virginia Library Historical Census Browser.

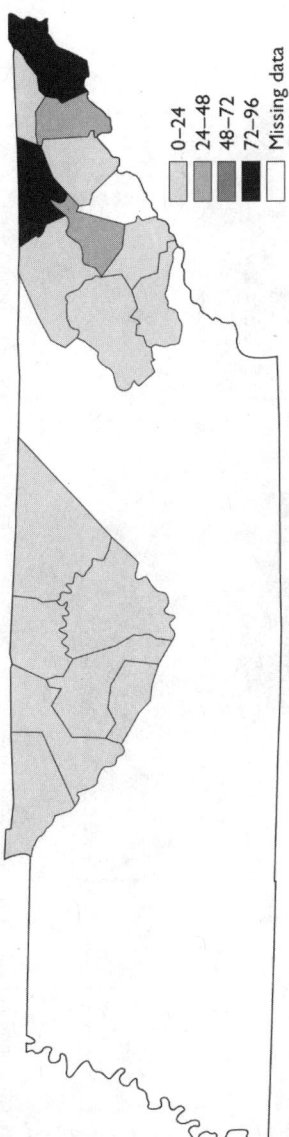

Tennessee counties in 1800, all other free persons. Based on data from University of Virginia Library Historical Census Browser.

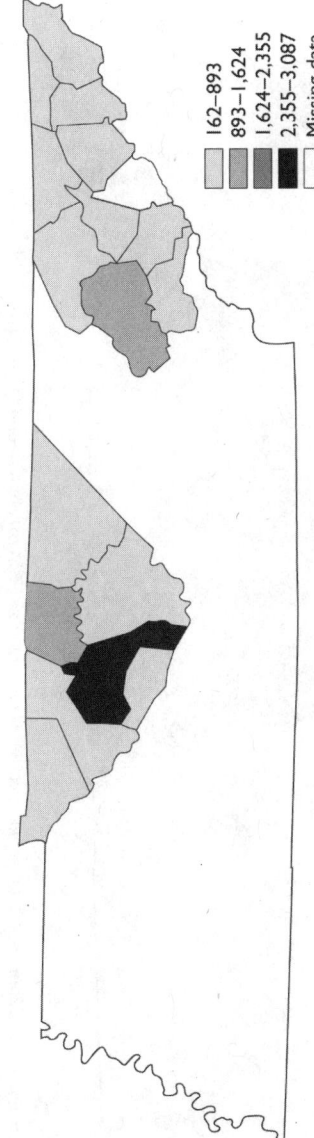

Tennessee counties in 1800, slaves. Based on data from University of Virginia Library Historical Census Browser.

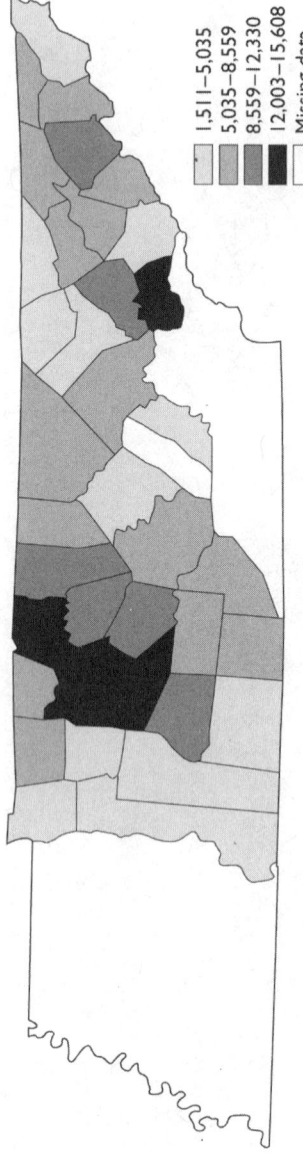

Tennessee counties in 1810, total population. Based on data from University of Virginia Library Historical Census Browser.

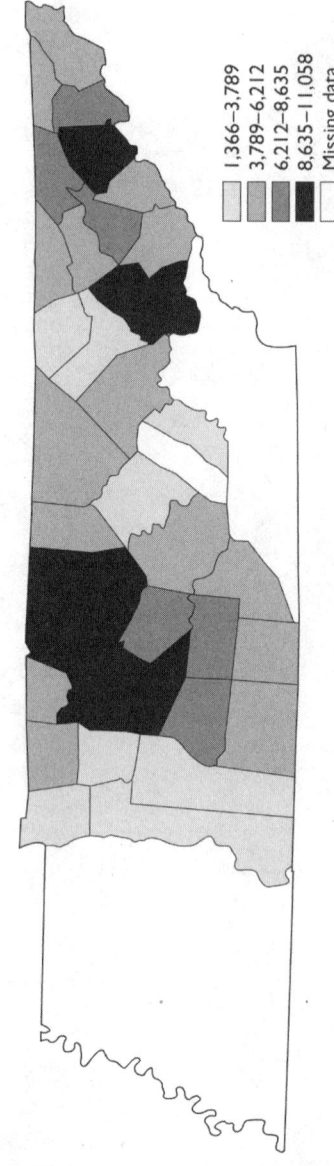

Tennessee counties in 1810, free whites. Based on data from University of Virginia Library Historical Census Browser.

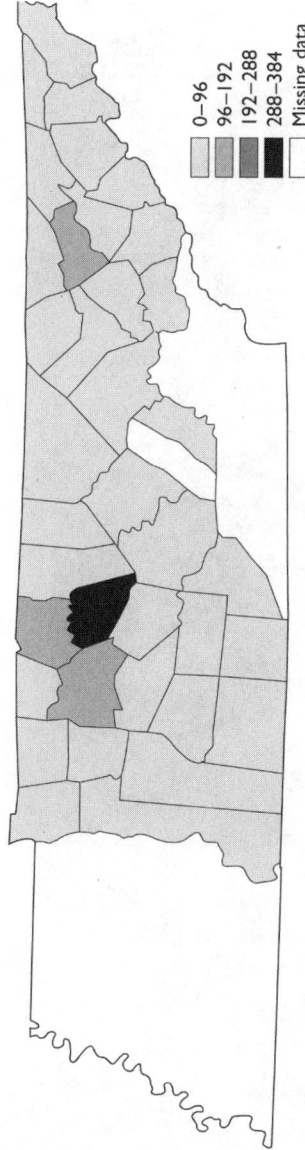

Tennessee counties in 1810, all other free persons. Based on data from *University of Virginia Library Historical Census Browser.*

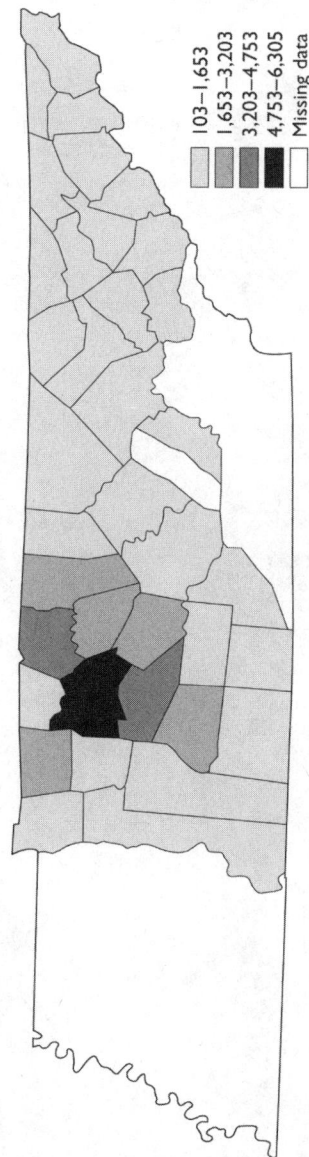

Tennessee counties in 1810, slaves. Based on data from *University of Virginia Library Historical Census Browser.*

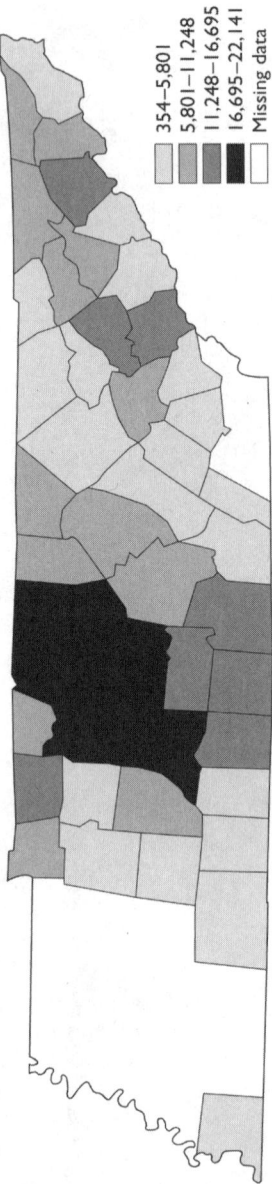

Tennessee counties in 1820, total population. Based on data from University of Virginia Library Historical Census Browser.

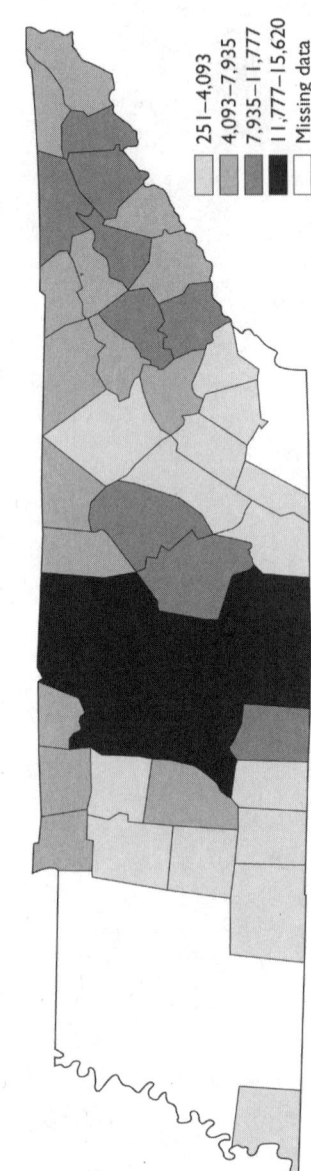

Tennessee counties in 1820, free whites. Based on data from University of Virginia Library Historical Census Browser.

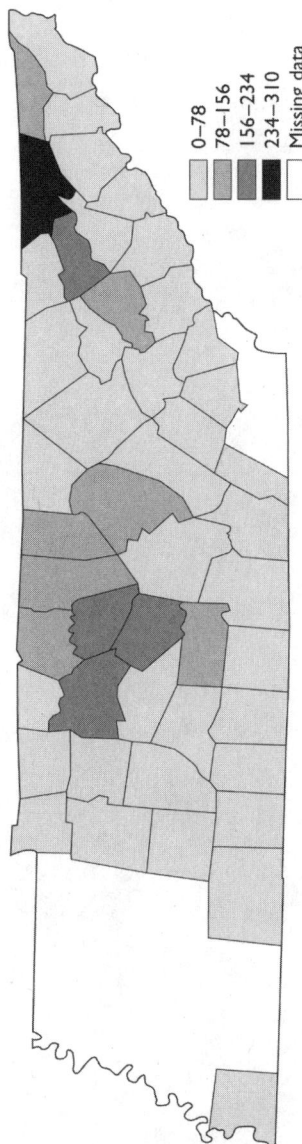

Tennessee counties in 1820, free blacks. Based on data from University of Virginia Library Historical Census Browser.

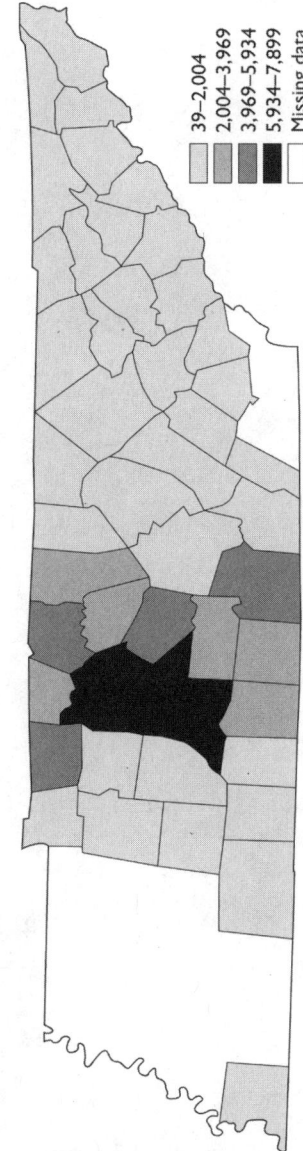

Tennessee counties in 1820, slaves. Based on data from University of Virginia Library Historical Census Browser.

Chapter 5

Ideological Division and American Nationalism in an Expanding Political Culture, 1796–1815

Arthur Campbell, a longtime resident of southwestern Virginia who had had extensive connections in Tennessee since the 1780s, was unhappy in the summer of 1810. While discussing various business activities with his son David, he lamented that expansive economic growth threatened the foundation of a stable society. "Our present pursuits, making Commerce and riches our chief goal," he argued, "is disease and death to our republican institutions; it is by a side wind joining the enemy, and may become a more odious treason than that of the ambitious Villain who foments open Insurrection."[1] No doubt many in Middle Tennessee would have agreed. As planters, merchants, and entrepreneurs pushed ever harder for commercial expansion, many ordinary folk found themselves falling deeply into debt. Concerned with its implications relative to their economic stability, they turned to the new political sphere to register their unhappiness.

Historians have argued that in the 1790s ordinary people used nascent democratic understandings both to join the political process and to establish links between local events and a new national political culture.[2] Nineteenth-century Middle Tennesseans certainly would have agreed. Public displays and newspaper debates fully demonstrated that power in Middle Tennessee was no longer exclusive to a single individual or group. Although they remained at the top of the political culture, the elite now had to negotiate their authority through the rituals of the public sphere.[3]

As the economy grew, this negotiation brought the planter, speculator, and entrepreneurial elements into conflict with a coalition of Tennesseans wanting greater control over extended commercial relations. Although no one wished to return to a subsistence-oriented economy, pressure for land, farm start-up costs, land payments and taxes, and merchant credit left many Tennesseans far enough in debt to help create a legitimate movement in favor of regulation or reform.[4]

In response to this concern a political position took shape that challenged more entrepreneurial elements in Middle Tennessee. In its earliest manifestation, it coalesced around two issues: judicial reform related to land distribution and debtors' rights connected with a lack of regional specie and President Jefferson's embargo. On the one hand, ordinary Tennesseans challenged expansive speculation because landed interests used contested claims and a confusing legal system to remove people from their land. Struggling to procure legal title not only left them potentially landless, but the expense involved in getting to court and paying legal fees drained already limited resources. On the other hand, Tennesseans were heavily influenced by the perception that a lack of specie threatened permanently to divide the region into a small class of wealthy creditors and a larger group of debtors.

As these issues became more entrenched, many Middle Tennesseans applied pressure on the state's governing representatives. No longer could the political sphere revolve around networks or personality clashes. No longer would temporary factions take care of the various interests that demanded some level of action. In effect, Tennessee's Jeffersonian party bifurcated, and both groups maintained a distinct interpretation of and commitment to economic progress.

Yet there was more to the region's political transformation, for the debate took place against a backdrop of militant nationalism that brought Tennessee permanently into the national political community. Where once the region's loyalty to the United States was rather tepid, the period from 1800 to 1815 cemented a strongly American identity. When combined with the emergent split over the nature and meaning of progress, this nationalism solidified the foundation for a permanent party structure in Tennessee.

Land and the Tennessee Court System

In the late eighteenth century there was a wide pattern of backcountry unrest over perceptions of distorted land distribution, legal protection for excessive speculation, and laws that favored creditors over debtors. In 1784 and 1785, for example, the Virginia General Assembly debated easing access to the court system as part of a broader discussion over debtors' rights.[5] And throughout the 1790s the question of judicial tyranny dominated the debate over political reform in Kentucky. As students of that state have noted, Kentuckians lacking clear title to their land, or who never were able to obtain any at all, "yearned for a more democratic legal system." By 1802 their cries reached such a fevered pitch that the Kentucky legislature replaced district courts with a system of circuit courts.[6]

Concerns over land led ordinary Tennesseans to distrust the judiciary as well. They took on added meaning, however, because they came at a time of unusual political, economic, and demographic expansion. As the civic sphere changed to reflect the needs of the new community, questions of land distribution and judicial reform could not help but make a serious political impression.

Tennesseans at the beginning of the nineteenth century faced an overwhelming number of land problems, mostly because of twenty-plus years of turmoil with regard to fraudulent purchases, military claims, and speculation. As early as 1780, surveyors had blurred boundaries, overlapped claims, and padded legitimate ones so that more land was given than appeared in the records. By the early nineteenth century, as "Manlius" pointed out, speculators had become particularly adept at throwing obstacles in the path of "honest people" and endeavored "to make as many dependent on their favor as possible."[7]

In later years things would improve, to be sure; as in other areas of the Southwest, landownership in Tennessee eventually rose to almost 50 percent of the adult population.[8] But obtaining clear title to land was more difficult at the turn of the century. And those who were able to get a tract were acutely aware of how easily they could lose it through writs of fieri facias and venditioni exponas.[9] Published by the hundreds in local newspapers, these writs acted as judicial notices of expulsion for people who could neither pay for lands nor the taxes on them.[10]

Those without clear titles had even bigger problems. Squatters, for example, found that speculators and planters consistently attempted to remove them, regardless of preemption laws or land improvement.[11] More often than not, these people had to purchase or rent their farms, or face removal by local government authorities.[12] Met with such bleak choices, most became tenants, moved into Indian territory, or went farther west. Although the destruction of all early census records make specific numbers impossible to obtain, historian Anita Goodstein has theorized that out-migration in Davidson County alone was as high as 70 percent during this early period.[13]

Those who stayed behind looked to the courts for relief. Yet the legal system as it stood in the early years of the nineteenth century only exacerbated tensions. In 1800 the court system was largely the same as it had been in the territorial period, when county courts had served as the most important and visible symbol of government authority. Comprised of a minimum of three justices of the peace, the courts met in quarterly sessions to hear most criminal cases and all civil cases involving sums over twenty dollars.[14] In so doing, they dispensed justice under the laws of North Carolina. When the region became a federal territory, and again when it achieved statehood, lawmakers merely legitimized the maintenance of the mother state's system.

During the territorial period the justices, all of whom were appointed by Governor William Blount, initiated building and internal improvement projects, meted justice for both criminal and civil cases, served as wards of the state for orphans and indigent people, and served as the probate court.[15] The county court also served as the register of preemptions and boundaries and, therefore, was the first court to which contested land claims went. Since the justices tended to be moderate to large speculators (the nineteen Davidson County justices of the peace between 1790 and 1795 held an average of 7,170 acres), they were careful to protect larger claims.[16] Poorer Tennesseans could appeal to a three-judge superior court of law and equity, which sat twice annually in Knoxville and Jonesboro in the East and Nashville in the West.[17] As often as not, however, such appeals were too expensive, and legal decisions would stand. As a result, "debt, ejectments and trespass" were the most common cases on the docket between 1790 and 1805.[18]

If this legal structure was awkward for anyone not near the courts, as "Pericles" noted in 1808, it nevertheless made sense in the territorial period. "In the midst of dangers the most terrific," he wrote, "justice could not be administered securely but in [Knoxville and Nashville] where the strength of the state was principally concentrated. Add to the thinness of population which had not extended far beyond these sanctuaries and we shall find that superior courts were then held in the center of every settlement."[19]

Changing circumstances, however, made it "absurd to say that any law should continue in force after the cause for which it was made no longer requires it."[20] And as the wars with the Cherokees, Creeks, and Chickamaugas ended and the population boomed, it became apparent how strongly the system favored the wealthy. First, there was the problem that the justices, Archibald Roane, David Campbell, and Andrew Jackson in 1800, were speculators themselves, which gave an inherent advantage to their colleagues. Since these men (and their successors) were appointed by the legislature for life, there was no chance of voting them out.

Equally important were the intertwined issues of cost and distance. In an 1806 petition, fifty-four men argued that they could not protect "their just rights against oppressors" because of the expense of pursuing appeals and the amount of time it took for "poor men" to reach the superior courts.[21] Petitioners also complained that most witnesses could not afford to make the trek either, while the law ensured that the most critical witnesses in terms of land would fall beyond their means: It required "the testimony of the Original Grantee Surveyor and Chain Carryers who in many cases are living in the extreme parts of the country."[22] Given that only speculators and their agents had ready access to surveyors, this requirement made it nearly impossible for poorer farmers to secure their claims.[23]

In 1808 young Thomas Hart Benton elaborated upon these issues.[24] Writing under the nom de plume "Oldcastle," he pointed out that "the enormous expense that attends the prosecution of a suit at law and the ruinous delays that are experienced at every stage betray the defects of a system radically wrong."[25] Something as simple as the distance between farmers and the major judicial centers made it clear how skewed the system had become, he argued:

> Rich folks may not feel this oppression but to farming men it is a serious calamity. Besides the loss of time it takes money out of their pockets for their personal expenses which they can but ill afford. When he attends the district court he has to put up at a tavern and there his personal expenses often exceed those which his law suit brings upon him in the court. When it is continued over four or five or six years in succession it amounts to an unjustifiable suppression and demands the reforming hand of the legislature."[26]

In a separate series of essays "Agricola" pointed to another way in which wealthy interests held a significant advantage: The technical and abstruse nature of legal procedure and jargon made it impossible for average Tennesseans to understand what was going on. To this end he argued that wealthy interests and their lawyers would ensure that suits became "as complicated as possible and carried to the highest and most remote courts, and kept off as long as possible, to render the decision intricate and expensive."[27] Agreed "A Farmer": "The present Judiciary of Tennessee is an intricate system of technicalities, twisted into a long and laboured chain of oppression and venality. Go where you will and the injured man complains of the tardy steps of the law—of its uncertainty—of its oppression."[28]

And because of their help in "enveloping [the temple of justice] in an atmosphere of awe, mystery, and repulsion, which forbids any who are unacquainted with the mysterious rites and ceremonies," Middle Tennessee's growing number of lawyers were labeled as unrepublican tools of aristocracy.[29] Attorneys drew fire for attempting to win cases on technicalities, delaying procedures until less wealthy litigants had to capitulate and tricking people into error through obscure jargon and legal phrases that distorted logic.[30]

Perhaps the *Carthage Gazette* best revealed prevailing sentiment in a satirical dialogue between lawyers "Slim" and "Avarice." Avarice opened the conversation by lauding the aristocratic nature of the legal profession. Could they achieve some measure of separation from the "vulgar and uninformed rabble, then we will go on progressively without interruption [and achieve titles]; but the titles must first be familiar and easy to the people's ear. We must be careful not to alarm those stubborn republicans; they must be gained upon by slow and progressive means."[31] Slim responded both by celebrating the complexities of the system and pointing to lawyers' sense of refined superiority. "I took a fee from a country clodhopper the other day for twenty dollars," he explained to his colleague, "for what two of his neighbors could have settled in half an hour—it was as much as I was able to bear the fellow's vulgarism—he addressed me in my own name, without any appearance of respect, and appeared to be as divested of manners as a Billingsgate stall keeper!!!"[32]

Disdain for the legal profession intensified as the 1809 legislative election approached. In the *Carthage Gazette*, "Detector" warned Smith County residents not to "elect lawyers to mend your judiciary, [otherwise] you will jump out of the frying pan and into the fire. [Rather,] be careful to elect farmers or mechanics, they will make plain laws."[33] In his 1811 race for Congress, Felix Grundy's mouthpiece, the *Nashville Clarion,* pointed out that "the only evidence that the people at large have that he will act from corrupt motives is his being a lawyer."[34] Even John Overton, the most politically and economically powerful figure in early national Tennessee, had to have his friends defend him against charges of legal corruption upon his 1811 candidacy for a seat in the U.S. House of Representatives.[35]

In short, many feared that the judiciary and its "temple priests" unfairly protected wealthy interests at a time when land had come to serve as a critical element in the people's economic stability.[36] But how could they solve the dilemma? As early as February 1808, Thomas Hart Benton made clear that a solution lay in the popular democracy of the new political culture. Reform, he noted, was "the easiest thing in the world. The people have nothing to do but to say 'we are tired of the present system and we want a new one.' If they will agree among themselves to utter this short sentence the whole work is accomplished and the power is in their own hands."[37] Agreed a "Friend of the People," "I will venture to affirm that 19 out of 20 of those Citizens of West Tennessee, whose living does not in some way or other grow out of the present system, are decidedly convinced that the present system is inadequate and oppressive."[38]

A flurry of public events, reproductions of key regional petitions, and newspaper editorials soon made reform a hot topic across the region. A Davidson County July 4 toast in 1808, for example, declared, "The Legislature of Tennessee—may they at their next session see the necessity of an alteration in the judiciary system."[39] Two weeks later four of the most populated counties in the region—Williamson, Rutherford, Maury, and Bedford—published grand jury reports that demanded legislative candidates take the question into consideration.[40] By early 1809, as "Simm" made clear, ongoing protests had made the judiciary "the touchstone at the approaching elections."[41] The time was ripe to affect change, agreed "Detector." Because the election would create a legislature that "will have a hand in correcting our Judiciary, which there is so much bustle about," he argued that Middle Tennesseans should carefully "inspect the candidates as soon as they declare themselves."[42]

Sympathetic politicians increasingly responded to this public pressure. During his 1809 race with Sampson Williams, Smith County candidate Thomas Harris specifically published a platform that revolved around the notion that "the present system was calculated to keep the wealth and circulating medium of the state concentrated in a few places to the injury of other parts of the country."[43] Williams did likewise—he made it clear in the *Gazette* that he was running on a platform of creating multiple new circuit courts that would feed into a state supreme court rather than into the biannual superior court sessions.

In the 1809 election this agitation helped send a majority of pro-reform statesmen to the legislature with the express mandate that they do something to alleviate the problem. In conjunction with pro-reform legislators from East Tennessee, this majority provided a powerful and sympathetic block of votes. Representative Thomas Harris set the tone for the session when he pointed out the necessity of heeding "the will of a large majority of the people [which] had been expressed in favor of a change . . . by the numerous memorials and petitions which were daily presented to the legislature."[44]

Building upon the suggestions in these "numerous memorials," Thomas Hart Benton proposed a bill that replaced the extant superior court with an appointed supreme court of errors and appeals—maintained by two "Judges in Error" and a circuit court judge. Although the county courts remained intact, the new state supreme court would meet in five judicial circuits, with the provision that each county in the circuit receive two court sessions per annum.[45] The logic was simple: Since small farmers were most affected by the distance to the old superior court, now they could have their appeals heard at their county seat.

Debate over Benton's bill showed that speculator-friendly elements would not fold easily, however. This opposition denied that more courts would reduce costs or administer equal justice. Specifically, they argued that a new judiciary would create a greater burden on "the people" by raising taxes to exorbitant levels.[46] An expansion of courts and court sessions would require new judges, increased salaries, and never-ending construction costs, to say nothing of the fact that there simply were not enough capable legal minds to handle the business of an expanded system.

Opponents feared that "the law might become unhinged by looseness and disorder" and that incompetent courts would increase the costs to the people by ensuring never ending appeals.[47] They also feared that the legislature was "sporting with the rights and liberties of our constituents, without . . . considering the consequences."[48] Besides, noted an anonymous author to the *Carthage Gazette,* judicial reform directly affected the lawyers, who "are a very numerous and respectable part of the community; and you will be certain of incurring the displeasure of the whole profession."[49]

Ultimately, the pro-reform elements carried the legislative debate, and despite a "last, struggling effort" by the opposition to suspend it by a year, Benton's bill passed in each house. Representative Harris spoke for many when he subsequently proclaimed to Middle Tennesseans, "You now have a court system that is well calculated to promote speedy, cheap and impartial justice to all descriptions of people in the state."[50] But if reformers won the battle, the war certainly was not over. The judges appointed by the legislature to the new courts were all of the gentry and in most cases were major speculators.[51] Their control of the new system ensured that "incompetent" lawyers and frivolous suits would be kept from clogging the system. A sign that reforms were not as successful as some had hoped, in 1811 Judge William Cocke was impeached in Grainger County because residents felt he was too partial toward his friends.[52] Thereafter Middle Tennesseans wanted changes to minimize the damage of corrupt judges, and judicial concerns ultimately even were a justification for the constitutional convention of 1834.[53]

Focusing on the mixed result of the reform battle, however, obfuscates its importance to political cultural development in Middle Tennessee. Indeed, judicial reform played a critical role in helping to establish two political forces in opposition. Court reform revolved around questions of land and economic stability. Purchasing real estate in a region with little specie meant that ordinary Tennesseans inevitably fell into debt.

And having to go to court to protect claims and fight insolvency proceedings frustrated their efforts at making enough money to discharge their obligations. Thus judicial reform was a way for poorer sorts and their political allies to establish themselves in opposition to what they felt were the unfair practices of speculators, planters, and their lawyers. In the new political culture, this would pave the way for subtle but growing distinctions between competing notions of progress.

Merchants, Debtors, and the Embargo

Debt stemming from merchant credit further established a restrained economic interest. Indeed, the commercial expansion of the first decade of the nineteenth century relied heavily upon extensive lines of credit. Specie simply was too rare and expensive for daily use. During the territorial period, when the economy was more self-contained, maintaining a debt at the local general store mattered for little. As often as not, bartered products would remove financial obligations, and what remained would carry over into other years. With the cotton and tobacco economy growing to global proportions, however, many local farmers found themselves dependent upon extensive credit. Recession or other economic changes made the situation more ominous, threatening property, future credit, and, ultimately, the entire system in which these people had come to operate.[54]

Early-nineteenth-century Tennesseans had reason to be concerned about contraction. By 1808 the Napoleonic conquests had engulfed Europe in war, and President Jefferson's reactions to them threatened to wreak havoc on debtors in the United States. Americans had benefited greatly by their trade with the major belligerents in the early years of the Napoleonic Wars.[55] After the naval battle of Trafalgar left Britain in control of the Atlantic, however, Napoleon embarked on a plan—known as the Continental System—that intended to cut off British trade with Europe.[56] The situation worsened for American commerce when in November 1807 the British responded with Orders in Council that barred any vessel from trading with Europe without first going through a British port.

President Jefferson decided that the best way to deal with the situation was to employ peaceable coercion. His policy was popular with many

Republicans because of the opinion that the world relied upon American shipping for vital goods. Taking it away, they thought, would force Britain and France to alter their policies and accommodate American demands. Thus Congress passed the Embargo Act of 1807, which dictated that American vessels could no longer trade with either Britain or Continental powers.

Jefferson's embargo had significant repercussions in Middle Tennessee. Perhaps most important was that because a large international market for its cotton and tobacco had disappeared, an already limited supply of hard money suddenly became nonexistent. Certainly many in the region saw it that way. In a petition to Governor John Sevier, several Middle Tennesseans pointed out that "the Embargo has entirely precluded us from the means of disposing of our produce at a foreign market, [meaning that] a scarcity of specie ensues, and an inability to meet our demands."[57] And inability to meet financial obligations meant that too often people's "property [was] taken by execution and sold for less than its value." A March 1809 petition published in the *Carthage Gazette* argued that specie had become so scarce that "in many instances good horses valued at from 40 to 50 dollars have been sold by virtue of executions for less than a dollar a piece, cows for half a dollar, and other property in proportion."[58] Perhaps Representative Thomas K. Harris best encapsulated the situation when he wrote to his legislative district, "It must be agreed that the amount of circulating specie in the state, would not be sufficient to pay the one-twentieth part of the peoples debt—that the most of these debts were contracted at a time when commerce was flattering HOPE—the fairest gift of heaven—and when it was reasonably expected that the surplus produce of the country would be amply sufficient to free the debtor from the fangs of the rude and unmerciful creditor."[59]

The embargo, in short, made the inability to pay debt disastrous. Certainly "A Reformer" thought so. In a petition to the legislature he hoped to make clear the "immediate urgency [which] arose from the distressed situation of the debtor class of community, and the sacrifice of property they were likely to experience, by the sudden check which had been given to the circulation of specie, by the embargo."[60] Another petition noted that there "have been an almost total stagnation or disappearance of that circulating medium which is considered as the index of property, this amongst a people who were acquiring strong commercial habits has produced resulting scenes of distress that could scarcely have been predictively imagined."[61] A Sumner County widow's tribulations put a more personal face on the problem. When Polly Young lost her husband Joseph, she wrote to her father-in-law, "My house once was the seat of peace and plenty but now instead of a consoling friend there are Merciless officers escorted by voracious creditors trying to sink me to the lowest degree of wretchedness and poverty."[62]

Debt, exacerbated as it was by the embargo, thus galvanized the public political voice as much as any issue. Many insisted that the best way to achieve relief was through systematic use of the new political culture, specifically, through petitioning and public debate.[63] Subsequent declarations extended to the embargo the "rich versus poor" rhetoric that had been part of the decade-long quest for judicial reform. "A Friend of the People," for example, lambasted "aristocratic Lawyers and Merchants" for taking over a public debate in Nashville and rejecting debtor relief, calling them "rabble" and arguing that they had "run away with the People's rights."[64] Rural folk in Davidson County agreed and countered the Nashville resolutions by reconvening and passing pro-relief resolutions of their own.[65] Another petition to Governor Sevier implored him to reject "any oppressive system which is calculated to add misery to the distressed—to distress the weak and elevate the strong, to make the poor poorer and the rich richer."[66]

Pointing out that distant merchants were as blameworthy as local ones for the region's problems, another group of petitioners to Governor Sevier argued, "It is most undoubtedly unfair to suffer the marchants of the atlantic cities who are themselves relieved from the pressure of the law, to have the advantage of the law here, to compel the payments of those sums from our marchants, which must at last be extracted by the unrelenting hand of the law, from the hard-earned property of our farmers and mechanicks."[67]

The increasing public outcry built upon a belief that Tennesseans had a "Constitutional right" to represent to the government "the peculiar inconveniences and difficulties under which we labour, and to beg leave that we be furnished with some mode, by which a redress of our grievances may be attained."[68] "Unless some speedy remedy is afforded," noted a group of petitioners to Governor Sevier, "incalculable calamity will be inflicted on those people who have been in the habit of looking to your excellency for protection in the day of vicissitudes and the hour of danger."[69] Even if, as a group of Smith County petitioners affirmed, "the act of the General Government [was] calculated for the good of the nation," it was clear that the local population had "a right to expect relief from constituted authorities."[70]

Most requests for relief asked for a law authorizing "magistrates to suspend the issuing of executions a certain number of days after giving judgment."[71] Formally known as a stay law, prodebtor writers called for one to remain in effect "during the continuance of the Embargo."[72] If they were not offered, feared some petitioners to the legislature, "general desolation must ensue. Men with their families must probably be stripped of all of their personal property and left destitute of subsistence on a naked piece of land without the means of cultivating it!"[73]

Entrepreneurial elements vociferously rejected stay laws. Their concerns primarily revolved around the sanctity of contract, for stay laws, they argued, denied creditors due process and undermined financial obligations. In 1808 Thomas Allen wrote to the *Impartial Review* his hope that no state constitution "be broken, so as to suspend the collection of honest debt."[74] An anonymous author later that month made clear that stay laws arbitrarily abrogated contractual responsibilities. He also added a new element into the debate: that stay laws protected those who lost money due to "neglect" and who intended to "defraud honest creditors."[75] In a letter to the *Impartial Review* "A Citizen" put it more forcefully when he noted that a stay law was "dishonest, because it legalizes knavery. Its avowed object is relief to the distressed, but it would leave it optional with everyone to pay his debts or not, as he might think proper. The dishonest would avail themselves of this privilege, the honest would not."[76]

Continuing to place their faith in boosterism, many entrepreneurs looked for innovations to replace international commerce with broader national markets.[77] For some, the answer to the region's economic travails was expanded agricultural output. "An Observer" provided merely one example. In late 1808 he attempted to impress upon the Middle Tennessee farmer that "raising hemp will be found of real advantage to them, in times of peace, embargo or war, and will always find a market."[78]

Others pointed to a program of manufactures, in the process reflecting a national trend among entrepreneurial Republican elements.[79] A petition signed by fifty-seven men, for example, asked for state support because "our country depends greatly on the promotion of its own manufactures, which alone gives life and vigor to commercial business, by which alone money is brought into our country."[80] A year later former legislator John Rhea argued, "At this time, when the commerce of the world is suspended, it behooves the people of the United States to attend to manufactures. Industry will supply the raw materials and the hand of the manufacturer will, if diligently exercised, prepare them for use, and diminish the importation of foreign merchandise."[81]

While popular with creditors and entrepreneurs, however, this position sparked noticeable public disapprobation. To the critics, expansion and new markets only indirectly addressed the immediate shortage of specie faced by indebted farmers. Moreover, it avoided the issue of government involvement in the economy: If it could do so to help boosters, then why not to help debtors as well? As one author to the *Carthage Gazette* put it, "If Government have a right to say 'you shall not carry your produce to such or such a market,' and no one disputes that right, they have certainly a right to say to the same citizens, 'you shall not have the use of the law, which is an instrument of our making and under our control, to enforce the payment of money from your neighbour, till the time arrives when we will suffer him to carry his produce to the market.'" Addressing the region's creditors, this anonymous writer pointed out that the loss of markets was a sacrifice that had been required by patriotic duty. As such, "the inconvenience of [not receiving payment was] a sacrifice required of [creditors] by their country."[82] "A Friend of the People" argued that any opposition to stay laws could only come from aristocratic sources. "The time has not yet come for such a measure to be popular with some people," he wrote. It would not be long, however, before "every poor man who owes a trifle is ruined, and none but large debts among rich men remain to be collected, all the odiousness of [stay laws] will disappear—it will then become a wise, virtuous, just and constitutional measure. Such is the magic of aristocracy."[83]

Most critical for the pro-relief camp was the need for their position to pass constitutional muster. Creditors and their allies pointed out that stay laws violated Article 1, Section 10 of the U.S. Constitution, which made clear that "no State shall . . . pass any law . . . impairing the obligation of contracts." Pro-debtor proponents felt that stay laws were acceptable because they did not actually abrogate contracts. Debtors maintained their financial responsibilities, they just received more time to come up with the necessary specie. Besides, the state legislature once before had authorized "every magistrate *to suspend the operation of executions,* commonly called staying of judgment, for 30, 60 and 120 days according to the magnitude of the sum." Was this not a firm precedent?[84] An anonymous writer in March 1809 thought so, and pointedly asked, "Is Tennessee to become the strong hold of avarice and barbarous cupidity? Is a monied aristocracy to be elevated by the effects of the embargo, while the poor people are to be sunk into the dust?"[85]

Ultimately, the legislature heard the cry. Building upon the longer-standing principle that allowed for staying executions, in 1809 it enacted laws that postponed payments and stayed legal executions.[86] Perhaps more important, when combined with land and judicial issues, questions of debtor relief significantly complicated long-term political-economic debates in Middle Tennessee.

By the outbreak of war in 1812, judicial reform and debtor relief had helped create competing political-economic camps. On the one hand, entrepreneurially minded merchants and planters had embraced technological innovation and wanted to use government institutions both to fund internal improvements and to protect investors from judicial reform and the destruction of financial contracts. On the other hand, many ordinary Middle Tennesseans and their political allies searched for greater control over an expansive economy through easier access to courts and government-sanctioned debtor relief. It was around these ideas of economic progress that political institutionalization evolved over the next few decades. By the 1830s they would form the backbone for Jacksonian politics in Tennessee.

Political Culture and the War of 1812

Yet there was more to this transformation. Judicial reform and debtors' rights became popular issues just as the Napoleonic conflicts enveloped the United States. And perhaps the most remarkable aspect of the embargo debate was that despite the division between creditors and debtors, both sides unanimously supported the embargo itself. The debate over the meaning of progress thus took place against a backdrop of increasingly militant nationalism that cemented Tennessee into the national political community. When combined with the gradual split within Tennessee's Jeffersonian coalition, this nationalism solidified the foundation for a permanent party structure in Tennessee.

A nascent American identity was noticeable by Jefferson's election in 1800, but it became more militant after the Chesapeake-Leopard affair. In 1807 the HMS *Leopard,* looking to find British sailors to impress into the Royal Navy, fired upon the USS *Chesapeake,* damaged it, and forced it to strike its colors. Royal marines then boarded the disabled vessel and removed sailors for service in His Majesty's Navy. Middle Tennesseans erupted with indignation when they heard the news, and their concerns culminated in a series of public meetings in which large numbers of people demanded some response by the government. A meeting under the control of John Overton and James Winchester even drew up formal protests.[87] Patriotic fervor, and a sense of belonging to an American community, would only grow from there.

Distaste for all things British was so strong that few people complained about Jefferson's embargo, even after it became clear how damaging it was to the regional economy. In 1808 Wilson Yandle (also spelled Yandell) of Murfreesboro prepared one of many Fourth of July toasts in support of Jefferson's decision: "The Embargo—May it have the desired effect."[88] In February 1809 the editor of the *Carthage Gazette* pointed out that "we never witnessed a greater unanimity to prevail in any considerable district of country, and relative to any important question, than now prevails throughout the State of Tennessee respecting the measures of the General Government. The voice of approbation is universal."[89]

Tennessee representative Thomas Harris reinforced the root cause of this support. "The perfidy of the British Government," he wrote to his constituents, "rendered our wish for the continuation of foreign commerce, vain and illusive; and the congress of the union wisely deemed it politic to lop it off."[90] An 1809 circular sent to President James Madison by a "Republican Meeting of Nashville" was equally clear. Pointing to British baseness, the attendees resolved, "We will support the constituted Authorities of our country in carrying into effect such measures as they may adopt for the purpose of inforcing a strict observance of the Non Intercourse Laws."[91] The attendees further noted that "should Congress in their wisdom determine that arms shall be resorted to against those, who have so often insulted, and injured us, we will risque our lives and fortunes to support the Cause of our country."[92]

Support for the embargo and non-intercourse informed an emerging nationalism quite different from the precarious American identity of the 1780s and 1790s, when first the Confederation and then the Washington and Adams administrations seemingly abandoned the region. Alluding to northeastern Federalist criticism of the embargo, in April 1809 Abram Murrey made clear that "by birth I am an American—by occupation and choice a farmer—and [I hope] that the time, may shortly arrive when the distinction of federalist, republican, &c. may be wiped away—when every true American will rally around the standard of his government."[93] An 1810 toast in Nashville further spoke to the question of identity: Over twelve hundred people listened to a blessing of "the union of the states" and the "speedy dissolution to the traitors who have, or may attempt to dissolve it."[94]

Besides the causes of the embargo, two other issues underlay Tennessee's distaste for the British, and therefore the surge of American nationalism: A desire to reconnect the younger generation with their revolutionary forebearers, through which Britain was a natural target, and the promise of acquiring land from Indians by flaming unsubstantiated fears that the British would incite them to attack the southwestern frontier.[95] As to the former, many Tennesseans had begun to feel that the legacy of the Revolution was in danger. A satirical dialogue between "Peter" and "Timothy," printed by the *Carthage Gazette*, directly addressed the issue. Pointing to the hollow nature of Fourth of July celebrations, Timothy argued, "So soon then, as the sons of independence lost their first love, they began to make this ever blessed day, an occasion of drunkenness, gluttony and blasphemy." He also felt that there was too much "trust in long speeches, noise and empty shew."[96] In other words, the political ritual offered by Fourth of July celebrations had become overextended, in the process threatening to render the Revolution meaningless.

No doubt many others agreed, for as the global situation deteriorated, people made direct connections to their Revolutionary forefathers. As early as 1801 Andrew Jackson was demanding that local politico William Dickson declare that he was "a true admirer of the whig principles of Seventy-six."[97] In 1810 the *Carthage Gazette* published a toast to the "heroes of '76—they have a place in the love and esteem of their countrymen more durable than statues of marble or monuments of brass."[98] Similarly, the *Nashville Clarion* lauded a group of "Patriotic Veteran" volunteers and declared, "He must deserve to be a slave whose pulse does not beat in unison with these grey-headed volunteers, called by the Genius of Liberty, once more from their peaceful dwellings to the tented field, to protect the independence they fought to purchase."[99] "A Citizen of Smith County" recounted a false alarm of a British-induced Indian assault on Tennessee and pointed out that in the expedition to meet them, "our venerable Revolutionary officers were first in heading the chosen band of virtues sons." He concluded his patriotic harangue by declaring *"Tories, Apostate Whigs and British Partizans!* Be cautious not to intrude upon our sacred rights and privileges any longer, for American liberty must not, shall not be imposed on with impunity."[100] A Fourth of July toast in 1812 that drew six cheers from a Smith County crowd was even more explicit: "The patriot heroes of America, whose blood was shed at the alter of liberty. May their sons emulate their noble example."[101]

The issue of land acquisition was more complicated, buried as it was beneath rhetoric of a British conspiracy. Concerns that Britain had pressed Indians to initiate a war were not rooted in any substantive evidence. But given the longstanding desire to obtain Creek land in Alabama and Chickasaw land in West Tennessee, the potential for British-inspired Indian attacks became a suitable pretext for initiating yet another assault on tribal sovereignty.[102]

Shawnee chief Tecumseh and his brother the Prophet were perhaps the most noted bogeymen in Tennessee. In 1811 Governor Willie Blount, an already significant speculator in Alabama, used isolated Creek incursions into southern Middle Tennessee (for hunting and to acquire livestock) to voice his belief that Tecumseh was stirring Creeks into attacking the frontier.[103] Other regional leaders, as well as the local media, followed suit at the first opportunity.[104] The *Nashville Clarion*, for example, expressed their horror at a British agent's order to Tecumseh-connected northern Indians: "Keep your eyes fixed on my tomahawk; [and] be you ready when

I give the signal." Echoing Governor Blount, the paper feared that such a command would be used to influence the Cherokees and Creeks on the southern frontier.[105] The *Carthage Gazette* made similar connections and remarked in astonished tones that the Cherokees, Choctaws, Chickasaws, and Creeks were "completely armed with new British muskets."[106] In the wake of the kidnapping of Martha Crawley by Creeks in 1812, Andrew Jackson raged that Tecumseh and the Prophet were little more than the "tools of England, [who had] caused our frontier to be stained with blood, and our peaceful citizens to fly in terror from their once happy abodes."[107]

More generally, the *Carthage Gazette* noted that it was evident "from the information we receive from the various parts of the Union, that the British spare no pains or expense to accomplish their diabolical design of setting the Indians at war with the whole of our frontier settlements."[108] In January 1812, David Campbell (a member of one of the most prominent speculation families in the Southwest) noted that "the British have made themselves justly odious to every good citizen, by pushing on the Indians to war against us."[109] An attack upon both the British and southwestern Indians was needed to address this problem.

The kidnapping of Martha Crawley only strengthened the demand for an attack.[110] Crawley, a resident of Humphreys County, was taken by a small band of Creeks in 1812. Retaliation for her kidnapping, as well as the death of five other women and children, was a must. As newly appointed Senator John Sevier pointed out, only through an attack would "those wretches . . . be reduced to reason." He also made clear his firm belief that "British emissaries are among them."[111] The *Nashville Clarion* invoked both the legacy of the Revolution and lingering memories of 1790s-era Indian attacks when it wrote in the wake of the Crawley affair that Middle Tennesseans had become "the sport of those who owe their existence to [white Tennesseans'] forebearance—to robberies innumerable every now and then the most shocking murders are added." Continuing, the editor made clear that Tennesseans should

> make the neighboring nations responsible for the acts committed in and through their territory. Teach double dealers your true character, and command the submission of the petty savages on your frontier. In times like the present forbearance will be construed as

pusillanimity. Act as your forefathers, and at the point of a bayonet subdue and extirpate the savage foe. The softer emotions of humanity are out of the question; it is folly to spare the viper that he may poison your family.[112]

The rarely spoken reality in this situation was that Americans stood to gain a lot of good cotton land out of Indian removal. Even as he demanded a retaliatory attack in the *Knoxville Gazette,* Senator Sevier wrote to President Madison that over 1.3 million acres of land was "not yet treated for" in Tennessee. He further noted,

> The situation, fertility of soil, and great local advantages attending that part of the Country, places it, if not on a superior point of View, on at least as desireable as any part of the Western Country. I beg leave to observe, that from the Acquaintance and knowledge I have of the Indian claimers, I am induced to believe, it would not be difficult to Acquire a relinquishment; and I am led to Anticipate that such an Accession of Territory will enter into the Views of the President, who I hope will unite in bringing About so desireable an object.[113]

Popular approbation for the embargo, emerging American nationalism, and the desire for more land both fed off of and fueled Tennessee's representatives in Congress to push a hard-line anti-British position. Out of Nashville, in fact, arose the one man arguably the most "hawkish" of anyone in Congress: Felix Grundy.[114] Grundy would later reappear in a critical post–Panic of 1819 debate that set the tone for Jacksonian politics in Tennessee, but in this period he was a driving force behind the national war effort.[115] Feeding off of Middle Tennessee's nationalism, Grundy helped direct the tenth and eleventh congressional sessions to expand American military power. His martial positioning, driven as it was by local sentiment, in turn fueled war talk in Tennessee. By January 1812 there was no looking back. David Campbell provides merely one example of Middle Tennessee sentiment. Pointing to his desire for a mass uprising to drive the British out of America, Campbell argued, "Fifty thousand men can do it, and if fifty thousand cannot, one hundred thousand can. If one hundred thousand cannot, certainly two hundred thousand would effect the work."[116]

Middle Tennesseans got what they wanted. On the eighteenth of June President Madison received from Congress a formal declaration of war against the British. Upon hearing of the development, the *Nashville Clarion* described a scene nearing pandemonium: widespread demonstrations of support, militia parades, toasts, and volleys of musket fire.[117] Felix Grundy made it clear that "the national legislature has done its duty. It now remains for the people of the United States to show themselves Americans."[118] Maj. Gen. Andrew Jackson certainly stood ready; upon hearing the war declaration he immediately offered twenty-five hundred volunteers to the president.

The War of 1812

Tennesseans maintained this martial spirit throughout the war, although the majority of their efforts were limited to attacks on southern Indian nations.[119] The Volunteer State's only real attempt directly to engage the British prior to 1815 came when Brig. Gen. James Winchester commanded part of William Henry Harrison's northwestern army. Unfortunately, in 1813 a combined British and Indian attack surprised and decimated his troops at the Battle of the River Raisin in Michigan. Winchester was taken prisoner, and he would spend the rest of his life fighting charges of cowardice for his conduct during the battle. That same year General Jackson marched two thousand volunteers down the Mississippi to support Gen. James Wilkinson at New Orleans. He was called off at Natchez, however, and eventually marched the entire army back to Nashville.

Tennessee's opportunity to get involved came late in 1813. In September of that year the Red-Sticks, a group of younger Creek warriors who wanted more offensive action in the Southwest, initiated a "punitive expedition" against errant Tensaw Creeks at Fort Mims, who, as historian Karl Davis has noted, "had become closely associated with the interests of the United States."[120] News of the "massacre," which included women and children, and which the media sometimes exaggerated as consisting of several hundred people, led Tennesseans to erupt in indignation.[121] Perhaps Thomas Craighead of Nashville best encapsulated regional sentiment when he argued that the "tocsin of war has sounded. Hundreds of our fellow brethren of the Mobile have fallen beneath the savage tomahawk. The martial sons of Tennessee do well to recollect the time when they and their fathers were isolated and exposed to the incursions of the same barbarians. Shall history register in the annals of our country that the friends and relatives of the people of Tennessee were slaughtered with impunity by the savages of the forest?" Shortly thereafter a committee of prominent Tennesseans, led by Governor Willie Blount and Andrew Jackson, recommended a war against the Creeks to "exterminate their Nation and [its] Abettors."[122]

Middle Tennesseans overwhelmingly supported offensive action. A petition from Franklin County, for example, argued that the "people on the frontiers feel more than they can say. Give them not reason to believe they are to be deserted. Let them not be induced . . . to imprecate the vengeance of heaven on the government and administration under which they live."[123] When the call was made for volunteers, around five thousand men agreed to march on the Creeks to ensure that, as Jackson put it, the "blood of our women and children [would] not call for vengeance in vain."[124]

On November 3, 1813, John Coffee led the first strike by slaughtering Creeks at Tallushatchee; as David Crockett later described it, many of them were "shot like dogs."[125] The following spring Jackson initiated a more decisive attack at the Horseshoe Bend of the Tallapoosa River. On March 27 Jackson's army charged Creek breastworks outside of the town of Tohopeka. The battle was bloody and lasted all day, but when it ended some nine hundred Red-Stick warriors, women, and children lay dead.[126] This battle effectively ended the Creek War.

Although Jackson received heavy criticism from the Federalist Party press for his brutal attack, his popularity in Tennessee shot through the roof.[127] Particularly helpful were the peace terms he forced upon the defeated Creeks. In the Treaty of Fort Jackson, he procured for speculators and settlers twenty million acres of prime agricultural land in central Alabama. An ulterior motive might have been suspected in late 1813, when Jackson took surveyors with him on his march to Horseshoe Bend. Certainly the *Nashville Clarion* hinted at other causes for the attack. In 1812 its editors had pointed out that Creek land was "extremely beautiful and finely watered with excellent springs and navigable rivers." A year later it made clear that the Fort Mims massacre provided a suitable "pretext for the dismemberment of their country."[128] Jackson himself noted to his troops that the "country to the South is inviting. The soil which now lies waste and uncultivated, may be converted into rich harvest fields to supply the wants of millions."¹²⁹ At any rate, southwestern residents sang Jackson's praises, as did the federal government, which made him a brigadier general in the U.S. Army and commander of the southwestern Seventh Military District.[130]

The Creek campaign made up the bulk of the Tennessee experience during the War of 1812. But far more famous was Tennesseans' final action, a natural extension of the Creek War: the Battle of New Orleans. On January 8, 1815, Jackson's army of Tennesseans and Kentuckians routed a formidable British force led by the Duke of Wellington's brother-in-law, Sir Edward Packenham. Although the Treaty of Ghent had ended hostilities two weeks earlier, this decisive victory restored American honor and brought about an immense nationalism that Jackson rode to prominence. No longer, it seemed, would the national character face assault—either from foreign disrespect or from internal dissension, such as the 1814 convention at Hartford, Connecticut, where unhappy Federalists met and discussed secession.[131] And for Jackson it was even more important. His popularity after the Battle of New Orleans was so great that it catapulted him into the forefront of national politics. Eventually, it helped put him in the White House.

༺✤༻

The nationalism espoused throughout the first decades of the nineteenth century made it easier for Middle Tennesseans eventually to accept a national party system. Whereas the region once had flirted with secession, the surge of American nationalism, combined with their commitment to Jeffersonian Republicanism, helped residents connect local issues with interregional and national political movements.[132] Indeed, the debate over progress found a home in a more general division emerging within the Republican Party ranks. On the one hand, "national republicans" fully endorsed entrepreneurial innovation and were beginning to press for tariffs, government-funded internal improvements, and generally expansive economic development. On the other hand, "democratic republicans" maintained a more restrained economic philosophy.[133] They were not averse to controlled economic development, but they (eventually) opposed tariffs and wanted the government out of the internal improvement business. These two groups formed the backbone of the national Whig and

Democratic Parties. And the ability of the two economic philosophies in Tennessee to connect with these emerging national movements made it far easier for Tennesseans eventually to accept the second-party system.

Stark political divisions were not yet in place in 1815, of course, although the events of the next few years firmly set Middle Tennessee down the path. After the end of the War of 1812 massive economic and demographic changes swept through the Southwest. By that point merchants and planters in Middle Tennessee had combined to become engines for economic expansion: "The commercial and agricultural capabilities of our country," noted the *Nashville Clarion*, "are every day opening to our view new sources of wealth and enterprise. A few years since and this portion of our country was a wild and trackless desart [sic], where nothing but savage inhabitants crossed the traveller's path—but now he is greeted by the busy face of the bustling merchant, and the steady *phiz* [sic] of the plodding and industrious planter who give to him a comfortable and hospitable reception."[134]

As before the war, such economic growth relied upon extensive credit schemes and optimism that the cotton market would continue to bring solid prices. Yet danger lurked behind this expansion. Should the market contract, many ordinary Tennesseans would face financial ruin. When it did, in late 1818 and early 1819, the resulting political debate reinforced the ideological divisions necessary for a viable two-party structure. The panic also prompted demands that something be done about banks, a set of new and seemingly out-of-control economic institutions. Virtually nonexistent during the embargo debates of 1808 and 1809, concern over banks helped democratic republican elements in Tennessee launch what would become the Jacksonian political philosophy.

Chapter 6

The Emergence of a Jacksonian Philosophy: Expansion, Banks, and Panic, 1815–1825

John Campbell was a man on the make in the fall of 1816. Interested in studying the law and having run out of opportunities in his native Virginia, Campbell set out for Nashville, Tennessee. What he found there surprised him. "I am delighted with the appearance of this flourishing little place," he wrote. "It is laid off with considerable taste and presents to the traveler at once the marks of polished society—activity in business and increasing wealth. It is worth all Tennessee besides that I have seen. To break from the wilderness when you see nothing but logg [sic] trails barren wilds and lonely deserts into Genteel Society and a Town of this appearance the affect upon the feelings is delightful."[1]

Campbell's observations are noteworthy for two reasons. First, they show that in only fifteen years the Cumberland River basin had become an area for "genteel society" through its reputation as "an elegant cotton country, [that] in a few years will be unendingly valuable."[2] Such highly regarded land had given local planters the means to access the profitable cotton and tobacco markets, and the resulting cash flow had created a class that significantly contributed to the image of local civility. Agreed Christopher Houston upon his arrival in Middle Tennessee, "People here are generally orderly, & in no part of the world, where I have been, are they more forward in encouraging literature. [For] a country so new, the cotton is excellent."[3]

Perhaps more important, Campbell's report provides palpable evidence that post-1815 economic dynamism solidified and expanded upon fifteen-plus years of already profound social transformation. Since 1796, Middle Tennessee had witnessed a tremendous wave of demographic and economic expansion. Because of this growth, the Cumberland River had become a highway for trade goods, which in turn created a mercantile class that relied upon local farmers to perpetuate the vibrant economy. The period from 1815 to 1819 saw particularly impressive expansion. As before the War of 1812, commercial growth revolved around land speculation, cotton, and entrepreneurial innovation. Yet even as planting and merchant interests were pushing economic boundaries, ordinary folk and their political allies continued to believe that unabated economic dynamism threatened to give them insurmountable levels of debt.

Their concern would grow louder after the Panic of 1819. When financial disaster finally struck after four years of unprecedented expansion, many people were crushed as never before. Now, anyone who had to deal even slightly with the market found that previously ubiquitous credit—which had driven land sales in Middle and West Tennessee and provided the backing for crop shipments and merchant exchanges—had severely contracted. Given the utter lack of any usable medium, many in the region faced ruin.

As before, ordinary Tennesseans used the contested and ideologically divided political culture to demand some level of relief. This time, however, there was a new wrinkle in the dialogue. In large measure, the debate revolved around banks, which had not existed in previous clashes over political-economic policy. Although Tennessee's first bank had appeared in 1807, new institutions were chartered at a brisk pace after 1815. And a shortage of specie combined with speculative mania and massive cotton production ensured that Middle Tennessee would become flooded by these new institutions' paper currency. As the panic hit, banks and bankers joined speculators and merchants as a focal point for ordinary Tennesseans' wrath. They also altered the nature of the political debate: Whereas in 1809 prodebtor politicians favored stay laws, after the panic they called for retrenchment rather than state-mandated relief. The difference was banks, and this difference would set the tone for Jacksonian politics in Tennessee.

The Postwar Economy

If the embargo and subsequent war had generally injured the regional economy, many Tennesseans would have agreed with the *Nashville Whig* that peace "re-animated the countenances of our merchants and various classes dependent on their patronage."[4] It particularly benefited the cotton trade. By early 1816 market prices for Tennessee cotton went as high as twenty-one dollars per hundredweight, which was six dollars higher than the best prices of the preembargo period.[5] Over the next two years it fluctuated between twenty and twenty-two dollars, although at times it would go as high as thirty.[6]

As long as the market in Europe remained solid, Tennessee producers could expect sizable profits. Lacking the necessary raw materials after twenty-plus years of commercial and military warfare, factories in Britain imported southern cotton at an astonishing rate.[7] Certainly the editors of the *Nashville Clarion* understood the importance of the foreign market. "What [will] most interest our readers in the news by this arrival," they wrote in 1818, "is the brisk prices which our staple productions of cotton [obtain] here in [the Liverpool] market; which are at least as high as could have been expected."[8]

Many entrepreneurs pushed to profit from the soaring national and international cotton prices. James Winchester and John Overton were merely two to do so. In 1817 they fronted a venture that hoped for state and federal funding to create a "Sumner Cotton Factory" complete with a "picking and carding engine that can pick and card from 30 to 35 pounds per day."[9] Caught in the postwar exuberance that gripped federal leaders such as John C. Calhoun and Henry Clay, Overton and his group argued, "Domestic Manufacturers, ought, as well on principle of Public consideration, as on those of private benefit, to receive the patronage, support, and protection of the legislature of every state in the union."[10] That same year Thomas Claiborne pointed out that he was "engaged as one of a company here in the building [of] a Steam Mill" for similar purposes.[11] Thomas King hoped to make money off smaller equipment. Announcing that his "Republican loom" was available for citizens to purchase stock in, he insisted that investors would find that it "very far surpasses any in America for ease and dispatch for weaving cloth."[12]

Getting the raw product to the mills, looms, and the wider market required an enhanced transportation infrastructure. After all, as Bishop Francis Asbury noted in 1815, Tennessee's turnpikes were "a disgrace to the State and to the undertakers, supposing they had any character to lose. It is a swindling of the public out of their money to demand toll on such roads as these."[13] Thus the quest for internal improvements became a critical part of the region's entrepreneurial growth. Within months of the Battle of New Orleans the legislature was inundated with petitions for turnpikes and river projects.[14] Within a few years there was enough underway that the *Nashville Whig* happily announced that "it must be truly gratifying to every person to witness the rage for internal improvements, which at present pervades the citizens of the west."[15]

Perhaps no transport innovation looked to take advantage of postwar cotton prices quite like the steamboat enterprise.[16] Steamboats had first appeared on the Mississippi in 1811, and since that point Nashville's entrepreneurs had struggled to incorporate them into their vision of commercial growth. Although no progress had been made by war's end, optimistic boosters nevertheless hoped that Tennessee soon would join the numerous "steam boat companies [that] are already formed and forming in every section west of the Alleghany." Thomas Jefferson certainly saw the advantages. To Nashville entrepreneur and congressman George Washington Campbell he wrote his congratulations on "the success of the steam boats. no part of the world can be more benefited by them than our Western states, and no river more than that of Tenissee."[17] "The spirit of Tennessee is up," observed the *Nashville Whig* in 1816, "and we hope in a few months to see the banks of the Cumberland lined with those powerful and useful engines."[18] Two years later it finally happened. In 1818 a group of investors, led by future governor William Carroll, attempted to send a steamboat up the Cumberland River. Impediments stopped them short of Nashville on that run, but rising waters helped them reach their destination in March 1819.

The arrival of that boat, christened the *General Jackson,* revolutionized cotton and other crop exportation to New Orleans. A trip that once took weeks to complete could now be achieved in seven days; the return trip took a little over two weeks.[19] Other investors quickly got involved. In 1819, for example, a group led by one Samuel Polk petitioned the legislature for incorporation of the Columbia Steamboat Company, with a capital stock of fifty thousand dollars.[20] That same year the Nashville Steamboat Company sought and received incorporation and had the *General Robertson* in operation by 1820. All told, by 1824 a dozen steamboats were making the trip from Nashville to New Orleans, and by 1825 over one million pounds of cotton had left the town for ports abroad.[21]

As could be expected, reduced transportation costs, combined with soaring cotton prices, encouraged Middle Tennesseans to engage in increasingly large-scale production, which in turn required extensive amounts of land. Thus of all the postwar economic activity in the Southwest, nothing so benefited from the "irrational exuberance" of the era quite like land speculation.[22] Farmers such as James B. Williams voiced their concern that "speculation without owning the land" threatened to remove more cautious members of the community from potentially valuable acreage. Williams made this point clear when he asked the general assembly for redemption of an old North Carolina grant, "not . . . as many others have done, for the purposes of speculation without owning the land," but so that he could obtain access to Stone's River and build a grist mill for the benefit of himself and his neighbors.[23] Maury County resident Christopher Houston echoed this sentiment. Although a speculator himself, he pointed out to his son Placebo, "There are always people here on alert for business, but a thousand eyes are open for this new land speculation. The way they manage it perhaps you know already. They bid up the prime lands to any price so that the poor people shall not get it."[24]

In a pattern similar to the prewar years, he also pointed out that speculators in Maury County made "land rights very uncertain."[25] Moses Fisk would have agreed. In 1815 he complained to the legislature that his original purchase of land in Davidson County had become meaningless because of earlier, overlapping claims. After having purchased new warrants, he found that these were contested and mostly useless as well. He thus asked the legislature to uphold the sanctity of his contracts and give him title to his twice-purchased land.[26] Only four years later, a group of Davidson County petitioners reinforced Fisk's concerns by pointing out that speculators "take our hard earned improvements from us through low cunning as they make it their business inperticular [sic] to locate every improvement in each neighborhood without exception, to profit by our labor which we have done on them."[27]

Although the heart of these men's complaints were true to the legacy of Tennessee land acquisition, behind the Davidson County petition's rhetoric lay a larger issue: For all intents and purposes, by 1815 there was little unclaimed land left in Middle Tennessee. Thus while they continued to harass poor landowners and squatters locally, many leading speculators moved on to the vast areas that would become Alabama and Mississippi. They also pushed to get a foothold in the fertile Chickasaw lands in West Tennessee, which speculators had coveted as early as 1784 when Stockley Donelson staked a claim there.[28]

Interest in West Tennessee justified a reconnection of older Indian antipathies, albeit this time directed toward the Chickasaws rather than Cherokees or Creeks. Shortly after the war ended an editorial in the *Carthage Gazette* pointed to the need to remove the Chickasaws before they "turn on our unsuspecting inhabitants and murder and steal, as outrageously as before." The following September a group of petitioners asked the legislature to use their influence with Congress to have "the Indian title to lands within the Charter limits of this State extinguished."[29] In 1818 the *Clarion* complained loudly that the Chickasaws had become "insolent" and wanted to know whether the government would do anything about it.[30] Ultimately, these pleas were successful. In 1817 and 1818 Andrew Jackson led a federally appointed commission that negotiated western Tennessee and Kentucky away from the Chickasaws. For approximately three hundred thousand dollars, the commission erased the remainder of Chickasaw influences in the region.[31]

The potential for profit seemed high for anyone willing to take a chance on these lands. In 1817, John Campbell pointed out that lawyer and surveyor Alfred Balch had "made about 60,000 dollars" on his speculation endeavors. He also trumpeted his belief that land near the Tennessee River would "rise in value two or three hundred per cent" and make southwestern Tennessee an ideal location for emigration and economic growth.[32] Christopher Houston readily agreed. In 1818 he pointed to Jackson's acquisition as a last ditch opportunity. "You have heard, I suppose, that General Jackson's purchase of land from the Chickasaws & Choctaws, include the

Obion river, the Forked Deer, the Hatchy &c., Rivers," he wrote to his son Placebo, "which has all along been reckoned the last in the United States. if you & your brother-in-laws ever intend moving to the Westward, now is the time to get land on this side of the Mississippi."[33] James Campbell seemed even more optimistic, arguing in early 1819 that "Jackson's late treaty with the Chickasaw & Choctaw tribes of Indians has widened the field for speculators so much in Tennessee that the capital of the state is almost entirely diverted from [speculation in] Alabama."[34] Noting that it was necessary to "secure success in public life," John Campbell made clear that "if these lands should sell low, immense fortunes will be made by buying them at the sales; and I am determined to avail myself of every opportunity I see presented."[35]

Yet the seemingly endless economic and political opportunities attached to these speculations, surveys, and sales came with an asterisk attached. All of it depended upon blind optimism in the expanding cotton market, the availability of Indian land—both achieved and anticipated—and the extensive use of generous credit terms. Looking to purchase as much land as possible, speculators rarely used actual specie in their transactions. And to obtain the credit necessary to pull off such large-scale purchases they had to have the support of Nashville's financial community, whose rapidly proliferating banking institutions rarely maintained the proper specie reserves. By 1817, the state's fifteen banks proved more than willing to open the door for a flood of paper currency to be used in financial transactions.[36]

The danger of so much paper was not lost on many Tennesseans. An important early debate over banking revolved around a proposed branch of the new Bank of the United States (BUS). In 1817, a cautious group of Middle Tennesseans favored locating a BUS branch in Nashville to check the speculation of local and state financial institutions. Opposing these men were a group of speculators and bankers led by John Overton, whose cronies controlled the Nashville Bank while he maintained the Nashville branch of the Knoxville Bank. Despite its inability to regulate banking practices at this early date, these men feared a BUS might force greater accountability in their land speculation enterprises.[37] Although Overton and his supporters were successful in keeping the BUS out until 1827 (by pushing through the legislature a fifty-thousand-dollar levy on any such institution), this miniature "bank war" showed that people were aware of the potential frailty of the economy. Any downturn might threaten to undermine the system upon which postwar Tennessee stood.

The Panic

In the late fall of 1818 and spring of 1819 the American economy came crashing to a halt. Suddenly, as banker John Summerville noted to investor Thomas Sumner, one could not "name a place in the least commercial, throughout the U. States & Europe but is suffering in the same way. History does not offer a parallel of distress equal to what the last 12 months have produced. The Manufacturer—the agriculturalist—the merchant— the bankers—and the speculators have all gone too far in trade. All have too much due for the circulating amount of medium."[38]

As Summerville intimated, the problem stemmed from an international economy in the midst of a painful contraction. In America, it grew out of a combination of unsound credit schemes offered by the newly re-created Bank of the United States and by state banks, as well as an unexpected drop in the value of the country's most important cash crops. Since the bank's founding, BUS president William Jones had left state banks free to create paper currency far in excess of their stores of specie.[39] Although this loose policy helped drive the frontier speculative mania, the situation had gotten out of hand by 1819. When British banks began to call in their transatlantic loans, the BUS had to call in state loans. This in turn forced state banks into the position of suspending specie payments and having to call in local loans, which ultimately trickled down to ordinary farmers who were forced to pay off debts with hard money.[40] As Christopher Houston noted, bank suspension made it "altogether uncertain how any one can be prepared to make payment."[41] John Summerville agreed: "Much distress prevails here in consequence of all creditors taking alarm & calling upon Nashville for their debts as they fall due, with a determination to have their money at every hazard. And as Nashville is the heart and soul of the trade of W. Tennessee, it of course suffers much without the possibility of relief for the present."[42]

Simultaneous to this sudden lack of a circulating medium was a plunge in the value of Middle Tennessee cotton. At twenty-seven dollars per hundredweight in the summer of 1818, within six months it had dropped to the 1805 price of seventeen dollars.⁴³ By early 1820 the price had sunk to seven to ten cents per pound and showed no sign of bottoming.⁴⁴ Unfortunately, other crops brought in little to alleviate financial strains. Tobacco, for example, dropped from ten to seven dollars per hundredweight, and then between two and three.⁴⁵ And as early as March 1819 the *Nashville Whig* pointed out, "We have it from authority to be relied upon, that articles similar to those now brought to our market, such as pigs, poultry, butter, vegetables, &c, were purchased last year, nearly one hundred percent [lower] than they are now obtained."⁴⁶ A year later James Houston lamented that he had "about forty fine hogs to sell and 150 bushels of wheat, but no money to be had for anything."⁴⁷

Perhaps Andrew Jackson put it best. In mid-1819 he noted that the "distressed state of the mercantile world has introduced its effects everywhere. Money has disappeared & has brought the great mass of mankind into Distress, from which there is no escape but industry and economy."⁴⁸ James Campbell went even further: "This country is literally at present in the d—ndest situation as it respects money that ever was heard of or read of. All the effects of banks and overtrading. The merchants have got in debt to the banks which debt they expect to pay when they sold their produce. That had fallen in price and remains a dead weight on their hands. They are now borrowing money in this way to keep up their credit hoping that some change may take place in the market which will save them."⁴⁹

Campbell's palpable anger was felt by many ordinary Tennesseans, who soon began publicly to meet to consider "the situation of our country [and recommend] a general retrenchment of expenses; of inculcating some uniform system of economy; of adopting means of relief against our present calamities; and of providing against future embarrassments."⁵⁰ In June 1819, reported the *Whig*, numerous citizens of "Nashville and its vicinage [met] at the Court-house, the object of which was to take into consideration the embarrassed state of the community."⁵¹ And the uproar made it clear that something had to be done about banks. Middle Tennessee banks' tendency toward unsafe speculation practices created an image in the post-panic period that they were, as one correspondent of the *Clarion* noted, "almost omnipotent in money matters, [and] their influence has been felt at our elections. They have ruined the country to build up towns—and ruined towns, to import goods. They have produced a monied aristocracy which makes the rich more rich—& the poor more poor. And what is worse, they have injured our circulating medium by making most erroneous loans to individuals, which they cannot pay; and of course, they cannot redeem their notes."[52]

"A Farmer" readily agreed. The fact that local institutions had over the last four years lost "sight of the public good," he noted in a letter to the *Whig*, meant "banks and bank paper was multiplied to a degree of madness—the value of money depreciated. As those institutions multiplied, public confidence was withdrawn."[53] After the panic, as "S. N. G." vividly illustrated, banks were among the least popular institutions in the state. "There was a ... species of buzzards," he noted in 1821, "which ... [have] hovered about Nashville. I know not the name by which they are distinguished in the nomenclature of naturalists, but the common people call them 'Banks.' The[se] banks are becoming weaker by the hour, whilst their opponents are growing in strength."[54]

The seemingly unwise policy decisions perpetrated by some regional bankers justified these public attacks. A petition from Smith County, for example, registered its concern that the Carthage Bank had blatantly disregarded explicit charter policy:

> When books were opened for the purchase of Bank stock in the year 1817 times were prosperous and your memorialists ... had reason to believe that the notes of those institutions at all times would be equal to the amount in specie promised on the face of the paper, that being an express condition in the charter. Now the paper received by your memorialists for causes unknown, but certainly not chargeable to them, cannot be converted into specie; or pay a foreign debt without a loss of twenty five percent.[55]

And then there was the case of John Summerville, an employee of the Nashville Bank. In 1817 he proclaimed to client Thomas Sumner that he could "make great—much beyond handsome profits for two years to come, if I had materials of consequence to work with." He thus asked Sumner to tie his money into silver, state bank note, and U.S. Bank note speculation, initially to the tune of approximately thirty-five hundred dollars.[56] Sumner agreed and added to the venture with some of his sister's savings. They received modest dividends in 1817 and 1818 but saw the floor fall out from beneath them when state banks and the BUS suspended specie payments in 1819.[57]

By creatively redistributing Sumner's and his sister's money across accounts and various states' notes, Summerville eventually recovered a large portion of their money, but up until that point he was as far as two thousand dollars in arrears for his speculations.[58] In an apologetic letter, he made it clear how unaware he was of the danger inherent in Middle Tennessee's evolving economy:

> I never knew until now what it was to feel keen distress of mind—To see honest industry and honorable [?] overtaken by such distress as now pervades the commercial community, and to be the innocent means of jeapordising the property of friends who confided in my foresight and prudence, proves too much for my feelings and occasions me a loss of sleep that I never supposed before, nor would suffer were the funds my own, nor would have suffered, if I could have foreseen even in distant prospect the difficulties and losses that has so suddenly burst upon us.[59]

Extensive internal trading such as Summerville's convinced many observers that a financial conspiracy existed, perpetrated by local banks to help an elite few avoid the disaster plaguing most other inhabitants of the region. "The monied aristocracy which has been produced by the shavers and banks of Nashville and their dependents," noted the *Clarion*'s editor to this end, "has destroyed with some, every moral feeling and every sentiment of consideration for the distresses of the people, they will overrun the country—It is an alarming evil not only as it regards individuals but as it respects society—would it not be well to know how it is that while the balance of the community feel so much distress, that bank directors, with few exceptions, feel none of it."[60]

"A Farmer" agreed. The "immediate effect of [establishing banks] is to withdraw specie from diffusive and general circulation; and its accumulation in vaults of the banks, thereby rendering it more accessible to brokers and others, who wish to get hold of it."[61] A group of petitioners from Warren County went so far as to say that by supporting banks the legislature had "ennobled a few of our fellow citizens by granting them hereditary Honours, Titles, Privileges and Emoluments, by which means they have monopolized and shut up in Banks, all our Gold and Silver coin, and left us no alternative. We must either receive their Bills of Credit in place of lawful money or go without. This we consider as inconsistent with our just and natural rights and destructive to our peace and happiness."[62]

Such a volatile political situation exposed the fact that something had to be done to help those people who had been wiped out by banks, specie suspension, and the panic. The problem was agreeing upon the best course of action.

Developing a Jacksonian Philosophy

Initially, those who were interested in protecting debtors employed rhetoric reminiscent of the embargo debate of 1809. In 1819, for example, the *Whig* noted, "Thousands of our unfortunate citizens, whose hopes are withered in the revolution which has taken place in the affairs of the commercial world, and in fact, many of those who have been engaged in the various pursuits of mankind, look to the benevolence of their Representatives in the adoption of a lenient Bankrupt Law."[63] A group of Davidson County petitioners asked the general assembly to pass a law "authorizing and allowing Defendants against whom executions have issued, and whom the Plaintiff will not receive current bills, to stay the execution on giving security for such time as your Honorable Body may think proper to give the Defendants an opportunity to raise the Specie—to save his property."[64]

Many politicians took advantage of this old embargo rhetoric. Led by Felix Grundy, they supported the notion that passing stay laws while simultaneously creating a new bank to expand the amount of paper in circulation would relieve the scarcity of money and therefore raise commodity prices to pre-panic levels. Not entirely unfriendly toward banking and mercantile philosophy, this position placed the panic debates squarely within the debtor/creditor framework of ten years before.

This group was in the public eye by the spring of 1819, when, as James Campbell noted, the "debtor party, as it may be aptly termed," threw their support behind laws that put a "stop to the collection of debts until the produce of the country would increase its capital to such a degree as would enable it to bear the burden of debt pressing upon it."[65] Through the summer and fall of 1819 the "debtor party's" anticreditor position reverberated through Middle Tennessee, and the exposed nerve they tapped helped them achieve a powerful interest in the legislature. In their first session the "party" quickly made good on the first part of their platform: They passed a law that provided for a stay of execution on acquiring debtor property for two years unless creditors accepted notes of leading banks at par.[66]

By tapping into public approbation for such measures these politicians temporarily managed to obtain a distinct legislative advantage. But they overplayed their hand on the question of banks by overlooking widespread discontent and attempting to create a lending institution that they thought would "make plenty of money which may perhaps alter prices and start trade again."[67] Said institution became known as the state "loan-office." It created over a million dollars in a circulating paper medium and made the bills legal tender for all taxes due the state and counties. Its only means of acquiring specie, however, was the vague promise of the sale of the newly acquired Cherokee lands in the Hiwassee District in East Tennessee. The loans it offered, moreover, were for one year at 6 percent interest, while personal loans were limited to five hundred dollars.

Not surprisingly, this measure was attacked on all sides as inadequate. From the debtor perspective, as James Campbell noted, the terms of loan required that agents

> take power of attorney from the borrowers and endorses the president [of the bank] to confess a judgement against them in favor of the bank in any of the courts of Nashville in the event that the terms of the loan are not punctually complied with. One of these terms is that 20 per cent on the amount loaned is to be paid in every 90 days & good security tendered to secure the payment of the residue. If these terms are rigidly enforced it will operate most seriously upon the people who will be foolish enough to borrow.[68]

In other words, the terms may have seemed excessively liberal by creditor standards, but those most in need of a loan seemingly would have a difficult time meeting their obligations. A group from Davidson County agreed. In an 1820 petition to the legislature, they blasted that body for allowing Grundy's loan office, but no others, to issue notes that were legal tender for "all debts due for taxes and individuals." By doing so, they argued, "many persons have been seriously injured, and the community deprived of a portion of a circulating medium, which at this time of embarrassment, is very interesting to them." They demanded that all "solvent" banks redeem in specie.[69]

Creditors were no more enthusiastic about the loan office, as Campbell made clear, because it attempted to collect

> and put in its vaults the notes of the [state's] other banks. In the first place the revenue of the state—the proceeds of the sales of the Cherokee lands & c. is in Nashville and Knoxville notes. By curtailing in the manner they do a considerable quantity of the notes of the old banks will be obtained. The intention I am told is that if the old banks refuse to give currency to their paper the new bank will sue them for the amount of their notes they may have collected into their vaults. This will pay hell in some way or other.[70]

Campbell was correct—the "old banks" saw through this attempt to force them into specie payments and refused to accept the new bank notes for any reason.[71] When combined with explicit concerns over the constitutionality of the loan office (and banks in general) these concerns had a profound impact on the institution. On the one hand, its notes quickly depreciated far below par; on the other hand debtors completely lost faith in the new bank that was supposed to help them.

Thus Grundy found his bank emasculated and mostly meaningless.[72] Although he and his allies tapped into the same impulses that had made the embargo so explosive ten years before, they entirely miscalculated the one significant difference in the two debates. By 1819, there had been such a proliferation of banks and bank notes that corruption seemed to exist on a much larger scale. Certainly "A Farmer" thought so. In tracing the history of banking in Tennessee, he noted that paper currency was not as important during the embargo and war years because "there were very few state banks, and consequently but a small portion of bank paper in circulation."[73] By 1820, however, the situation was entirely different, thus requiring a new solution to the old dilemma.

Andrew Jackson agreed, making public his belief that through banks "the imprudent speculator may be enabled to extricate himself from his pecuniary embarrassments but the burthen must ultimately fall upon the honest farmer and industrious tradesman."[74] Privately, he was even more explicit. "Let every honest man take care of himself," he wrote John Donelson, "and have nothing to do with the new raggs of the State, for be assured that the Interest of Speculators will be alone consulted during [its] existence."[75]

The older embargo position was eclipsed by a relief movement combining widespread antibank, prospecie sentiment with creditor-friendly elements under the argument that "the industrious and prudent have no need of legislative aid in complying with their contracts."[76] It built upon the belief that all legislative solutions were illusory because they did not actually alleviate ordinary Tennesseans' problems; rather, they protected banks and others who had gone too far in land and monetary speculation. Representative Robert Allen best summarized this emerging position in 1819:

> I know of no class of men who have less claim upon the paternal indulgence or gracious favor of the government than most of the purchasers of public land—I mean that portion most clamorous for relief, and the most to be benefited by a bill. They associated themselves in companies, with all the money the banks (with whom they were mostly connected) could lend, and at the auction sales put down all competition from actual settlers; the prudent man's home was bought over his head, at a price he could not give for it. It is now in the hands of one of these speculators, who has other lands adjoining.[77]

This coalition became particularly visible shortly after Grundy overplayed his hand with the loan office. A Sumner county grand jury led the charge when in 1820 it convened to discuss the financial difficulties plaguing the region and proclaimed that instead of helping small farmers, stay laws and specie suspension mostly benefited large businesses and speculators who had overextended bank credit.[78] In short, they argued, only wealthy debtors would benefit from Grundy's bank.[79] The state supreme court agreed, ruling that the stay law of 1819 provided an illegal advantage to debtors over creditors by compelling the latter to accept the depreciated new bank notes in payment.[80]

At the same time, a significant number of leaders argued that banks failed constitutional muster. Nowhere in the 1796 Tennessee constitution was there a provision that explicitly endorsed the creation of a bank. And section twenty-three of article eleven vaguely declared that "perpetuities and monopolies are contrary to the genius of a free state, and shall not be allowed."[81] Andrew Jackson spoke for many across the region when he proclaimed that "the constitution of our State, as well as the Constitution of the United States prohibited the establishment of Banks in any state,—

and that such a thing as loan offices by a state for the purpose of creating a fund out of the property of the State for the payment of individual debts certainly is not a power granted by any provisions of the state constitution."[82]

For the leading figures of this new political movement, which included Jackson and William Carroll, the answer to the financial recession was clear: Tennessee needed to engage in a program of "industry and economy" without resorting to expanding the region's paper base or allowing anyone out of the contract between debtor and creditor.[83] As early as February 1819 the *Nashville Clarion* called on Tennesseans to "set about a general retrenchment of your expenses. You can be œconomising in your dress and in your living. Lop off your redundancies."[84] Moreover, as a petition from Smith County made clear, many common Tennesseans "would heartily concur in any just measure that could be adopted to undo all that has been done in relation to banking in the State of Tennessee, satisfied such institutions always create a monopoly at war with the soundest principles of political freedom."[85]

"Pindar" went so far as to offer a plan to avoid future "hard times." In 1820 he warned his fellow Tennesseans, "When you see a *Bank* door, consider it as the gate to destruction, and beware of entering thereat. When you see a *Store*, consider it as a mansion of pestilence, and run for your lives. Never run in debt for personal property—bear well in mind—yea—observe particularly from this time hence forward, what the apostle says— *Owe no man anything.*"[86] By 1823 there seemed to be no looking back, as "Neckar" made clear in the *Whig:* "Public opinion," he noted, "is no doubt firmly and unequivocally fixed in favor of a sound metallic currency."[87]

This antipaper, antibank policy converted the restrained definition of progress into a policy of retrenchment and specie payments. It would become the hallmark of the Jacksonian political perspective.[88] As early as 1819 the message provided powerful political fodder, as Henry Bryan made clear in his successful legislative campaign. "Banking in all its forms," he noted, "under every disguise, is a rank fraud upon the laboring and industrious parts of society; it is in truth a schem[e], whereby, in a silent and secret manner, to make idleness productive and filch from industry, the hard produce of its earnings."[89] James Campbell pointed out that electoral victory would hinge on how to respond to "the state of the diseases produced by bank mania—& speculation."⁹⁰ Andrew Jackson, meanwhile, implied to his nephew that two local politicians were unacceptable as candidates because although they were "men of talents—they both have been taken with the Bank mania, which has [proved] the adage that there are no great men without their weaknesses."⁹¹

Scores of candidates charged into this lively political atmosphere, as James Campbell pointed out in 1819: "We are getting . . . on in our electioneering here. This county we have no less than seven candidates for the legislature and but one to elect. In the adjacent congressional district Trimble & Cannon are up. It will probably be a closer election than any that has ever taken place in that district."⁹² Campbell concluded by noting the relative oratorical strength of these legislative candidates: "If oratory were to improve by the number of speeches that are made we would excel Greece or Rome. But we have no Ciceroes [sic] tho we have many Jim Meeks."⁹³

Ordinary people also actively supported specific candidates and issues, just as they had done ten years earlier with debtor relief and judicial reform. Certainly the 1821 gubernatorial race followed this pattern. As James Campbell pointed out, the race was "more warmly contested than they have ever been before in Tennessee. The old & the new banks are the touchstone of political orthodoxy. Our stump orators are already declaring on their respective sides."⁹⁴ Agreed one John McLemore a few months later: "Considerable interest is already manifested about the election. I expect it will be a very warm one, the relief expected from the Banks."⁹⁵ By the summer of 1821 Middle Tennessee had become so embroiled in the election that Campbell wrote, "I never have seen so deep an interest manifested by the people in state politicks as is now."⁹⁶

The two gubernatorial candidates, William Carroll and Edward Ward, further stimulated popular involvement by canvassing the countryside for votes to an unprecedented degree. Carroll, a war hero turned merchant who had incurred heavy losses in the panic, gained the upper hand by calling for statewide financial retrenchment and a return to hard specie. He also denounced the slave-owning land speculator Ward as a monied and probank "aristocrat."⁹⁷ The slur appealed to regional sensibilities to such a degree that, regardless of Ward's lukewarm support for banks, his supporters began to despair. "Carroll has been here and 'spoke a speech' well calculated to win him votes," wrote John McAlister to Ward supporter John Overton. "I wish to Heaven I could write you that Ward would get a majority, and hope as sincerely as any man that the account of his having a majority in this county might reach me. But all this I fear, will not be according to either of our desires."[98]

McAlister was correct: Carroll was indeed elected in a landslide of 41,244 to 11,171 (the Middle Tennessee count was 27,496 to 6,709). These numbers represented a spike in votes compared with the previous and next gubernatorial elections. In 1819 the total vote count was 45,620, of which Middle Tennessee accounted for 25,436. In 1823, by contrast, when Carroll ran unopposed, only 32,597 turned out to vote. Interestingly, 23,795, or 73 percent of all votes, were cast in Middle Tennessee. The regional vote, in other words, remained consistently high throughout these years of economic turmoil.[99]

Not everyone in Middle Tennessee subscribed to the prevailing notion of industry and economy. Although proponents of commercial growth temporarily faltered, they nevertheless attempted throughout the period to kick-start the economy through entrepreneurial innovation. At the outset of the panic, "A Farmer" lamented the "reprehensible" and seemingly backward state of Tennessee agriculture, insisting that "liberality in the farmer, is the best economy he can pursue. The more industrious he is in cultivating and manuring his fields, the more abundant will be his harvests. The better keeping he affords his cattle and horses, the more labour they will perform and the higher will be their price in the market." He also demanded that the legislature consider improving the roads, pointing out that they were "intimately connected with the interests of every farmer who frequents the market."[100] Late in 1818, moreover, investors in Nashville publicized the availability of bridge stock. In January 1819 a group of Nashville entrepreneurs showed their support for internal improvements by having the *Clarion* reprint glowing reports of European canal ventures.[101]

Even as the panic spiraled out of control, in October 1819 a petitioner argued that improving the Cumberland River was essential to the growth of the cotton trade and that "fifty or perhaps seventy five thousand Dollars would make the river passible [sic] at all seasons."¹⁰² A year later a *Whig* correspondent suggested the propriety of state aid for manufacturing as a means of correcting "those evils, which are now so severely felt by the people."¹⁰³ And throughout the spring of 1820 "Bogtrotter" infuriated more conservative editorialists by supporting the notion of purchasing land on extensive credit.¹⁰⁴

Speculators seemed to act in a particularly decisive manner. In 1819 John Campbell wrote that declining cotton prices and limited specie made "now the time for speculation" in western land. "Five or six hundred dollars in specie will buy 1000 acres of land at two dollars an acre," he pointed out to his brother, which was "one fourth of [regular] prices. These lands in four or five years will sell for 50 or 60 $ and acre."¹⁰⁵ That same year a group of speculators came up with a way to reignite the land business: They called for "a wonderful lottery in Nashville, drawing for the priority of entry in the Western District." They proposed offering twelve thousand acres of their own as a means of getting started.¹⁰⁶

This entrepreneurial element strongly opposed measures that in any way regulated the region's financial institutions. To them, specie suspension was a measure "calculated to relieve against that general embarrassment and distress which pervades the commercial world."¹⁰⁷ Perhaps John Summerville best summarized this position. Banks and other entrepreneurial activity needed no real regulation, he continually argued to Thomas Sumner, because the financial scene was shortly to improve; "all that is asked is a continuance of confidence for a few months—and all will end honestly. This is the well founded belief of the directors of the three [Nashville] banks."¹⁰⁸

The confidence of this "national republican" element proved accurate. As the world market slowly reopened for southern commodities, Middle Tennessee producers found prices for cotton and tobacco climbing from $8.00 and $1.00, respectively, in early 1823 to $11.00 to $12.50 and $2½ to $3.00 by November.¹⁰⁹ By the fall of 1824 cotton and tobacco prices had risen to 23 cents per pound, and 5.5 cents per pound, respectively, thus heralding the beginning of a new round of economic expansion.¹¹⁰ Prices in 1825 reinforced this new boom. Cotton, as Thomas Scott wrote his father, sold "for a good price now. I think our house (that is the house I do business in) will make something like from 10 to 20 thousand dollars on cotton this Season. They have bought about 1500 bales."[111] Burgeoning steamboat and internal improvement activity further facilitated market growth.[112] By 1826, the year banks finally resumed specie payments, over $1 million in cotton left Nashville via the Cumberland for ports at New Orleans, Louisville, and Pittsburgh.

As the economy returned to pre-panic strength, national republicans grew more confident. Now they had control of Nashville, and they generally had a visible presence throughout the region.[113] The recent economic contraction was but a hiccup, something that might happen again, but that was worth the risk. John Campbell, for example, made it clear that his "plans and schemes may all fail but he who will never attempt anything will never succeed in anything. If I make nothing I shall still be satisfied."[114] By 1829 there was enough support for commercial endeavors that the legislature organized an internal improvements board and appropriated $150,000 for its use.[115]

Entrepreneurial elements also realized the danger in the political perspective followed by the increasingly popular Jackson and his allies. Although Jackson remained personal friends with Overton, Ward, John Coffee, and other speculators, he distanced himself from their speculative and banking tendencies and generally did not get along with the merchants and heads of financial institutions in his hometown of Nashville.[116] In the 1824 presidential election Henry Clay and John Quincy Adams both had a noticeable following in Middle Tennessee, while Newton Cannon became known as a loud pro–William H. Crawford and anti-Jackson man.[117] He was the first politician in Tennessee eventually to run under the Whig label. A speculator, planter, and merchant, as early as 1815 Cannon represented the four counties with the highest concentration of industry and commercial activity in the state—Davidson, Williamson, Maury, and Rutherford.[118] And he was certainly not alone in his distaste for Old Hickory. By 1827, as B. T. Martin noted, Jackson had become such a political lightning rod that the legislature was a hot-bed of "Anti-Jacksonism."[119] Even if he received nearly unanimous support statewide, the general nevertheless faced noticeable opposition within his home region, and his hometown.[120]

James K. Polk's 1825 congressional race is particularly instructive for its ideological and personal divisions. His primary opponent that year was

Andrew Erwin, a longtime enemy of Andrew Jackson. Erwin also was personal friends with Henry Clay, readily endorsed the "American System," and lambasted Polk for his timidity on the question of internal improvements. From the outset the campaign was public and issue-driven: Polk employed regular pamphlets and writing campaigns, while Erwin used the *Nashville Whig* to advance his positions (his son owned the paper). Polk further helped his campaign when "he traversed and canvassed [his district] again and again. Before the canvas was half over he had displayed so much activity and energy in his movements that he was regarded by his competitors as the most formidable opponent."[121]

Meanwhile, after twenty-plus years of demographic flux the Middle Tennessee population began to stabilize. As it did so, most ordinary Tennesseans continued to engage the market but came to realize that cotton presented as many difficulties as opportunities. Over the 1820s and into the Jacksonian years, Middle Tennessee commercial agriculture emphasized diversification: Grain, corn, tobacco, cotton, and livestock all had a presence in the regional economy.[122] And a considerable number of these ordinary Tennesseans feared that an excessively national republican polity would become "filled with purse-proud, technical fools whose thimblefull of brains will be displaced by the mere forms of law; but whose wealth will enable them to look down with indifference on the little suits of the poor. Justice will be stayed, and probably in many instances left without redress."[123]

The shameless pursuit of money was the root of the entrepreneurial problem. As Christopher Houston noted, "In truth, I had rather see my children seeking the true riches, with just a competency, and walking in the ways of virtue, than to be lords of a whole country. Let the dead preach to us, what is all Colonel Work's 100,000 worth to him? What is impires [sic] to Napoleon the Great? Death is a great leveller."[124] Many ordinary Tennesseans agreed with Houston and stood firmly behind a more restrained definition of progress. By minimizing contact both with banks and with the expansive market, many hoped to avoid excessive debt and thus the economic catastrophe that wiped out the region in 1819.

Middle Tennessee's intense political-economic debate was not unusual for a southwestern community. Historian Daniel Dupre, for example, has shown that in northern Alabama a transportation revolution created a cotton economy of international proportion. In the wake of the Panic of 1819, however, common yeomen feared for their economic independence and came together as part of a Democratic coalition to fight elite interests. This struggle, says Dupre, created clear political and social interests in Madison County: one identified as the "Royalists," or money interest (successful cotton growers enamored of market growth and internal improvements), and the other identified with those individuals less successful in weathering the storm of the panic. These groups became the foundation for the second-party system and remained ideologically separated until threatened by northern abolitionism.[125]

Similarly, historian Stephen Aron has shown that high land prices in the early nineteenth century made money a greater imperative in central Kentucky. It also reduced the likelihood that ordinary families could achieve either personal independence or easier provision for dependents and descendants. Even as these people were forced to engage the market or move farther west, however, the land situation allowed slaveholding farmers to take advantage of the national (and international) economic developments. Merchants in Lexington facilitated this new commercialism. As in Nashville, they undermined traditional economic exchanges by discriminating in favor of cash customers, and their far-flung connections for a time made Lexington a major economic hub for the Southwest. Commercialism in turn sparked a meaningful debate over the state's future. Could the economy ever again cater to households generating modest marketable surpluses or would it continue to favor men of more substantial means whose land and slave hands produced commodities on a larger scale? Ultimately, the latter position carried the debate. While the Panic of 1819 shook many Kentuckians and made Henry Clay's nascent concept of an American System more vulnerable, Aron shows that by the 1820s there was no real economic alternative to fall back on.[126] The best that could be done was to put a restraint on economic development, a position from which politicians such as Kentucky expatriate and Tennessee congressman Felix Grundy made their careers.

Like its geographic cousins, understanding Middle Tennessee during the early national period requires the illumination of the tension between those advocating expansive development and those who were interested in a more restrained economy. The resulting ideologically divided civic sphere comprised the state's antebellum political moorings and is one that modern scholars have typically discussed as little more than a preamble to the years after Andrew Jackson and his cohort became a national political force.[127] Studying Jeffersonian Tennessee is critical because the popular democratic political culture that emerged during these years established a foundation for the explosion in voting and contested ideological perspectives that defined life in Jacksonian Tennessee.

Epilogue

Slavery and the Transition to Jacksonian Politics

The early national debate over progress and popular democracy took place against a backdrop of increasingly codified racial discrimination. Indeed, the institution of slavery exerted enormous influence over Middle Tennessee's social and geographic identity. As we have seen, slaves had been an integral part of American settlement from the outset. At that point the tiny white population needed as much help as they could muster, meaning that slaves maintained complex relationships with their masters that allowed access to firearms and independent agricultural production.[1]

That, combined with Revolutionary-era misgivings about the institution, made some Tennesseans uneasy about its nature. And at the turn of the nineteenth century, white perceptions of slavery and black autonomy remained somewhat ambiguous.[2] Many slaves performed common functions such as buying and selling goods for their masters. Urban slaves, moreover, maintained a measure of independence through the hire-out system, while free blacks used the 1796 constitution to participate in such important community events as militia musters and civil elections. And both slaves and free blacks benefited from a wave of evangelical awakening, which gave Middle Tennesseans, regardless of color, opportunities to play a role in church affairs.[3]

As the century progressed, however, slaves' condition changed. The combination of rebellion, rumors of rebellion, an emerging antislavery impulse, and an ever-expanding black population led many white Tennesseans to fear for the continuity of the region's economic and social order. The contested black condition thus gave way to a society defined by racism and restrictive slave laws. And by the 1820s hardening legal and social racism had become part of the political consciousness. Two developments served as the catalyst for this politicization: the Missouri crisis of 1819–20 and an antislavery movement that emerged immediately prior thereto. Missouri was scary enough—many slaveholders and their supporters feared that abolition would lead to insurrection and economic catastrophe, which amid the Panic of 1819 was a dismal thought. But antislavery activity made the threat even worse. Between 1814 and the late 1820s dozens of petitions calling for emancipation made their way to the legislature, while manumission societies popped up all over East Tennessee. Middle Tennessee's concerns were compounded by antislavery agitation within the Methodist Church.

Where once restricting the African American population was not of general political-economic concern, by the 1820s white residents were insisting their representatives do something. The legislature was more than receptive. Unlike in other "southern" states, where nonslaveholders seemed to control early-nineteenth-century assemblies, Tennessee slaveholders dominated the government from the outset of statehood. Their control would continue well into the antebellum period: The statewide percentage of slaveholding legislators never dropped below 65 percent through 1861 and usually hovered around 80 percent. These numbers are remarkable when one considers that less than 25 percent of the population in 1830 controlled the 141,603 slaves in the state. In other words, a slaveholding minority easily was able to impose its will when necessary to secure the peculiar institution.[4]

And impose their will they did, particularly after Missouri and antislavery ensconced the institution within the political consciousness. Culminating in constitutional revisions in 1834, they tightened slave codes, took away free blacks' right to vote and serve in militias, and even took steps to remove that population from the state entirely. Their actions ensured that the black experience in Jacksonian Tennessee would be far different than the one the blacks had understood thirty years earlier. Tennessee by then had become a *herrenvolk* society—one that defined its political and economic reality by the subjugation of the black population.[5]

Epilogue: Slavery and the Transition to Jacksonian Politics

In short, the inexorable development of the institution of slavery had serious effects on Middle Tennessee's social development, and over time it could not help but wind its way into the political consciousness. And if it did not directly affect political institutionalization in Jeffersonian Tennessee, by the Jacksonian years it had become a critical characteristic of the region's political, economic, and social world view.

Slavery, Insurrection, and the Free Black Population

Slave rebellions, the explosion of cotton, and the increasing black population provided the initial catalyst for social and legal changes to Middle Tennessee's atmosphere of contested race relations. After the 1792 Haitian revolt, and particularly after Gabriel Prosser's failed 1800 rebellion, slaveholding Tennesseans began to fear that a loosely controlled and expanding black population threatened social order.[6] Thus they began to emphasize legal avenues to maintain order.

In 1799, for example, the legislature minimized the possibility of masters facing trial for physical abuse. Although slaves had legal standing in extreme cases, the state provided the loophole that owners would not face charges should a slave die while resisting or during "moderate correction."[7] To reduce the possibility that a revolt might stem from mass gatherings, meanwhile, the 1799 legislature sanctioned the dispersal of "unauthorized" slave meetings and allowed for the prosecution of the property owner where the meeting took place. Whereas the 1741 North Carolina slave code merely fined people who encouraged insubordination or rebellion, the Tennessee legislature placed upon such an individual a twenty-year prison sentence. Active participation in an insurrection was punishable by death.[8]

It soon got stricter. In response to the Virginia conspiracies of 1800 and 1802, the state assembly passed a law forbidding "words in the hearing of a slave or person of colour, either publicly or privately, that may have a tendency to inflame their minds, or induce them to insurrection."[9] Thereafter they made it illegal either for a white or free black person to be in the company of a slave for any reason, unless specifically approved by the slave's master.[10] That same year the legislature more formally altered the older, North Carolina–based statute on slave patrols.[11] Thenceforth, militia captains would have the authority to appoint patrols to search suspect places at night, and could punish slaves without passes with "fifteen stripes."[12]

Securing white social control made the institution more violent and arbitrary as the nineteenth century progressed. In 1804, for example, Andrew Jackson advertised a reward for a runaway and offered "ten dollars extra, for every hundred lashes any person will give him, to the amount of three hundred."[13] In 1807 a mob on the Duck River lamented that they had to hang a "Negro found guilty of murder" rather than burn him as vengeance demanded—the ground was too wet for a fire to set.[14] In 1815 it was rumored that one John Lanier consciously rounded up "a parcel of free Negroes" and sold them into slavery as a means of paying off debt.[15]

There were more brutal examples. In 1825 David Leach faced expulsion from the Zion Presbyterian Church for "chastising a Negro boy named Arch in a most unchristian and Inhuman manner, giving the said Arch to the amount of one hundred and fifty Paddles and one hundred and fifty lashes, on his naked hips back and thighs." In his defense Leach put forward that Arch had engaged "in conduct highly provoking" before running away. Once captured, he felt a harsh punishment would serve both as a corrective measure and as a deterrent for other slaves living in the region. The church agreed with him, and he was acquitted.[16]

Similarly, little was said in 1821 when Andrew Jackson, in an effort to break Mrs. Jackson's maid Betty of "bad habits," directed "that at the first impertinence, or the first disobedience of orders, that she be publicly whipped." More specifically, Jackson declared that "the first cloaths she attempts to wash for any person but the family—without the express permission of her mistress, that [she be taken] to the public whipping post and given fifty lashes."[17] John Campbell grew so concerned by increasing white violence that he chose not to put his slave Jerry up for hire in Nashville, despite the fact that he could bring as much as "$200 per annum." For him the risk was too great, because Jerry could well fall "into the hands of an unfeeling scoundrel who would treat him with inhumanity."[18]

Whites grew particularly concerned about the free black population. Because they maintained a level of autonomy, white Tennesseans increasingly saw a disconnect between freedmen's lifestyles and their desire for greater social control. It did not help that there was a large and ongoing in-migration of free blacks. In 1791 there were fourteen in Davidson County, the only real community in the region. By 1800 the number in Davidson had grown to seventeen, with the next two in size, Sullivan County and Wilson County, holding seventeen and nine, respectively. The total free black population in Middle Tennessee that year was fifty-one. Reflecting the general trend of population growth, the number of free blacks in Middle Tennessee dramatically rose by 1810, to a total of 809. The largest communities were the 384 in Wilson County, 130 in Davidson, and 97 in Sumner.[19] Given that as of 1812 Middle Tennessee slaveholders had manumitted only 11 slaves, these numbers indicate a large in-migration.[20]

Early on the legislature enacted measures designed to regulate free blacks' daily lives. In 1806, for example, it required that "every free Negro or mulatto [be] registered in a Book to be kept by clerks of counties—specifying age, name, color, stature, marks, if any; when and how he became free."[21] These Tennesseans had to keep a copy of this registration on their person at all times. Without it they were treated as runaways and sold back into slavery.[22]

The legislature also made it harder for free black Tennesseans to get a leg up in the evolving economy. At the turn of the nineteenth century, as we have seen, men such as Jetro Locklier and Robert Rentfroe had had enough autonomy to pursue rather prominent economic endeavors. A limited number of particularly "trustworthy" men had even received white sponsorship for legislative approval for full citizenship, and in some cases they had been allowed by the legislature to "prove their accounts" in order to obtain debts from delinquent white patrons.[23] These sorts of petitions became increasingly rare, however, and when they did come in front of the legislature, they lacked political weight. An October 1815 petition requesting that one Sherwood Bryan, a resident of Davidson County, be granted citizenship "in every respect as if he were a white man" was read and tabled; ultimately nothing came of it. In 1822 Smith County resident Jacob Stone's petition to prove his accounts was found "unreasonable" and ignored.[24]

Over the next few decades the legislature considered removing the free black population from the state. In 1816 legislators endorsed a congressional plan to establish a settlement for free blacks in Liberia. In 1819, Benjamin Ingram followed upon this initiative by petitioning to move free blacks to the state of Alabama. Fourteen years later the American Colonization Society in Franklin County did the same.[25] In the interim the Tennessee Manumission Society formally endorsed the colonization position, and in 1829 the Tennessee Colonization Society came into existence. In 1833, the society even received from the state ten dollars for each free black resident it relocated.[26]

Ultimately, however, the colonization impulse amounted to little, mostly because of slaveholders' fear that giving up their work force would lead to economic catastrophe.[27] Moreover, there was a genuine belief that manumission for the purposes of colonization would "deluge Society with a set of miserable beings who must & would result to every species of depredation upon the whites for means of support."[28] Social order, in other words, was of the utmost importance, and manumission would do little other than destroy it. All told, fewer than three hundred free black people ever left the state, and most of those did so in the mid-1850s.[29]

Threats from Within and Without

In 1816 the *Carthage Gazette* provided a lurid account of a failed slave revolt in South Carolina, deeming it "very important intelligence" because of the light it shed on potential activity in Middle Tennessee.[30] This "intelligence" showed the paranoia to which white citizens were increasingly susceptible. Fear of insurrection had certainly been a justification for anti-black legislation between 1796 and 1815. By the late 1810s it, and the concomitant fear of chaos it engendered, made it easy for the defense of slavery to join the debate over progress as an important part of the Middle Tennessee political culture. All that was needed was a catalyst to make common Middle Tennesseans more concerned about the issue. It came in the form of two interrelated developments: the Missouri crisis and the emergence of a local antislavery movement.

In 1817 the Missouri Territory petitioned Congress for statehood. Two years later the issue was officially debated, at which time New York representative James Tallmadge Jr. proposed an amendment requiring the new state to abolish slavery. His proposal touched off a sectional firestorm, and although the House of Representatives narrowly passed the amended bill, the Senate destroyed it in March 1819. In March 1820 Congress finally negotiated a compromise. First, they allowed slavery in Missouri but admitted Maine to keep the proper ratio of free to slave states, and second, they abolished the peculiar institution north of latitude 36 degrees 30 minutes. This compromise effectively put the issue to rest in 1820, although it would reemerge during the sectional debates of 1850–61.[31]

Middle Tennessee firmly believed that Tallmadge's and his supporters' position raised the specter of insurrection and social chaos. Some even feared that it might undo the bonds of union. Andrew Jackson, for example, wrote that the "Missouri question, so called, has agitated the public mind, and what now I see, will be the entering wedge to separate the union. It is even more wicked, it will excite those who is subject of discussion to insurrection and massacre—it is a question of political ascendancy and power, and the Eastern interest are determined to succeed regardless of the consequences, the constitution or our national happiness."[32] A year later the *Nashville Whig* minimized regional culpability for the institution in an attack on northern merchants who supported Tallmadge's amendment. "Which is worse," asked the editor, "to tolerate the existence of servitude, inherited from our fathers with the soil, on which we were born; or to be actively engaged in the traffic which produced this servitude?" Continuing, he pointed out that "in the face of these facts our pharisaical brethren can pronounce the 'stand off—we are holier than ye.' They can bellow and rave in favor of Missouri restriction in public, and in private employ their wealth and enterprise in this unrighteous business."[33]

Simultaneous to the Missouri crisis emerged a homegrown antislavery movement. Given that their climate and soil minimized the usefulness of slavery as an institution, it is no surprise that manumission societies popped up all over East Tennessee, the first in 1814. In that year eight people in Jefferson County, led by Quaker minister Charles Osborn and Presbyterian reverend John Rankin, established the Tennessee Manumission Society. By 1816 there were sixteen branches with four hundred seventy-four members; by 1825 there were twenty-five with one thousand members.[34] One prominent antislavery advocate, Elihu Embree, even established a newspaper, the weekly *Manumission Intelligencer*, which remained in publication until his death in 1820.[35] Benjamin Lundy subsequently published the *Genius of Universal Emancipation* from Greeneville. He continued until 1824, when pressure from proslavery advocates convinced Lundy to move to Baltimore.[36]

Tennessee antislavery was further fueled by the Methodist Church. In 1808 Bishop Francis Asbury noted that Tennessee Methodists at the Western Annual Conference "made a regulation respecting slavery: it was, that no member of society, or preacher, should sell or buy a slave unjustly, inhumanly, or covetously."[37] A guilty examinee faced expulsion from the group. Tennessee Methodists reinforced this law in 1812, when they broke from the Western Conference to start their own.

In 1815 the Tennessee Conference disqualified anyone from the office of deacon who refused to express disapproval of slavery and declare a willingness to emancipate their slaves when practicable. It also passed a regulation requiring preachers to manumit children of slaves at the age of twenty-five. Only two years later, the church set a limit on the amount of time new preachers could keep slaves they formerly may have owned, and in 1818 the church's annual conference devolved into a boisterous debate between antislavery and proslavery elements.[38]

Yet despite a lot of sound and fury in the East and from Methodists, antislavery made little headway in Middle Tennessee. Manumission societies never took root because of their conservatism. They emphatically rejected extralegal forms of abolition, never maintained a solid plan for bringing about their objectives, and did little more than endorse the idea of colonization. They also were undermined by the fact that their most committed advocates went north in search of safer environs. By 1820, for example, men such as Rankin and Osborn were long gone from the Volunteer State, with Benjamin Lundy not far behind.[39]

Without a forceful position and clear objectives, antislavery concerns could not overcome fears that emancipation, even if gradual, was not economically feasible. As Nashvillian John Summerville put it in 1819, "There is no plan that can ameliorate the condition of our slaves effectually but that of universal emancipation, and this plan cannot be executed with success unless they can be colonized, and in this there are so many obstacles to be over come that it will require ages to succeed."[40] Fourteen years later Representative Edward Littlefield of Maury County and Representative Leonard Sims of Rutherford and Williamson made an identical argument. Slavery and free black marginalization were the only means of maintaining order as long as there was a sizable black population in Tennessee.[41]

Methodist leaders, meanwhile, decided to tone down their antislavery rhetoric in order to procure greater numbers of converts.[42] The high point of Methodist antislavery came between 1819 and 1822, when the Conference refused to ordain slaveholders and, under East Tennessee preacher James Axley, even denied them the ability to exhort and lead public prayer meetings.[43] Axley's policies were so rigid that they turned moderate Methodists against him, and by 1822 he had been replaced by a more lenient preacher named George Ekin. Soon thereafter the Conference ordained deacons and preachers without reference to slave property, and by the Tennessee Conference of 1824 the church only would endorse the principle that slavery was an abstract evil. Thenceforth, little was done actively to undermine the institution.[44]

Missouri and the nascent antislavery movement nevertheless placed concerns over the African American population firmly within the Middle Tennessee political consciousness. Free blacks were particularly scrutinized. By the mid-1820s many white residents felt they had a negative effect on the slave population and believed it was becoming too difficult to deal with this growing and potentially unruly community.[45] In 1825 ninety-four Rutherford County petitioners accused free black families of encouraging slaves to steal and of instilling "into their minds views of liberty." Another petition that year argued that free blacks should be taxed at high rates and have guardians "to direct their conduct." It also argued that free blacks should no longer vote or serve in militias. Thirty-two others commented that they were insolent toward whites and thus "hurtful to society and especially to the rising generation." These petitioners requested a law compelling free blacks to leave Tennessee, or at the very least that something be done to keep them from controlling militia company elections.[46]

Tennessee's racial assumptions hardened just as Nat Turner's rebellion exploded into the southern consciousness. In 1831 Turner, a preacher in Southampton, Virginia, led slaves on a march that ultimately killed nearly sixty whites. The shock of the attack was compounded shortly thereafter by the rumor of an insurrection in Tennessee.[47] Although the plot was foiled before anything could happen, the two scares, combined with an emerging northern abolition movement (spearheaded by William Lloyd Garrison) left proslavery Tennesseans reeling. Slavery and racial discrimination were no longer abstract questions; now they were necessary means of social control.[48]

Shortly after news of these rebellions (and northern threats) made the rounds, the legislature passed a law that would consent to manumission only if freedmen agreed immediately to leave the state.[49] That same session legislators prohibited free blacks from moving to Tennessee.[50] They also tightened slave codes by requiring that "unusual numbers" of slaves who congregated at "suspicious times and places" be dispersed immediately. Moreover, they made it a capital offense for a slave to conspire or rebel; the chief instigator could be killed on the spot rather than go through a trial if he showed any inclination toward resisting arrest. And any slave convicted even of indirect involvement in a conspiracy faced whipping, jail, pillorying, and even death, without any hope for appeal.[51] The state also increased the remunerative aspects of slave patrolling by giving the men who served three-month terms a one-year exemption from public road work, militia musters, and jury duty.[52]

These new laws clearly reflected the desire to keep slaves and free blacks under control. And by the 1830s many in East Tennessee agreed with these restrictions. After Nat Turner's rebellion they, too, saw the social danger inherent in servile insurrection and gradually stifled the antislavery impulse.[53] The heady years from 1827 to 1829, when over four thousand East Tennesseans signed petitions calling for emancipation, were gone.[54] By the late 1830s there was no indigenous antislavery pressure anywhere in the state.[55]

The Constitution of 1834 perfectly encapsulated Tennessee's entrenched political commitment to slavery. Even as the convention pushed a constitutional provision encouraging internal improvements, a committee on slave issues declared that "the African slave . . . bears upon his forehead a mark of separation which distinguishes him from the white man—as much after he is a free man as while he was a slave."[56] The legislature then attacked what little freedom remained for the free black population by writing their ability to vote and serve in the militias out of the Tennessee constitution. As delegate William Loving put it, it was "an evil example to our slaves to allow free Negroes to exercise the right of suffrage." Others feared it would make Tennessee a destination point for free blacks and runaways, thereby destroying social order and undermining Jacksonian understandings of democracy.[57]

Sociologist Pierre L. van den Berghe has defined *herrenvolk* democracy as "regimes that are democratic for the master race but tyrannical for subordinate groups."[58] Certainly this definition would have applied to mid-

Epilogue: Slavery and the Transition to Jacksonian Politics

nineteenth-century Tennessee. Although white residents enjoyed a level of democracy they could not have imagined forty years earlier, by the constitutional convention of 1834 it had come to rest upon the subjugation of the black population. Slavery was so firmly entrenched and fear of insurrection so strong that enslaved Tennesseans lost most symbols of autonomy. And for the free black population, subordination included a strong element of exclusion as well. The removal of their right to vote and participate in militia activity effectively marginalized them and implicitly endorsed their removal altogether.

Between 1775 and 1825 Middle Tennessee transformed from a contested zone of interaction between Spanish, Indians, and a small number of slaves and white settlers to a region with a dynamic commercial market and an entrenched commitment to the institution of slavery. This vibrant commercial society reshaped the region's political culture from one of nascent democratic institutions controlled by a paternal leadership to one that included issue-driven electioneering, high-volume legislative petitioning, public political rituals, and, in contested elections, high voter turnout. It also established a clear political debate between competing understandings of progress, one that was parlayed in the wake of the Panic of 1819 into broader National Republican and Democratic Republican movements. Eventually, these movements became the foundation for the second party system in Tennessee.

Alongside this political and commercial expansion, however, evolved a *herrenvolk* society. First apparent because of fears of population growth and servile insurrection, it grew stronger and closed inward as more threats to the peculiar institution seemed to emerge. Initially not a force in the region's political culture, Middle Tennesseans by 1820 insisted that governing institutions do something to protect the regional economic and social structure.[59]

Simply put, slavery became too entrenched through the course of Middle Tennessee's early national transformation to have anything but a major effect on Jacksonian political and economic institutions. By the 1820s local Tennesseans, both prominent and common, agreed that the region's economy was inextricably bound to it. Andrew Jackson, for example, defined his income as coming from "farming and Negro sales."[60] Edward Ward, meanwhile, supplemented his planting and speculation income by offering "several Negroes for hire, consisting of men, women and boys."[61] John Shofner, a small-time operator from Bedford County, managed to blend his fealty to slavery with a solid streak of progressivism. Shofner owned five or six slaves whom he used to help maintain the farm's agricultural position within the market economy. Not surprisingly, given his level of economic success, Shofner became a devoted Whig and proponent of entrepreneurial growth.[62] His experience certainly indicates, however, that the region's entrepreneurial impulse by the 1830s had come to refract through the prism of slavery.

Ultimately, then, Middle Tennessee's story encompasses far more than the twenty-one counties that fell within its boundaries during this period—it is one of how a region of the upper Southwest evolved from frontier to southern society. Indeed, examining Middle Tennessee's early national political-economic evolution allows us to explore the issues, values, and visions around which politics coalesced, as well as how and why a more open (white male) political democracy emerged in the early American Southwest. In so doing, it shows that the popular democratic political culture that emerged during these years established a foundation for the explosion in voting and contested ideological perspectives that defined life in Jacksonian Tennessee. This vibrant and contested civic sphere allowed a two-party system eventually to formalize around competing notions of progress. But it also undermined Indian cultural and economic prerogatives and hemmed in an increasingly large population of slaves and free black residents. Democracy, in other words, was not the clean, positive parade once described by historian Frederick Jackson Turner as the hallmark of the American experience.[63]

Studying the early national political culture in Tennessee thus helps scholars clarify the ways in which a broad southern community defined and came to grips with the question of "progress." In so doing, it sheds light on the process by which the democratic impulse affected the social construction of the Old South.

Introduction

1. Douglas Bradburn, "Revolutionary Politics, Nationhood, and the Problem of American Citizenship, 1787–1804," PhD diss., Univ. of Chicago, 2004, 5.
2. Charles Sydnor, *Gentlemen Freeholders: Political Practices in Washington's Virginia* (Chapel Hill: Univ. of North Carolina Press, 1952). For more on colonial political understandings, see Gordon Wood, *Creation of the American Republic, 1776–1787* (Chapel Hill: Univ. of North Carolina Press, 1969); Gordon Wood, *The Radicalism of the American Revolution* (New York: Knopf, 1992); Richard Beeman, *The Varieties of Political Experience in Eighteenth-Century America* (Philadelphia: Univ. of Pennsylvania Press, 2004); and Bernard Bailyn, *The Ideological Origins of the American Revolution* (Cambridge: Harvard Univ. Press, 1967). For more on colonial southern political culture, see William Cooper, *Liberty and Slavery: Southern Politics to 1860* (New York: McGraw-Hill, 1983); and Bertram Wyatt-Brown, *The Shaping of Southern Culture: Honor, Grace and War, 1760s–1880s* (Chapel Hill: Univ. of North Carolina Press, 2001). For conservative political traditions as transferred into the early national period, see Joanne B. Freeman, *Affairs of Honor: National Politics in the New Republic* (New Haven, Conn.: Yale Univ. Press, 2001); Richard Buel Jr., *Securing the Revolution: Ideology in American Politics, 1789–1815* (Ithaca, N.Y.: Cornell Univ. Press, 1972); Joyce Appleby, *Capitalism and a New Social Order: The Republican Vision of the 1790s* (New York: New York Univ. Press, 1984); Stanley Elkins and Eric McKitrick, *The Age of Federalism: The Early American Republic, 1788–1800* (New York: Oxford Univ. Press, 1993); James Rogers Sharp, *American Politics in the Early Republic: The New Nation in Crisis* (New Haven, Conn.: Yale Univ. Press, 1993); Lance Banning, *The Jeffersonian Persuasion: Evolution of a Party Ideology* (Ithaca, N.Y.: Cornell Univ. Press, 1978); and Richard Beeman, "Deference,

Republicanism and the Emergence of Popular Politics in Eighteenth-Century America," *William and Mary Quarterly* 49 (1992): 401–30.
3. Arthur Campbell to Archibald Stuart, Feb. 27, 1786, Campbell Family Papers, Rare Books, Manuscripts, and Special Collections, William R. Perkins Library, Duke Univ. (hereafter cited as Campbell Family Papers).
4. See John R. Finger, *Tennessee Frontiers: Three Regions in Transition* (Bloomington: Indiana Univ. Press, 2001), 126–28; and Thomas Perkins Abernethy, *From Frontier to Plantation in Tennessee: A Study in Frontier Democracy* (Chapel Hill: Univ. of North Carolina Press, 1932), 133. For more on the Northwest Ordinance, see Peter Onuf, *Statehood and Union: A History of the Northwest Ordinance* (Bloomington: Indiana Univ. Press, 1987).
5. William Blount to John Gray Blount, Nov. 7, 1790, in *The John Gray Blount Papers*, vol. 2, *1790–1795*, ed. Alice B. Keith (Raleigh, N.C.: State Department of Archives and History, 1959), 131. Blount's declaration supports Donald Ratcliffe's observation that the peculiar climate created by the Northwest Ordinance severely restricted party development. The territorial governor simply was independent of local controls of any form. See Ratcliffe, *Party Spirit in a Frontier Republic: Democratic Politics in Ohio, 1793–1821* (Columbus: Ohio State Univ. Press, 1998), chap. 1.
6. See, for example, Ratcliffe, *Party Spirit in a Frontier Republic*; and Patricia Watlington, *The Partisan Spirit: Kentucky Politics, 1779–1792* (Chapel Hill: Univ. of North Carolina Press, 1972).
7. As defined by Jürgen Habermas, the public sphere is a place for mediation between the state and the people in their private capacities. Or as John L. Brooke has put it, it is "the place where matters of shared importance unfold in early modern and modern societies." Of course, this sphere is limited to white participants. See John L. Brooke, "Consent, Civil Society, and the Public Sphere in the Age of Revolution and the Early American Republic," in *Beyond the Founders: New Approaches to the Political History of the Early American Republic*, ed. Jeffrey Pasley, Andrew Robertson, and David Waldstreicher (Chapel Hill: Univ. of North Carolina Press, 2004), 207–8; and Jürgen Habermas, *The Structural Transformation of the Public Sphere: An Inquiry into a Category of Bourgeois Society*, trans. Thomas Burger (Cambridge: Harvard Univ. Press, 1989).
8. This reflects many historians' contention that ritual and celebration facilitated cross-regional political links. See, for example, David Waldstreicher, *In the Midst of Perpetual Fetes: The Making of American Nationalism, 1776–1820* (Chapel Hill: Univ. of North Carolina Press, 1997); or Simon Newman, *Parades and the Politics of the Street: Festive Culture in the Early American Republic* (Philadelphia: Univ. of Pennsylvania Press, 2000). For more on Tennessee's early divided loyalties, see chapter 1. See also James Lewis, *The American Union and the Problem of Neighborhood: The United States and the Collapse of the Spanish Empire, 1783–1829* (Chapel Hill: Univ. of North Carolina Press, 1998); Robert Remini, *Andrew Jackson and the Course of American Empire, 1767–1821* (New York: Harper and Row, 1977); William Masterson, *William Blount* (Baton Rouge: Louisiana State Univ. Press, 1954); and Buckner Melton, *The First Impeachment: The Constitution's Framers and the Case of Senator William Blount* (Macon, Ga.: Mercer Univ. Press, 1998).
9. *Oxford English Dictionary* online, www.oed.com.

10. "The Savage and the Civilized Man," *Knoxville Gazette,* May 19, 1792.
11. David Hackett Fischer, *The Revolution of American Conservatism: The Federalist Party in the Era of Jeffersonian Democracy* (New York: Harper, 1965), xi.
12. Sean Wilentz, *The Rise of American Democracy: Jefferson to Lincoln* (New York: Norton, 2005), xviii.
13. For more on the *"new* new political history," as it has recently been dubbed, see Pasley, Robertson, and Waldstreicher, *Beyond the Founders;* Waldstreicher, *In the Midst of Perpetual Fetes;* Newman, *Parades and the Politics of the Street;* Len Travers, *Celebrating the Fourth: Independence Day and the Rites of Nationalism in the Early Republic* (Amherst: Univ. of Massachusetts Press, 1997); and Albrecht Koschnik, "The Democratic Societies and the Limits of the American Public Sphere, circa 1793–1795," *William and Mary Quarterly* 57 (2001): 615–36.
14. Slavery long has been understood to underpin Jacksonian, and southern, politics. See, for example, Eugene D. Genovese, *The Political Economy of Slavery: Studies in the Economy and Society of the Slave South* (New York: Vintage, 1965); Elizabeth Fox-Genovese and Eugene D. Genovese, *Fruits of Merchant Capital: Slavery and Bourgeois Property in the Rise and Expansion of Capitalism* (New York: Oxford, 1983); Cooper, *Liberty and Slavery;* John Ashworth, *Slavery, Capitalism, and Politics in the Antebellum Republic,* vol. 1, *Commerce and Compromise, 1820–1850* (New York: Oxford Univ. Press, 1995); William Freehling, *The Road to Disunion: Secessionists at Bay, 1776–1854* (New York: Oxford Univ. Press, 1990); Manisha Sinha, *The Counterrevolution of Slavery: Politics and Ideology in Antebellum South Carolina* (Chapel Hill: Univ. of North Carolina Press, 1999); and Stephanie McCurry, *Masters of Small Worlds: Yeoman Households, Gender Relations, and the Political Culture of the Antebellum South Carolina Low Country* (New York: Oxford Univ. Press, 1995).
15. For more on slave life during the territorial period, see chapter 4, this volume. See also Cynthia Cumfer, "'The Idea of Mankind Is So Various': An Intellectual History of Tennessee, 1768–1810," Ph.D. diss., Univ. of California at Los Angeles, 2001; William Toomey, "Prelude to Statehood: The Southwest Territory, 1790–1796," Ph.D. diss., Univ. of Tennessee, 1991; and William Alphonso Walker, "Tennessee, 1796–1821," Ph.D. diss., Univ. of Texas, 1959.
16. David Grant to John Owen, Sept. 3, 1790, Campbell Family Papers.
17. Cumfer, "Idea of Mankind Is So Various," 537. See also Ellen Eslinger, *Citizens of Zion: The Social Origins of Camp Meeting Revivalism* (Knoxville: Univ. of Tennessee Press, 1999), 41; and Ellen Eslinger, "The Shape of Slavery on the Kentucky Frontier, 1775–1800," *Register of the Kentucky Historical Society* 92, no. 4 (Winter 1994): 1–23.
18. Anita Shafer Goodstein, "Black History on the Nashville Frontier, 1780–1810," *Tennessee Historical Quarterly* 38, no. 4 (Winter 1979): 401–20. See also Anita Shafer Goodstein, *Nashville, 1780–1860: From Frontier to City* (Gainesville: Univ. Press of Florida, 1989), chap. 4.
19. *Carthage Gazette,* Aug. 17, 1809.
20. Bobby J. Lovett, *The African-American History of Nashville, 1780–1930: Elites and Dilemmas* (Fayetteville: Univ. of Arkansas Press, 1999), 4. Other free black men who served with Jackson during the Creek War include Christopher Christian, Caesar Prince, and Philip Thomas (8).

21. Petition 145-1825, Reel 9, Legislative Petitions, Tennessee State Library and Archives, Nashville (hereafter cited as TSLA).
22. Lacy Ford, "Making the 'White Man's Country' White: Race, Slavery, and State-Building in the Jacksonian South," *Journal of the Early Republic* 19, no. 4 (Winter 1999): 719. See also George M. Fredrickson, *The Black Image in the White Mind: The Debate on Afro-American Character and Destiny, 1817–1914* (New York: Harper and Row, 1971); and Freehling, *Road to Disunion*.
23. For more on this question, see Joyce Chaplin, *An Anxious Pursuit: Agricultural Innovation and Modernity in the Lower South, 1830–1815* (Chapel Hill: Univ. of North Carolina Press, 1993), esp. chap. 2.
24. See Michael F. Holt, *The Rise and Fall of the American Whig Party: Jacksonian Politics and the Onset of the Civil War* (New York: Oxford Univ. Press, 1999). See also Michael F. Holt, *The Political Crisis of the 1850s* (New York: W. W. Norton, 1978); and Ashworth, *Slavery, Capitalism and Politics*.
25. Finger, *Tennessee Frontiers*, chap. 1.
26. Ibid., 3–4.

Chapter 1

1. Daniel Smith, "The Journal of Daniel Smith, September 25, 1779," *Tennessee Historical Magazine* 1 (Mar. 1915): 51.
2. Tribes throughout the Southwest faced a shift in economic understandings. Greg O'Brien, for example, has shown the extent to which commercial prowess improved the ability of some leaders to command respect. O'Brien, *Choctaws in a Revolutionary Age, 1750–1830* (Lincoln: Univ. of Nebraska Press, 2002). See also Erik Hinderaker, *Elusive Empires: Constructing Colonialism in the Ohio Valley, 1673–1800* (New York: Cambridge Univ. Press, 1997).
3. John Haywood, *The Civil and Political History of the State of Tennessee from Its Earliest Settlement up to the Year 1796* (1823; reprint, Knoxville: Tenase Press, 1969), 188, 144.
4. Arthur Campbell to Samuel Purviance, Nov. 18, 1784, Arthur Lee Campbell Papers, Filson Historical Society, Louisville, Ky. (hereafter cited as Arthur Lee Campbell Papers).
5. See Andrew Cayton, "'When Shall We Cease to Have Judases?': The Blount Conspiracy and the Limits of the 'Extended Republic,'" in *Launching the "Extended Republic": The Federalist Era*, ed. Ronald J. Hoffman and Peter J. Albert (Charlottesville: Univ. of Virginia Press, 1996), 156–89. On the regional importance of the Mississippi River, see John May to Samuel Beall, Apr. 15, 1780, quoted in Stephen Aron, *How the West Was Lost: The Transformation of Kentucky from Daniel Boone to Henry Clay* (Baltimore: Johns Hopkins Univ. Press, 1996), 117.
6. James Robertson to Alexander McGillivray, Aug. 3, 1788, in "Correspondence of James Robertson," *American Historical Magazine* 1 (Jan. 1896): 81.
7. Eslinger, *Citizens of Zion*, 93–94. See also Waldstreicher, *In the Midst of Perpetual Fetes*, 158–59; Albert J. Tillson, "The Militia and Popular Political Culture in the Upper Valley of Virginia, 1740–1775," *Virginia Magazine of History and Biography* 94, no. 3 (July 1986):

259–64; Cumfer, "Idea of Mankind Is So Various," chap. 6, esp. 404–5, 433; and Richard Beeman, *Evolution of the Southern Backcountry: A Case Study of Lunenburg County, Virginia, 1746–1832* (Philadelphia: Univ. of Pennsylvania Press, 1984), 134.

8. For years prior to the Revolution, Indian tribes in Tennessee participated in what historian Richard White has called a middle ground—a zone of interaction in which Indians were neither dominant nor dominated by white settlers. See Richard White, *The Middle Ground: Indians, Empires and Republics in the Great Lakes Region, 1650–1815* (New York: Cambridge Univ. Press, 1991). See also John R. Finger, "Tennessee Indian History: Creativity and Power," *Tennessee Historical Quarterly* 54, no. 4 (Winter 1995): 296; Finger, *Tennessee Frontiers*, chap. 2; and Cumfer, "Idea of Mankind Is So Various," chap. 4. Although first contact took place in 1540 with Hernando de Soto's expedition, there was little meaningful interaction before the seventeenth century. It came at the tail end of a long period of white-Indian interaction that had altered basic tendencies on both sides. Starting in the 1670s, the Iroquois tribe pushed into the area below the Ohio River to satisfy the demands of the fur trade. The Cumberland basin thus became an area for extended hunts, used by multiple tribes. The result was that once indigenous groups such as the Shawnee were forced out of the region by 1730, the land became one shared by several groups. For more on first contact, see Lawrence Clayton, Vernon Knight Jr., and Edward Moore, eds., *The De Soto Chronicles: The Expedition of Hernando de Soto to North America in 1539–1543*, 2 vols. (Tuscaloosa: Univ. of Alabama Press, 1993). See also "De Soto Expedition," in *The Tennessee Encyclopedia of History and Culture*, ed. Carroll Van West (Nashville: Rutledge Hill Press, 1998), 862–63. For more on the emergence of the middle ground in the late seventeenth century, see Hinderaker, *Elusive Empires*, chap. 1. See also Finger, *Tennessee Frontiers*, chap. 1.

9. Usufruct understandings of property were common throughout the native world. John Philip Reid, *A Law of Blood: The Primitive Law of the Cherokee Nation* (New York: New York Univ. Press, 1970), 123–41. See also Claudio Saunt, *A New Order of Things: Property, Power and the Transformation of the Creek Indians, 1733–1816* (New York: Cambridge Univ. Press, 1999); and William Cronon, *Changes in the Land: Indians, Colonists and the Ecology of New England* (New York: Hill and Wang, 1983).

10. See Cumfer, "Idea of Mankind Is So Various," chap. 1.

11. William G. McLoughlin, *Cherokee Renascence in the New Republic* (Princeton, N.J.: Princeton University Press, 1986); Reid, *Law of Blood*; Theda Perdue, *Cherokee Women: Gender and Culture Change, 1700–1835* (Lincoln: Univ. of Nebraska Press, 1998); and Cumfer, "Idea of Mankind Is So Various," chap. 1.

12. Unknown author, Campbell Family Papers.

13. Hinderaker, *Elusive Empires*, 165–66; Finger, *Tennessee Frontiers*, chap. 2.

14. Hinderaker, *Elusive Empires*, preface.

15. Hinderaker, *Elusive Empires*. See also Aron, *How the West Was Lost*; and Fred Anderson, *Crucible of War: The Seven Years' War and the Fate of Empire in British North America, 1754–1766* (New York: Knopf, 2000).

16. On treaties, see Finger, *Tennessee Frontiers*, 42. For more on Henderson and the Transylvania Company, see Aron, *How the West Was Lost*; and Mark Miller, "Richard Henderson:

The Making of a Land Speculator" (master's thesis, Univ. of North Carolina at Chapel Hill, 1975). For more on the Chickamaugas, see James Pate, "The Chickamauga: A Forgotten Segment of Indian Resistance on the Southern Frontier," Ph.D. diss., Mississippi State Univ., 1969.

17. One explanation for the sale of the land was that it provided a means by which elder Cherokees could control younger members of the tribe. Cherokee matrilineal tradition dictated that men had little to no formal control over younger men from different clans. One way to keep them in line was for tribal elders to provide them with gifts. From this perspective, elders were merely trying to keep younger warriors—whose masculinity was already under attack from white expansion—from starting an all-out war. See Nathaniel Sheidley, "Unruly Men: Indians, Settlers, and the Ethos of Frontier Patriarchy in the Upper Tennessee Watershed, 1763–1815," Ph.D. diss., Princeton Univ., 1999, 74–78. For more on Cherokee gender relations, see Perdue, *Cherokee Women*, and Theda Perdue, "Women, Men and American Indian Policy: The Cherokee Response to 'Civilization,'" in *Negotiators of Change: Historical Perspectives on Native American Women*, ed. Nancy Shoemaker (London: Routledge, 1995), 90–114.
18. Talk by Old Tassel, in *American State Papers: Indian Affairs*, vol. 1, ed. Walter Lowrie and Arthur St. Clair (Washington, D.C.: GPO, 1932), 42. See also David Andrew Nichols, "Red Gentlemen and White Savages: Indian Relations and Political Culture After the American Revolution, 1784–1800," Ph.D. diss., Univ. of Kentucky, 2000, 87.
19. For more on the concept of stilling crying blood, see Cumfer, "Idea of Mankind Is So Various," chaps. 2 and 3.
20. See, for example, O'Brien, *Choctaws in a Revolutionary Age*.
21. Chickasaws also were actively attacking the Cumberland settlements prior to 1783. Finger, *Tennessee Frontiers*, 70. See also Pate, "Chickamauga."
22. John Sevier to Alexander Martin, Mar. 22, 1785, in *State Records of North Carolina*, vol. 17, *1781–1785*, ed. William Clark (Wilmington, N.C.: Broadfoot, 1994), 624.
23. See William S. Powell, *North Carolina Through Four Centuries* (Chapel Hill: Univ. of North Carolina Press, 1989).
24. Finger, *Tennessee Frontiers*, chap. 3.
25. The 1782 law fixed the amount of land offered to veterans at 640 acres for privates; 1,000 acres for noncommissioned officers; subalterns, 2,560; captains, 3,840; majors, 4,800; lieutenant colonels, 7,200; colonels, 7,200; and brigadier generals, 12,000. Laws of North Carolina, 1782, chap. 3, North Carolina State Library and Archives, Raleigh.
26. Abernethy, *From Frontier to Plantation*, 58.
27. Finger, *Tennessee Frontiers*, 101. Such swindling and questionable land grabbing explain why James Madison opposed Alexander Hamilton's plan for funding the domestic debt in 1790. Hamilton wanted to repay bondholders at par; Madison, looking over the unscrupulous nature of the land business, believed that the original holders deserved some compensation. For more on the debate over funding and assumption, see Elkins and McKitrick, *Age of Federalism;* Joseph Ellis, *Founding Brothers: The Revolutionary Generation* (New York: Knopf, 2000); and Forrest McDonald, *The Presidency of George Washington* (Lawrence: Univ. of Kansas Press, 1974).

28. For more on conquest theory, see Stuart Banner, *How the Indians Lost Their Land: Law and Power on the Frontier* (Cambridge: Harvard Univ. Press, Belknap Press, 2005); Reginald Horsman, *Expansion and American Indian Policy* (Norman: Univ. of Oklahoma Press, 1992); and Sharon Korman, *The Right of Conquest: The Acquisition of Territory by Force in International Law and Practice* (New York: Oxford Univ. Press, 1996).
29. Finger, *Tennessee Frontiers*, 105–6; Abernethy, *From Frontier to Plantation*, chap. 4. The closest exchange-rate comparison dates to a slightly later period, 1791. See Lawrence H. Officer, "Exchange Rate between the United States Dollar and the British Pound, 1791–2004," Economic History Services, EH.Net, www.eh.net/hmit/exchangerates/pound.php (2004).
30. Index to North Carolina and Tennessee Land Grants, TSLA.
31. Thomas Polk to John Gray Blount, July 5, 1783, in *John Gray Blount Papers*, vol. 1, *1764–1788*, ed. Alice B. Keith (Raleigh, N.C.: State Department of Archives and History, 1952), 68.
32. John Sevier's migration to the frontier serves as another example. See Carl Driver, *John Sevier: Pioneer of the Old Southwest* (Chapel Hill: Univ. of North Carolina Press, 1932). Tennessee's young surveyor-speculators were similar to those trying to establish themselves in Kentucky during the same period. See Watlington, *Partisan Spirit*, 36.
33. Walter Durham, "Isaac Bledsoe," in *The Tennessee Encyclopedia of History and Culture*, online edition, Tennessee Historical Society, www.tennesseeencyclopedia.net.
34. Kevin E. Smith, "Bledsoe's Station: Archeology, History and the Interpretation of the Middle Tennessee Frontier, 1770–1820," *Tennessee Historical Quarterly* 59 (Fall 2000): 175–87. See also Goodstein, *Nashville, 1780–1860*, chap. 1. Stations also served as a visible display of distrust of Indians: settlers knew their activity would bring a reaction, and stations served as symbols of defense and even strength. Hinderaker, *Elusive Empires*, 164.
35. Waldstreicher, *In the Midst of Perpetual Fetes*, 157. See also Newman, *Parades and the Politics of the Street*.
36. On census enumeration, see "Circular Letter from Governor Blount," in *The Territorial Papers of the United States*, vol. 4, ed. Clarence E. Carter (Washington, D.C., 1936), 49–50.
37. Eslinger, *Citizens of Zion*, 93–94; and Waldstreicher, *In the Midst of Perpetual Fetes*, 158–59. Moreover, their potentially unruly character put them in tension with the elite's inclinations toward dominance. See Tillson, "Militia and Popular Political Culture." See also Cumfer, "Idea of Mankind Is So Various," chap. 6, esp. 404–5, 433; and Beeman, *Evolution of the Southern Backcountry*, 134.
38. Carroll Van West, "Kasper Mansker," *Tennessee Encyclopedia of History and Culture*, online edition. See also Walter T. Durham, "Kasper Mansker: Cumberland Frontiersman," *Tennessee Historical Quarterly* 30 (1971): 154–77.
39. The fact that station communities tended to be interrelated certainly helped expedite the democratic process. See Eslinger, *Citizens of Zion*, 17–21.
40. W. Calvin Dickinson, "Watauga Association," *Tennessee Encyclopedia of History and Culture*, online edition.
41. *Three Pioneer Documents: John Donelson's Journal, Cumberland Compact, and the Minutes of the Cumberland Court* (Nashville: Tennessee Historical Society, 1964); Kenneth Feith, "Cumberland Compact," in *Tennessee Encyclopedia of History and Culture*, online edition.

Although eight stations were initially planned for the Cumberland District, only four existed as of the writing of the compact.

42. Sevier to Caswell, May 14, 1785, in Clark, *State Records of North Carolina* 17:447. In fact, many in the Franklin experiment genuinely operated under the assumption that the North Carolina General Assembly's actions had authorized them to set the ball in motion. John Sevier to Richard Caswell, May 14, 1785, in Clark, *State Records of North Carolina* 17:446.
43. See Remini, *Course of American Empire*, chap. 4. As Nathaniel Sheidley has noted, most prominent North Carolinians were not concerned without reason; Sevier, in an effort to shore up his control over the region, readily advocated taking land "by the sword." Sheidley, "Unruly Men," 182.
44. John Sevier to Evan Shelby, Feb. 11, 1787, MF 678, Reel 7, Box 14 s-17, Tennessee Historical Society Miscellaneous Files, TSLA (hereafter cited as THS Miscellaneous Files). Anthony Bledsoe to Richard Caswell, Mar. 26, 1787, in *State Records of North Carolina*, vol. 22, ed. William Clark (Raleigh, North Carolina: P. M. Hale, 1905), 677.
45. See Phillip Hamer, *Tennessee: A History, 1673–1932*, vol. 1 (New York: American Historical Society, 1933), 130–31.
46. Samuel Cole Williams, *History of the Lost State of Franklin* (Johnson City, Tenn.: Watauga Press, 1924); James W. Hagy, "Democracy Defeated: The Frankland Constitution of 1785," *Tennessee Historical Quarterly* 40 (Fall 1981): 239–56; Jerry Alan Sayers, "Disunited States: The Lost State of Franklin and Frontier State Movements at the Dawn of the American Republic" (master's thesis, Univ. of Virginia, 2002); and Remini, *Course of American Empire*, 47.
47. This particular reference was made by the 256 signers of the Cumberland Compact. Goodstein, *Nashville, 1780–1860*, 2.
48. Campbell to Samuel Purviance, Nov. 18, 1784, Arthur Lee Campbell Papers.
49. See Craig Symonds, "The Failure of America's Indian Policy on the Southwestern Frontier, 1785–1793," *Tennessee Historical Quarterly* 35 (Spring 1976): 29–45.
50. John P. Brown, *Old Frontiers: The Story of the Cherokee Indians from the Earliest Times to the Date of their Removal to the West, 1838* (Kingsport, Tenn.: Southern Publishers, 1938), 217–19.
51. J. G. M. Ramsey, *Annals of Tennessee to the End of the Eighteenth Century* (1853; reprint, Knoxville: East Tennessee Historical Society, 1967), 514.
52. Washington's Memoranda on Indian Affairs, 1789, in *The Papers of George Washington: Presidential Series*, vol. 4, *September 1789–January 1790*, ed. William W. Abbot and Dorothy Twohig (Charlottesville: Univ. of Virginia Press, 1993), 481.
53. Spaight to Alexander Martin, as quoted in Sayers, "Disunited States."
54. Andrew Cayton, "'Separate Interests' and the Nation-State: The Washington Administration and the Origins of Regionalism in the Trans-Appalachian West," *Journal of American History* 79, no. 1 (June 1992): 58. Through the course of the 1780s, eight out of nine delegates to the North Carolina legislature from the western district were major speculators. See Goodstein, *Nashville, 1780–1860*, chap. 1.
55. Campbell was pointing to the brief period in 1784 when North Carolina ceded its western land to the confederation. Campbell to Samuel Purviance, Nov. 18, 1784, Arthur Lee Campbell Papers. The situation was similar to that found by Rachel Klein in South Caro-

lina, where the coastal elite did little to help their backcountry counterparts during their Cherokee war in the early 1760s. See Klein, *Unification of a Slave State: The Rise of the Planter Class in the South Carolina Backcountry, 1760–1808* (Chapel Hill: Univ. of North Carolina Press, 1991), 38.

56. Ibid. Craig Friend has pointed out that there may have been another reason for federal reluctance: sectional rivalry. From this perspective, easterners feared that unrestricted use of the Mississippi River would disconnect the West from Philadelphia, Baltimore, and other supply towns. Policies that benefited the West, in other words, threatened eastern commercial interests and were therefore to be avoided. See Friend, "Inheriting Eden: The Creation of Society and Community in Early Kentucky, 1792–1812," Ph.D. diss., Univ. of Kentucky, 1995, 79. See also Fredrika Teute, "Land, Liberty and Labor in the Post-Revolutionary Era: Kentucky as the Promised Land," Ph.D. diss., Johns Hopkins Univ., 1988.

57. Cherokees, seeing a possibility for a new, peaceful relationship with Americans, endorsed Confederation efforts by revising kinship relations with frontier leaders: they downgraded locals from fathers and elder brothers to brothers and designated Congress as their new father. Cumfer, "Idea of Mankind Is So Various," 113, 123–24.

58. Symonds, "Failure of America's Indian Policy," 30.

59. In this sense, Tennesseans supported David Waldstreicher's contention that "the lack of national incorporation did not prevent frontierspeople from claiming national rights." Waldstreicher, *In the Midst of Perpetual Fetes*, 280. See also Cooper, *Liberty and Slavery*, 54–55.

60. Daniel Smith, "A Short Description of the Tennassee Government," in *Tennessee Beginnings, Combining a Short Description of the Tennessee Government (by Daniel Smith) 1793; The Constitution of the State of Tennessee, 1796; and A Catechetical Exposition of the Constitution of the State of Tennessee, by Willie Blount, 1803*, by Daniel Smith and Willie Blount (Spartanburg, S.C.: Reprint Company, 1976), 22–26. In 1796 the Tennessee Constitution made it clear that the new state's right to Mississippi navigation was nonnegotiable. Tennessee Constitution, in *Messages of the Governor's of Tennessee*, vol. 1, *1796–1821*, ed. Robert White (Nashville: Tennessee Historical Commission, 1952), Appendix A. Similar alienation occurred in Kentucky. See Eslinger, *Citizens of Zion*, 145.

61. Thomas Purson to James Robertson, May 23, 1787, in "Correspondence of James Robertson," *American Historical Magazine* 1 (Jan. 1896): 78.

62. Jo Tice Bloom, "Establishing Precedents: Dr. James White and the Southwest Territory," *Tennessee Historical Quarterly* 54 (Winter 1995): 326. White's activities were simultaneous to James Wilkinson's attempts to unify Kentucky with Spain. See Haywood, *Civil and Political History*, chap. 6; and Thomas P. Abernethy, *The South in the New Nation, 1789–1819* (Baton Rouge: Louisiana State Univ. Press, 1961), chap. 3. Malcolm Rohrbough has noted that flirtation with the Spanish was a common phenomenon for western speculators of all types. See Rohrbough, *The Trans-Appalachian Frontier: People, Societies, and Institutions, 1775–1850* (New York: Oxford Univ. Press, 1978), 45.

63. Andrew Jackson to Daniel Smith, Feb. 13, 1789, as quoted in Robert Remini, *Andrew Jackson and His Indian Wars* (New York: Viking Press, 2001), 31.

64. Daniel Dovenbarger, "Land Speculation in Early Middle Tennessee: Laws and Practice" (master's thesis, Vanderbilt Univ., 1981), 111.

65. Powell, *North Carolina Through Four Centuries*, 227–29.

66. Carter, *Territorial Papers* 4:3–8, 13–17, 18. See also Finger, *Tennessee Frontiers*, 125–27; and Onuf, *Statehood and Union*.
67. See Frederick Jackson Turner, "The Significance of the Frontier in American History," *Annual Report of the American Historical Association for the Year 1893* (Washington, D.C., 1894). See also John Mack Faragher, ed., *Rereading Fredrick Jackson Turner: The Significance of the Frontier in American History and Other Essays* (New York: Henry Holt, 1994).
68. Elizabeth Perkins, *Border Life: History and Memory in the Revolutionary Ohio Valley* (Chapel Hill: Univ. of North Carolina Press, 1998), chap. 4; and Eslinger, *Citizens of Zion*, 93–94.
69. See Masterson, *William Blount*; Toomey, "Prelude to Statehood"; and Cumfer, "Idea of Mankind Is So Various." For more on Tennessee's expectations of federal protection, see chapter 2, this volume.
70. For more on the territorial appointments, see "Recommendations for Federal Offices in North Carolina and the Southwestern Government," in *The Papers of Thomas Jefferson*, vol. 16, ed. Julian P. Boyd et al. (Princeton, N.J.: Princeton Univ. Press, 1961), 476–78.
71. William Blount to John Steele, July 10, 1791, in Carter, *Territorial Papers* 4:30–31. See also Remini, *Course of American Empire*, 51.
72. William Blount to John Sevier, July 6, 1798, MF 678, THS Miscellaneous Files. See also Remini, *Course of American Empire*.
73. Carter, *Territorial Papers* 4:430–60. See also Index to North Carolina Land Grants, TSLA.
74. The legislators were Leroy Taylor, John Tipton, George Rutledge, Joseph Hardin, William Cocke, Joseph McMinn, Alexander Kelly, John Beard, Samuel Wear, George Doherty, James White, David Wilson, and James Ford. Carter, *Territorial Papers* 4:430–60. Tipton was perhaps the only renegade. Unhappy with the inability of the territorial government to respond to Indian threats, he distanced himself from Blount's machine.
75. In 1790 the region was comprised of lands used by Chickasaws, Cherokees, and Chickamaugas and held white settlements totaling 28,649 residents in the eastern portion and 7,049 in the Cumberland. Carter, *Territorial Papers*, vol. 4. See Rohrbough, *Trans-Appalachian Frontier*, and Onuf, *Statehood and Union*.
76. Samuel Cole Williams, "The Clarksville Compact of 1785," *Tennessee Historical Quarterly* 3, no. 3 (Sept. 1944): 236–47. The state of Franklin provides a fine example from the east. Recent scholarship has shown that while Franklinites were angered by North Carolina's leadership, they looked to the Confederation Congress for legitimacy and greater oversight for their day-to-day operations. Sayers, "Disunited States."
77. Text taken from Williams, "Clarksville Compact," 243.
78. Text of the Cumberland Compact taken from A. W. Putnam, *History of Middle Tennessee; or, Life and Times of Gen. James Robertson* (Nashville, 1859), 94–100.
79. The others: five held between five and ten thousand acres, five more held between one and five thousand acres, and the remaining five held between five hundred and one thousand acres. Goodstein, *Nashville, 1780–1860*, 8.
80. Hinderaker, *Elusive Empires*, 236. See also Peter Onuf, *Jefferson's Empire: The Language of Nationhood* (Charlottesville: Univ. of Virginia Press, 2000), 41; Onuf, *Statehood and Union*; and Onuf, *The Origins of the Federal Republic: Jurisdictional Conflicts in the United States, 1775–1787* (Philadelphia: Univ. of Pennsylvania Press, 1983).

Chapter 2

1. I. H. Williamson to James Robertson, Aug. 31, 1789, in "Correspondence of James Robertson," *American Historical Magazine* 1 (Jan. 1896): 89–90.
2. Ibid.
3. George Washington's memorandum on Indian affairs, Dec. 1789, *Papers of George Washington* 4:480. See also Cherokee Chiefs to Washington, 19 May 1789, in *Papers of George Washington: Presidential Series*, vol. 2, *April–June 1789*, ed. William W. Abbot, et al. (Charlottesville: Univ. of Virginia Press, 1987), 325–26.
4. Federalists at the time were cognizant that this policy might create "separate interests in the Trans-Appalachian West." See Henry Knox, "Report to George Washington," Jan. 22, 1791, quoted in Cayton, "'Separate Interests' and the Nation-State," 41.
5. See, for example, Ratcliffe, *Party Spirit in a Frontier Republic*; Alan Taylor, *William Cooper's Town: Power and Persuasion on the Early American Frontier* (New York: Vintage, 1995); and Watlington, *Partisan Spirit*.
6. The Virginia, South Carolina, and Tennessee Companies made up the early Yazoo land speculation interests. Although initially unsuccessful, a 1795 revival of some of their claims became famous in the Supreme Court case *Fletcher v. Peck*, in which Chief Justice John Marshall upheld the principle of the sanctity of contract regardless of the means by which the land grants were obtained. See C. Peter Magrath, *Yazoo: Law and Politics in the New Republic: The Case of Fletcher v. Peck* (New York: Norton Press, 1967). Blount's interest in the Muscle Shoals went back a few years. Together with Sevier, John Donelson, and Richard Caswell, he had attempted as early as 1783 to obtain access to the "Great Bent." See William Blount to John Donelson, May 17, 1783, and John Sevier to William Blount, Oct. 7, 1785, *John Gray Blount Papers* 1:57, 221. Their activity was so extensive that it garnered the notice of leading men outside of the territory. See, for example, Benjamin Logan to Benjamin Harrison, Aug. 11, 1783, Bullitt Family Papers—Oxmoor Collection, Filson Historical Society, Louisville, Ky.
7. Henry Knox to George Washington, Mar. 10, 1791, in Carter, *Territorial Papers* 4:50–52.
8. Cumfer, "Idea of Mankind Is So Various," 133–34.
9. Nichols, "Red Gentlemen and White Savages," 82–83.
10. Finger, *Tennessee Frontiers*, 135.
11. According to Briton George Welbank, Cherokee leaders claimed not really to understand the treaty they signed. This sort of white manipulation certainly fits with Henderson's 1775 treaty and other white efforts to procure land. Cumfer, "Idea of Mankind Is So Various," 144.
12. James Carey to William Blount, Mar. 19, 1793, *American State Papers: Indian Affairs*, vol. 1; and Henry Knox to George Washington, Jan. 17, 1792, in Carter, *Territorial Papers* 4:114. See also Toomey, "Prelude to Statehood," chap. 3; and Remini, *Andrew Jackson and His Indian Wars*, 31.
13. Bloody Fellow to William Blount, Sept. 10, 1792, in "Correspondence of James Robertson," *American Historical Magazine* 2 (Jan. 1897): 70–71.
14. Nichols, "Red Gentlemen and White Savages," 248.

15. This was not a new practice. As early as the seventeenth century, Illinois used slave raids as a form of commercial exchange in the Ohio Valley. See Hinderaker, *Elusive Empires,* chap. 1.
16. James White to James Monroe, Aug. 9, 1792, in *Papers of James Monroe,* vol. 2, *Selected Correspondence and Papers, 1776–1794,* ed. Daniel Preston (Westport, Conn.: Greenwood Press, 2006), 556.
17. *American State Papers: Indian Affairs* 1:276.
18. See also Cumfer, "Idea of Mankind Is So Various," 307; and Toomey, "Prelude to Statehood," chap. 3. For more on slavery in early Tennessee, see chapter 4, this volume.
19. Treaty of Holston, printed in Carter, *Territorial Papers* 4:63. See also *American State Papers: Indian Affairs* 1:52.
20. Carter, *Territorial Papers* 4:72–73.
21. James White to James Monroe, Aug. 9, 1792, *Papers of James Monroe* 2:556.
22. Carter, *Territorial Papers* 4:365. Arthur Lee Campbell to William Preston, Oct. 9, 1774, MS 3QQ117, Draper Collection (microfilm edition), TSLA (hereafter cited as Draper Collection). See also James Seagrove to William Blount, Feb. 10, 1794, in "Correspondence of James Robertson," *American Historical Magazine* 3 (July 1898): 284–85.
23. For more on Creek social, economic, and political life during this period, see Saunt, *New Order of Things,* chaps. 1 and 2.
24. Quote taken from Tom Kanon, "The Kidnapping of Martha Crawley and Settler-Indians Relations Prior to the War of 1812," *Tennessee Historical Quarterly* 64, no. 1 (Spring 2005): 14.
25. Henry Knox to Washington, July 7, 1789, *American State Papers: Indian Affairs* 1:52.
26. John Speed to Isaac Shelby, June 21, 1793, MS A S544, Folder 1, Isaac Shelby Papers, Filson Historical Society, Louisville, Ky. (hereafter cited as Isaac Shelby Papers).
27. Haywood, *Civil and Political History,* 359. See also Barnard to Seagrove, July 13, 1792, William Blount Papers, Filson Historical Society, Louisville, Ky. (hereafter cited as William Blount Papers); and "Extracts from the Minutes of Information Given to Governor Blount by James Carey, One of the Interpreters of the United States to the Cherokee Nation, 8th November 1792," William Blount Papers. Creeks also used the Spanish to create buffer zones. See Nichols, "Red Gentlemen and White Savages," 94.
28. Petition of Tennessee County to General James Robertson, in "Correspondence of James Robertson," Feb. 1, 1792, *American Historical Magazine* 1, no. 3 (July 1896): 284.
29. Henry Knox to Alexander McGillivray, Aug. 11, 1792, *American State Papers: Indian Affairs* 1:257.
30. James White to James Monroe, Aug. 9, 1792, *Papers of James Monroe* 2:556.
31. William Blount to James Robertson, Sept. 21, 1791, in Carter, *Territorial Papers* 4:82.
32. William Blount to Henry Knox, *American State Papers: Indian Affairs* 1:276.
33. William Blount to Daniel Smith, June 17, 1793, in Carter, *Territorial Papers* 4:274–75.
34. William Blount to James Robertson, Oct. 27, 1792, in "Correspondence of James Robertson," *American Historical Magazine* 2 (Jan. 1897): 83.
35. Blount to Robertson, Mar. 12, 1793, in "Correspondence of James Robertson," *American Historical Magazine* 2 (Jan. 1897): 279.
36. Ibid. See also Abernethy, *From Frontier to Plantation,* 142; and Watlington, *Partisan Spirit,* chap. 3. For more on Citizen Genet's activity on behalf of the Girondist government

in France, see Harry Ammon, *The Genet Mission* (New York: Norton Press, 1973); and Albert Hall Bowman, *The Struggle for Neutrality: Franco-American Diplomacy During the Federalist Era* (Knoxville: Univ. of Tennessee Press, 1974).

37. Bradburn, "The Problem of Citizenship," 173–74.
38. Blount to Robertson, Sept. 25, 1793, in "Correspondence of James Robertson," *American Historical Magazine* 3 (July 1898): 75.
39. Blount to Robertson, Aug. 28, 1793, in "Correspondence of James Robertson," *American Historical Magazine* 2 (Jan. 1897): 371–72.
40. Toomey, "Prelude to Statehood," chap. 1.
41. James Seagrove to William Knox, May 24, 1792, *American State Papers: Indian Affairs* 1:296.
42. John Nichols to William Lytle, May 8, 1793, William Lytle Papers, 445-z, Southern Historical Collection, Wilson Library, Univ. of North Carolina at Chapel Hill (hereafter cited as Lytle Papers). No doubt also speculating when "killed and scalped by Indians" were Col. Hugh Tenan, John Brown, and William Grimes, a nephew of North Carolina congressman Alexander Mebane. As a general in the North Carolina line, Mebane was granted five thousand acres of Tennessee land for his services. *Knoxville Gazette*, Jan. 9, 1795.
43. Davidson County tax receipts, Nov. 16, 1795, and June 11, 1796, Lytle Papers. Lytle owned title to 6,000 acres in Davidson County, while his brother Archibald held another 2,010.
44. Martin Armstrong and Stockley Donelson to James Glasgow, June 12, 1794, Microfilm AC 814, Reel 6, Box 15, Folder 15, Dyas Collection, John Coffee Papers (Tennessee Historical Society), TSLA (hereafter cited as Dyas Collection, John Coffee Papers).
45. Blount to Robertson, Jan. 19, 1794, in "Correspondence of James Robertson," *American Historical Magazine* 3 (July 1898): 282–83. Blount simultaneously was involved in heavy speculation in Kentucky land. See Blount to John Smith, Jan. 20, 1794, *John Gray Blount Papers* 2:350–51. In 1795 he found just the acreage for which he was looking, and together with John Sevier (and others), he attempted to purchase the four-million-acre Muscle Shoals area. Although the land was clearly under the control of the Creeks, and the Georgia legislature would in 1796 repeal the purchase authorization, this revival of the Tennessee Company hoped to attract European buyers and jump-start a land industry that had stagnated under the weight of Indian attacks.
46. Carter, *Territorial Papers* 4:93.
47. Henry Knox to William Blount, Aug. 15, 1792, in Carter, *Territorial Papers* 4:162–64.
48. Knox to Blount, Aug. 26, 1793, in Carter, *Territorial Papers* 4:299–300. Knox was such a notorious speculator that he was alternately honored and despised by those living in the Maine district of Massachusetts. See Alan Taylor, *Liberty Men and Great Proprietors: The Revolutionary Settlement on the Maine Frontier, 1760–1820* (Chapel Hill: Univ. of North Carolina Press, 1990).
49. A Philadelphia gentleman to his correspondent in Knox County, Mar. 19, 1795, *Knoxville Gazette*, Apr. 24, 1795. See also *Knoxville Gazette*, Feb. 27, 1795.
50. Harriet Simpson Arnow, *Flowering of the Cumberland* (New York: Macmillan, 1963), 20, 197.
51. William Blount to Henry Knox, in Carter, *Territorial Papers* 4:231.

52. *Knoxville Gazette*, Apr. 6, 1793, as quoted in Masterson, *William Blount*, 241.
53. Daniel Smith to Henry Knox, July 19, 1793, in Carter, *Territorial Papers* 4:280–83.
54. Haywood, *Civil and Political History*, 307, as quoted in Symonds, "Failure of America's Indian Policy," 40. One of the more critical vigilante assaults came in the form of Capt. Hugh Beard's militia attack on Cherokee chief Hanging Maw's family. The massacre not only infuriated the administration but also increased the level of frontier assaults initiated by local tribes. See Masterson, *William Blount*, chap. 9.
55. Finger, *Tennessee Frontiers*, 144. Sevier's attack was similar to Benjamin Logan's 1786 Kentucky expedition. For more on Logan's Kentucky expedition, see Hinderaker, *Elusive Empires*, 240–41.
56. William [?] to Isaac Shelby, Aug. 13, 1794, Folder 1, Isaac Shelby Papers.
57. Andrew Jackson to John McKee, May 16, 1794, in *The Correspondence of Andrew Jackson*, vol. 1, ed. James Spencer Bassett (Washington, D.C.: Carnegie Institution, 1926), 13. See also James Robertson to William Blount, Nov. 15, 1794, *American State Papers: Indian Affairs* 1:542.
58. *Knoxville Gazette*, Dec. 13, 1794.
59. James Taylor to William Lytle, Mar. 5, 1794, Lytle Papers.
60. Val Sevier to John Sevier, Aug. 9, 1794, MS 1DD118, Draper Collection.
61. Toomey, "Prelude to Statehood," 140. See also Masterson, *William Blount*, and Ramsey, *Annals of Tennessee*.
62. The Washington and Adams administrations were so unhappy with Sevier's campaign that for years they refused to provide the funding to pay for it. It was not until Andrew Jackson cajoled Congress into it that they finally paid for it, in 1798. For more on this, see chapter 3, this volume.
63. Bradburn, "The Problem of Citizenship," chap. 4.
64. Vans Murray on the floor of the House of Representatives, Jan. 29, 1795, *Annals of Congress*, 3d Cong. (Washington, D.C.: Gales and Seaton, 1834–56), 1154–55.
65. Secretary of War Pickering to William Blount, Mar. 23, 1795, *American Historical Magazine* 4 (Apr. 1899), 182.
66. Ibid., 184–85.
67. Bloom, "Establishing Precedents," 331. See also James White to William Blount, Mar. 19, 1795, and White to Blount, Mar. 29, 1795, "Correspondence of James Robertson," *American Historical Magazine* 4 (Apr. 1899): 178.
68. Mutiny would not have come at the expense of the leaders of the territory. The threat was to the federal government—in the form of separate settlements with Spain or Britain. As Malcolm Rohrbough has noted, when "abandoned," frontier residents always turned to local institutions for protection. In this case it would have ensured that the territorial elite would have remained in control of the small but growing population. Rohrbough, *Trans-Appalachian Frontier*, 45.
69. Bloody Fellow to William Blount, Jan. 3, 1795, in "Correspondence of James Robertson," *American Historical Magazine* 4 (Apr. 1899): 93.
70. Blount's conspiracy was abetted by the fact that he and other major speculators were plunged into a recession in 1796 and 1797. Frontier conspiracy, then, underscored the

connection between economics and American identity: Settlers engaged in Spanish intrigue in the 1780s to protect settlers and speculation enterprises from Indian raids; Blount's conspiracy in 1796–97 would revive speculator fortunes by opening new land for sale and under the protection of the British Empire. See Cayton, "When Shall We Cease to Have Judases," 160, 163; and Melton, *First Impeachment*. See also Remini, *Course of American Empire*, chap. 10.

71. Blount to Robertson, Nov. 22, 1794, in "Correspondence of James Robertson," *American Historical Magazine* 3 (July 1898): 374.
72. Blount had begun to ponder the question of statehood early on and in 1793 had authorized a legislature with an eye toward just such a resolution. By 1795, he might also have had another goal in mind: positioning himself for the U.S. Senate. The evidence is shaky, but it is curious that he was careful to place all of his close political allies in the Constitutional Convention, where they could approve his measures and then go to their various districts and support his candidacy. See Walker, "Tennessee, 1796–1821," chap. 1. See also Masterson, *William Blount*, and Finger, *Tennessee Frontiers*.
73. *Journal of the Proceedings of the House of Representatives of the Territory of the United States South of the River Ohio, 1795* (Knoxville, 1795).
74. Carter, *Territorial Papers* 4:404–5. The contrast in regional population, however, is startling—since the 1791 census, the territorial population had gone from thirty-three thousand to seventy-seven thousand, but the middle district had gone from seven thousand to only eleven thousand. Such a pronounced difference bred significant political tension between eastern and central Tennessee, and as we shall see, the population explosion of the early nineteenth century would only magnify the problem. See Remini, *Course of American Empire;* and Abernethy, *From Frontier to Plantation*.
75. Amy H. Sturgis, "'Charged with Republican Notions': Western Constitutions, 1775–1796" (master's thesis, Vanderbilt Univ., 1995).
76. Chauncey Goodrich to Oliver Wolcott, May 13, 1796, in *Memoirs of the Administrations of Washington and John Adams, Edited from the Papers of Oliver Wolcott, Secretary of the Treasury*, vol. 1, ed. George Gibbs (New York, 1846), 338–39, as quoted in Samuel C. Williams, "The Admission of Tennessee into the Union," *Tennessee Historical Quarterly* 4 (Winter 1945): 313. Blount and William Cocke provide further insight into the situation: "It is generally believed that the State of Tennessee would have experience no difficulty on the admission of her senators if it had not been understood that George Washington would not again accept the Presidency and that that State would throw its weight into the Southern Scale against Mr. Adams." Cocke and Blount to John Sevier, June 2, 1796, reproduced in Williams, "Admission of Tennessee into the Union," opposite 312–13. See also Mary-Jo Kline, ed., *The Political Correspondence and Public Papers of Aaron Burr*, vol. 1 (Princeton, N.J.: Princeton Univ. Press, 1983), 257–63.
77. William Loughton Smith's speech, in U.S. Congress, *The Debates and Proceedings in the Congress of the United States; with an Appendix Containing Important State Papers and Public Documents*, 4th Cong., 1st sess. (Washington, D.C.: Gales and Seaton, 1834), 1300–1304. See also Kline, *Papers of Aaron Burr* 1:257–63.
78. William Cocke to Thomas Jefferson, Aug. 17, 1796, in *The Papers of Thomas Jefferson*, vol. 29, ed. Barbara Oberg et al. (Princeton, N.J.: Princeton Univ. Press, 2002), 169–70.

79. Blount to John Sevier, Sept. 27, 1796, as quoted in Masterson, *William Blount*, 298.
80. Contrary to what Donald Ratcliffe noted for the Ohio Territory: He points out that statehood was an essential step toward the development of a modern party contest. Ratcliffe, *Party Spirit in a Frontier Republic*, chap. 1.
81. See Reginald Horsman, "The British Indian Department and the Resistance to General Anthony Wayne, 1793–1795," *Mississippi Valley Historical Review* 49, no. 2 (Sept. 1962): 269–90. See also Elkins and McKitrick, *Age of Federalism*, 438–39.
82. See Stanley J. Folmsbee, "Sectionalism and Internal Improvements in Tennessee, 1796–1845," Ph.D. diss., Univ. of Pennsylvania, 1939; and St. George L. Sioussat, "Some Phases of Tennessee Politics in the Jackson Period," *American Historical Review* 14, no. 1 (1908): 51–69.
83. "Savage and the Civilized Man."
84. Thomas Jefferson to John Adams, 11 June 1812, in *The Adams-Jefferson Letters: The Complete Correspondence Between Thomas Jefferson and Abigail and John Adams*, ed. Lester Cappon (Chapel Hill: Univ. of North Carolina Press, 1959), 307–8. See also Onuf, *Jefferson's Empire*, 18–52.
85. Onuf notes that this vision of Indian "backsliding" helped Jefferson contradict the philosophical position staked out by men such as George-Louis Leclerc, Comte de Buffon, who believed that New World inhabitants naturally degenerated into a savage state. Jefferson in effect turned this argument on its head: It is not the environment but contact with European depravity that is the source of degeneration. Onuf, *Jefferson's Empire*, 20, 25–33. For an example of Jefferson's thoughts on the matter, see Memoranda to James Madison, circa 4 Mar. 1809, in *The Papers of Thomas Jefferson: Retirement Series*, vol. 1, *4 March 1809 to 15 November 1809*, ed. J. Jefferson Looney (Princeton, N.J.: Princeton Univ. Press, 2004), 6–7.
86. For more on Federalists' civilization strategy, see Nichols, "Red Gentlemen and White Savages."
87. David Campbell to Thomas Jefferson, Jan. 1, 1804, Thomas Jefferson Papers Series 9: Collected Manuscripts, 1783–1822, Library of Congress.
88. Timothy Pickering to Rufus King, June 4, 1795, in *The Life and Correspondence of Rufus King*, vol. 1, ed. Charles King (New York: G. P. Putnam's Sons, 1971), 106–7.
89. Perhaps Indian agent Benjamin Hawkins best summarized the Federalist position regarding the Southwest Territory when he stated that the Blount conspiracy would "eventually be productive of service to the U.S. by an exposure of those dirty intriguers and their villainous plots to involve the government in confusion, difficulties, and distress." Benjamin Hawkins to David Henley, June 4, 1797, David Henley Papers, Rare Books, Manuscripts, and Special Collections, William R. Perkins Library, Duke Univ. The local population responded by admiringly electing Blount to a term in the state senate, where his peers quickly elevated him to Speaker. For more on Federalists and the Blount impeachment, see Melton, *First Impeachment*. Federalists' reactions show the extent to which the "first party system" hinged upon fears that political opponents were bent on destroying the new constitutional order. See Joanne B. Freeman, "The Election of 1800: A Study in the Logic of Political Change," *Yale Law Journal* 108, no. 8 (June 1999): 1959–94. See also Freeman,

"Dueling as Politics: Reinterpreting the Burr-Hamilton Duel," *William and Mary Quarterly* 53, no. 1 (Apr. 1996): 289–318; and Sharp, *American Politics in the Early Republic*.

90. William Peters to William Preston, Jan. 12, 1798, Preston Family Papers—Joyes Collection, Filson Historical Society, Louisville, Ky. (hereafter cited as Preston Family Papers—Joyes Collection). A few months later the orders became even more specific: William Preston was ordered to march "up the Tennessee to the Settlements where Archibald Lackey lives, and apprehend and remove all persons that you may find without passports on the Indian lands. And also, all those who may have passports that you find cultivating or otherwise labouring on the Cherokee lands." Thomas Butler to Preston, Apr. 25, 1798, Preston Family Papers—Joyes Collection.

91. Benjamin Howard to William Preston, Mar. 13, 1798, Preston Family Papers—Joyes Collection.

92. Ibid. See also Benjamin Hawkins to John Sevier, Feb. 17, 1797; John Sevier to Captain Sparks, Feb. 17, 1797; and John Sevier to the inhabitants of Powell's Valley, Feb. 17, 1797, GP-2, Reel 1, Box 1, Folder 3, John Sevier Papers, First Administration, TSLA (hereafter cited as John Sevier Papers, First Administration).

93. Andrew Jackson to John Overton, Jan. 22, 1798, Microfilm, No. 812, Reel 2, Box 5, Folder 4, Claybrooke Collection (Tennessee Historical Society), TSLA (hereafter cited as Claybrooke Collection). This is a seemingly odd play, given that Tennessee was no longer part of North Carolina. Upon further reflection, however, Jackson's report to Ashe is not all that surprising—the corruption, after all, was directly connected to North Carolina land warrants, North Carolina land offices, and members of the North Carolina elite.

94. Edward Jones to Samuel Ashe, Mar. 17, 1798, *Governor's Papers: Samuel Ashe, 1796–1798*, vol. 21, North Carolina State Library and Archives, Raleigh.

95. H. O. Tatum to Samuel Ashe, Feb. 9, 1798, *Governor's Papers: Samuel Ashe, 1796–1798*.

96. Report of Gaither, Graham and Locke to Samuel Ashe, Mar. 24, 1798, *Governor's Papers: Samuel Ashe, 1796–1798*.

97. John Murrin, "The Jeffersonian Triumph and American Exceptionalism," *Journal of the Early Republic* 20, no. 1 (Spring 2000): 12. See also Lewis, *American Union and the Problem of Neighborhood*; and Richard Ellis, "The Market Revolution and the Transformation of American Politics, 1801–1837," in *The Market Revolution in America: Social, Religious and Political Expressions, 1800–1880*, ed. Melvyn Stokes and Stephen Conway (Charlottesville: Univ. of Virginia Press, 1996), 153.

98. See Onuf, *Jefferson's Empire*.

99. In many cases the derogatory use of "federalism" supplanted the use of "aristocracy" as the epithet of choice, although as the nineteenth century progressed the terms tended to be used interchangeably. See, for example, the *Carthage Gazette and Friend of the People*, June 29, 1810.

100. Nichols, "Red Gentlemen and White Savages," 207.

101. As Arthur Campbell put it, indigenous nations made "infractions" of treaties on a whim; thus, he reasoned, treaties should be little more than a general law, subject to local modification if necessary. Campbell to the Virginia Independent Chronicle, June 1788, MS 9DD48, Draper Collection.

102. Cynthia Cumfer, "Local Origins of National Indian Policy: Cherokee and Tennessean Ideas about Sovereignty and Nationhood, 1790–1811," *Journal of the Early Republic* 23, no. 1 (Spring 2003): 23–24.
103. "Address of James Lyon to the Electors of the Congressional District, Composed of the Thirteen Counties on the Waters of the Cumberland River, in Tennessee," in *Early American Imprints, Series II: Shaw–Shoemaker, 1801–1819*, no. 12958.
104. Bureau of the Census, *Second Census of the United States*, 1800 (Washington, D.C.: Gales and Seaton, 1801). Bureau of the Census, *Fourth Census of the United States*, 1820 (Washington, D.C.: Gales and Seaton, 1821). See also Goodstein, *Nashville, 1780–1860*, appendix table 1.

Chapter 3

1. The state was not unanimously behind Aaron Burr, however. In December 1800 Thomas Jefferson wrote Burr that at least one Tennessee elector planned to cast his second vote for Albert Gallatin. Jefferson to Burr, Dec. 15, 1800, James Madison to Jefferson, Dec. 18, 1800, and Jefferson to Thomas Mann Randolph, Dec. 19, 1800, all in *The Papers of Thomas Jefferson*, vol. 32, ed. Barbra Oberg, et al. (Princeton, N.J.: Princeton Univ. Press, 2005), 306, 322–24.
2. *Tennessee Gazette*, Feb. 18, 1801.
3. See, for example, Ratcliffe, *Party Spirit in a Frontier Republic*; and Watlington, *Partisan Spirit*.
4. This position was reminiscent of Kentucky's "Court" party, as described by Watlington in *Partisan Spirit*.
5. Arthur to David Campbell, Jan. 29, 1799, Campbell Family Papers. See also Ebenezer Brooks to Arthur Campbell, July 6, 1798, Campbell Family Papers. For more on colonial political understandings, see Wood, *Creation of the American Republic*; Wood, *Radicalism of the American Revolution*; Bailyn, *Ideological Origins of the American Revolution*; and Sydnor, *Gentlemen Freeholders*.
6. *Tennessee Gazette*, July 8, 1801.
7. Waldstreicher, *In the Midst of Perpetual Fetes*, 157. See also Newman, *Parades and the Politics of the Street*; and Koschnik, "Democratic Societies," 615–36.
8. In the most visible cases, attempts at gaining public approval led competing politicians to the dueling ground. See Freeman, *Affairs of Honor*. See also Wyatt-Brown, *Shaping of Southern Culture*.
9. This reinforces historian Rachel Klein's contention that even "if ambitious backcountry men found ways to enhance their local influence, they were almost entirely without avenues to [territory-wide] power." Klein, *Unification of a Slave State*, 41.
10. Census Schedule, 1795, in Carter, *Territorial Papers* 4:404; and Davidson County Militia Election Returns, Militia Election Returns, Reel 1, Box 1, Folder 5 RG 131, TSLA.
11. Cumfer, "Idea of Mankind Is So Various," chap. 6, esp. 404–5, 433. See also Remini, *Course of American Empire*, 15–16; Toomey, "Prelude to Statehood"; Trevor A. Smith, "Pioneers, Patriots, and Politicians: The Tennessee Militia System, 1772–1857," Ph.D. diss., Univ. of

Tennessee, 2003, chap. 4; Rohrbough, *Trans-Appalachian Frontier*, chap. 2; and Goodstein, *Nashville, 1780–1860*.

12. See also Tillson, "Militia and Popular Political Culture." For more on the unruly nature of the lower sorts on the Virginia frontier, see Beeman, *Evolution of the Southern Backcountry*.
13. See Robert Prince to John Sevier, Sept. 20, 1796, GP-2, Reel 3, Q-28, John Sevier Papers, First Administration. For more on the importance of militia positions to elite political aspirations, see Lorman Ratner, *Andrew Jackson and His Tennessee Lieutenants* (Westport, Conn.: Greenwood Press, 1997).
14. Prince to Sevier, Sept. 20, 1796, as quoted in Walker, "Tennessee, 1796–1821," 129.
15. Thomas Johnson to John Sevier, GP-2, Reel 3, Q-46, John Sevier Papers, First Administration.
16. Johnson to Sevier, Sept. 23, 1796, GP-2, Reel 3, Q-29, John Sevier Papers, First Administration.
17. Jackson to Sevier, May 8, 1797, in *The Papers of Andrew Jackson*, vol. 1, *1770–1803*, ed. Sam B. Smith and Harriet Chappell Owlsley (Knoxville: Univ. of Tennessee Press, 1980), 136–37.
18. James Robertson to John Sevier, Oct. 14, 1796, GP-2, Reel 1, Box 2, Folder 1, John Sevier Papers, First Administration. See also Isaac Roberts to Sevier, Nov. 22, 1796, GP-2, Reel 1, Box 2 Folder 1, John Sevier Papers, First Administration.
19. For more the confrontational nature of Federalist era politics, see Freeman, *Affairs of Honor*. See also Wyatt-Brown, *Shaping of Southern Culture*; Buel, *Securing the Revolution*; Appleby, *Capitalism and a New Social Order*; Elkins and McKitrick, *Age of Federalism;* and Sharp, *American Politics in the Early Republic*.
20. John Tipton and John Sevier had engaged in a significant battle over control of eastern Tennessee during Sevier's tenure as governor of Franklin. See Williams, *History of the Lost State;* and Abernethy, *From Frontier to Plantation*.
21. The 1797 election for major general was a contest between Jackson and George Conway. Jackson and his allies knew ahead of time that Sevier would interfere, and they unsuccessfully did what they could to upset the outcome. See Sevier to George Conway, Mar. 8, 1797, GP-2, Reel 1, Box 1, Folder 3, John Sevier Papers, First Administration.
22. Quoted by Jackson in Jackson to John Sevier, May 8, 1797, *Papers of Andrew Jackson* 1:136.
23. Sevier to Jackson May 8, 1797, *Papers of Andrew Jackson* 1:138.
24. William Cocke to Andrew Jackson, Apr. 18, 1797, *Papers of Andrew Jackson* 1:131. In short order, Jackson and Cocke would have a falling out of their own. In 1798 the two men competed for Cocke's Senate seat, and after a relatively heated campaign, Jackson won. Cocke soon thereafter published a private letter from Jackson that put his political intentions in a negative light, and Jackson was quick to take offence. Issuing an immediate and powerful rebuke, the new senator continued a persistent harassment for several months. Their relationship never recovered. See Remini, *Course of American Empire*, chap. 4.
25. Sevier to Jackson, May 8, 1797, *Papers of Andrew Jackson* 1:138.
26. W. C. C. Claiborne to Andrew Jackson, July 20, 1797, as quoted in Remini, *Andrew Jackson and His Indian Wars*, 39.

27. Jackson's case was helped by influential letters from William Blount and his half brother and future governor, Willie. See William Blount to Sevier, July 6, 1798, Reel 1, Box 2, B-158, THS Miscellaneous Files; and Willie Blount to Sevier, Aug. 18, 1798, Reel 1, Box 2, B-159, THS Miscellaneous Files.
28. Numerical List of Regiments of the Militia of Tennessee, 1796–1836, Militia Election Returns, Reel 22, Box 46, Folder 36, RG 131, TSLA; for the 1796 vote count, see Reel 1, Box 1, Folder 4. For the 1795 vote, see Carter, *Territorial Papers* 4:405.
29. See Ratner, *Andrew Jackson and His Tennessee Lieutenants*. See also Eslinger, *Citizens of Zion;* Watlington, *Partisan Sprit;* and Perkins, *Border Life*.
30. William Nash, Governor's Petition, August 1796, GP-2, Reel 2, Box 2, Folder 4, John Sevier Papers, First Administration.
31. William Tyrell Lewis to John Sevier, Aug. 11, 1796, GP-2, Reel 3, Q-43, John Sevier Papers, First Administration. Robert Weakley of Sumner County submitted a similar petition on behalf of Nash, proclaiming to Sevier that "if Justice takes place Nash [will be] the Major." Weakley to Sevier, Aug. 14, 1796, GP-2, Reel 1, Box 2, Folder 1, John Sevier Papers, First Administration. Other reports of fraudulent activity appeared throughout the early years of statehood. See also James Robertson to Sevier, Aug. 10, 1796, GP-2, Reel 3, Q-42, John Sevier Papers, First Administration; James Winchester to Sevier, Aug. 14, 1796, GP-2, Reel 3, Q-27 Thomas Buckingham to Sevier, Oct. 10, 1796, Militia Election Returns, and Robert Hays to Sevier, both in Reel 1, Box 1, Folder 5, RG 131, TSLA.
32. George Blackmore to John Sevier, Oct. 19, 1796, Militia Elections Returns, Reel 1, Box 1, Folder 5, RG 131, TSLA. Leeroy Taylor to Sevier, Oct. 2, 1796, Q-31.
33. Thomas Johnson to John Sevier, Jan. 28, 1797, Militia Election Returns, Reel 1, Box 1, Folder 30, RG 131, TSLA.
34. James McQuestion to John Sevier, Sept. 8, 1797, Militia Election Returns, Reel 1, Box 1, Folder 20, RG 131, TSLA.
35. James Nichols to John Sevier, Sept. 7, 1797, Militia Election Returns, Reel 1, Box 1, Folder 20, RG 131, TSLA.
36. Davidson County and Smith County Petitions to Governor Sevier, GP-4, Box 1, Folder 12, John Sevier Papers, Second Administration, TSLA (hereafter cited as John Sevier Papers, Second Administration); *Nashville Clarion*, Feb. 7, 1809; and the *Carthage Gazette*, Feb. 18, Mar. 6, 1809.
37. John Hane to John Sevier, Dec. 18, 1798, GP-2, Reel 1, Box 2, Folder 3, John Sevier Papers, First Administration.
38. Petition 8-2-1801, Reel 1, TSLA.
39. Specifically, the counties were Jackson, Dickson, Stewart, Rutherford, Overton, White, Warren, Bedford, Hickman, Franklin, Maury, Humphreys, Lincoln, and Giles. Bureau of the Census, *Second Census of the United States,* and Bureau of the Census, *Third Census of the United States,* 1810 (Washington, D.C.: Gales and Seaton, 1811). See also Tennessee Counties: Dates of Formation and Parent Counties, handout, TSLA.
40. *Impartial Review and Cumberland Repository,* Aug. 9, 1806.
41. Cynthia Cumfer has provided these numbers by systematically going through the three reels of microfilm that comprise the legislative petitions of the period. Furthermore, the

Governor's Papers microfilm series chronicles the dozens going to Sevier and Roane over this eleven-year time frame. Both numbers are estimates of the total number, however, as petitions have been lost or misfiled. Cumfer, "Idea of Mankind Is So Various," 441; and Governor's Papers, GP-2, GP-3, GP-4, TSLA.

42. Petition 16-2-1799-1, Reel 1, TSLA.
43. Petition 16-2-1809, Reel 3, TSLA.
44. John Sevier noted in a letter to Judge John Overton that Williams's "dispute with Harris was decided in favor of the election of the latter." Sevier to Overton, Nov. 2, 1809, AC 803-2, Murdock Collection, John Overton Papers, TSLA (hereafter cited as Murdock Collection, John Overton Papers). A similar incident occurred in Humphrey County in 1812, when a defeated candidate for sheriff successfully applied to the circuit court for a new election. GP-5, Folder 4, Willie Blount Papers, TSLA.
45. There even were celebrations on behalf of the Lewis and Clark expedition. See, for example, the Mechanical Society proceedings, *Tennessee Gazette*, July 20, 1803. The Mechanical Society also erected a liberty pole at that year's Fourth of July celebrations. On parades: *Impartial Review and Cumberland Repository*, Jan. 31, 1807. On effigy burning: Aaron Burr found himself (figuratively) on fire over his alleged treason. See, for example, the *Impartial Review and Cumberland Repository*, Jan. 3, 1807. On the toasting and celebration of Lewis and Clark: *Impartial Review and Cumberland Repository*, Oct. 23, 1806, Feb. 14, 1807. See also the *Carthage Gazette*, Feb. 9, Sept. 16, 1809. For toasting and parades, see, for example, *Nashville Gazette*, May 20, 1801, July 8, 1803, and *Nashville Clarion*, July 20, 1808. For more on the concept of politics and ritual, see Waldstreicher, *In the Midst of Perpetual Fetes*; Newman, *Parades and the Politics of the Street*; and Travers, *Celebrating the Fourth*.
46. "Journal of John Sevier," *Tennessee Historical Magazine* 6, no. 1 (Apr. 1920): 24.
47. For Fourth of July celebrations, see, for example, *Tennessee Gazette*, July 8, 13, 1803; *Nashville Clarion*, July 20, 1808; and *Impartial Review and Cumberland Repository*, July 12, 1806.
48. *Carthage Gazette*, Apr. 5, 1811.
49. Newman, *Parades and the Politics of the Street*, 79.
50. John L. Brooke, "Ancient Lodges and Self-Created Societies: Voluntary Association and the Public Sphere in the Early Republic," in *Launching the "Extended Republic": The Federalist Era*, ed. Ronald J. Hoffman and Peter J. Albert (Charlottesville: Univ. of Virginia Press, 1996), 281. The label "imagined community" draws from Benedict Anderson, *Imagined Communities: Reflections on the Origins and Spread of Nationalism* (London: Verso Press, 1983).
51. Roy R. Glashan, ed., *American Governors and Gubernatorial Elections, 1775–1978* (Westport, Conn.: Meckler Books, 1979), 290–97.
52. *Tennessee Gazette*, Feb. 18, 1801. A Fourth of July toast that was simultaneously cheered and given cannon fire further solidified Sevier's universal acclaim: "Our fellow citizen John Sevier, governor of Tennessee," toasted William C. C. Claiborne. "May his future life be serene and happy, under the influence of approving virtue." *Tennessee Gazette*, July 8, 1801.
53. As Lorman Ratner has noted, the military label was one of two ways of achieving an explicit mark of gentry status—the other being to become a judge. See Ratner, *Andrew Jackson and His Tennessee Lieutenants*.

54. For more on the Glasgow Conspiracy, see Kristofer Ray, "Land Speculation, Popular Democracy and Political Transformation on the Tennessee Frontier." See also *Governor's Papers: Samuel Ashe, 1796–1798*; and Report of Gaither, Graham and Locke to Samuel Ashe, Mar. 24, 1798, *Governor's Papers: Samuel Ashe, 1796–1798*.
55. Andrew Jackson to Benjamin Bradford, July 15, 1803, *Papers of Andrew Jackson* 1:343.
56. John Carter to Benjamin Bradford, July 19, 1803, *Papers of Andrew Jackson* 1:337.
57. John Carter to Benjamin Bradford, July 19, 1803, *Papers of Andrew Jackson* 1:338.
58. The rhetoric used by political underlings reinforces the idea that protection of honor also meant promotion of self and allies at the expense of the political "other." For more on the nature of these rituals, see Greenberg, *Honor and Slavery*; and Freeman, "Dueling as Politics," 297.
59. For the vote count in the gubernatorial race, see Glashan, *American Governors and Gubernatorial Elections*, 290–97. Continuing, Campbell made clear that despite his position as a gentleman, he considered dropping the facade of disinterested service, remarking, "Altho very weak the day of the election at this Place I had a mind to step into the Court-Yard to canvass for Mr. Roane. I saw he had not fair play and I have understood the carrying on at most other Court Houses in this District was much the same." Arthur Campbell to David Campbell, Aug. 22, 1803, Campbell Family Papers.
60. At one point Sevier agreed to an immediate interview but apparently changed his mind and called for a later date and place, much to Jackson's dismay. See Jackson to Sevier, Oct. 9, 1803, *Papers of Andrew Jackson* 1:375; and Sevier to Jackson, Oct. 9, 1803, *Papers of Andrew Jackson* 1:375.
61. Sevier to Jackson, Oct. 10, 1803, *Papers of Andrew Jackson* 1:381; "For the Knoxville *Gazette*," reprinted in the *Tennessee Gazette*, Nov. 23, 1803.
62. Oath of Josiah Nichol, Oct. 23, 1803, No. 678, Reel 6, Box 11, N-38, THS Miscellaneous Files.
63. Bertram Wyatt-Brown and Lorman Ratner have observed that this protection of lesser associates bespoke of a "thane" relationship. Carried over from Scotland, a thane relationship was one where codependent leaders and underlings mutually protected and promoted reputation. See Wyatt-Brown, "Andrew Jackson's Honor," in Wyatt-Brown, *Shaping of Southern Culture*, chap. 3; and Ratner, *Andrew Jackson and His Tennessee Lieutenants*.
64. "For the Knoxville *Gazette*," reprinted in the *Tennessee Gazette*, Nov. 23, 1803.
65. Sevier had had his reputation besmirched and nearly destroyed because of his leadership in the short-lived Franklin experiment. To restore his name, he marched the remnants of the Franklin Militia into Cherokee country, where he successfully attacked and looted several villages. These raids seemingly proved Sevier's commitment to those settlers who were ignored by other political outlets. His reputation was subsequently restored to such a degree that a committee of Washington County loyalists met and reconciled with him, and he received a pardon from the North Carolina government. In 1789 he was even elected to represent the Western district in the assembly. For more on Franklin, see Williams, *History of the Lost State*; Finger, *Tennessee Frontiers*; and Abernethy, *From Frontier to Plantation*.

66. Sevier did allow some Mero District Militia to serve, to be sure, but they were under the command of James Winchester and mustered on a far smaller scale than their eastern counterparts. Sevier was careful, moreover, to see to it that Winchester and not Jackson had control of the Mero militia. See Military Order Book of John Sevier, 1796–1804, GP-2, Reel 2, Box 2, Folder 9, John Sevier Papers, Second Administration, 67. Jackson and his friends did not passively accept Sevier's actions. See, for example, Archibald Roane to Arthur Campbell, Dec. 12, 1803, Campbell Family Papers; William Maclin to John Overton, Jan. 22, 1804, AC 803-2, Murdock Collection, John Overton Papers; and John Sevier to Henry Dearborn, Feb. 8, 1804, GP-4, Box 1, Folder 1, John Sevier Papers, Second Administration. See also Remini, *Course of American Empire;* and Walker, "Tennessee, 1796–1821."
68. Jackson also engaged in confrontations with Newton Cannon and John Cocke, although the only other bullet wound he received came as a result of a shootout with Thomas Hart Benton and his brother in 1813. See Walker, "Tennessee, 1796–1821," 160. See also Charles Sellers, "Banking and Politics in Jackson's Tennessee, 1817–1821," *Mississippi Valley Historical Review* 41 (1954–55): 63; Abernethy, *From Frontier to Plantation,* 292–93.
69. The most solid hypotheses regarding various factional alignments come from Walker, "Tennessee, 1796–1821," chaps. 4 and 5; Abernethy, *From Frontier to Plantation,* 124–28, 164–81, 194–222; and Remini, *Course of American Empire.* On the general population and their early-nineteenth-century political tendencies, see "The Recollections of John Hillsman, Esq., an Aged Gentleman Residing a Few Miles from Knoxville, in 1849," 8, Reel 4, Box 7, H-98, THS Miscellaneous Files, TSLA (hereafter cited as "Recollections of John Hillsman"). Sevier himself pointed to the blurry nature of the political split between himself and Jackson in an 1803 letter to mutual ally James Robertson. See James Robertson, "Correspondence of James Robertson," *American Historical Magazine* 4, no. 4 (Oct. 1899): 373–74.
70. Willie Blount had served as investigator during the 1803 collection of evidence that was presented to Roane by Jackson. Willie Blount and Patrick Campbell to Archibald Roane, Sept. 12, 1803, No. 678, Reel 1, Box 2, B-160, THS Miscellaneous Files. That did not diminish their seeming ties, however. In 1811 Blount even went so far as to provide Sevier with a personal letter of introduction to Henry Clay, then Speaker of the House of Representatives. See "Journal of John Sevier," *Tennessee Historical Magazine* 6, no. 1 (Apr. 1920): 41. As to Sevier's other friendships, see Sevier to Overton, July 22, 1810, John Sevier Papers, Rare Books, Manuscripts, and Special Collections, William R. Perkins Library, Duke Univ.; and Sevier to Overton, Nov. 2, 1809, AC 803-2, Murdock Collection, John Overton Papers. For similar connections in a slightly later period, see Joseph McMinn to Robert Whyte, Oct. 5, 1817, I-C-4, Box 2-11, Robert Whyte Papers, TSLA.
71. "Recollections of John Hillsman," 9–10. See also "Journal of John Sevier," *Tennessee Historical Magazine* 6, no. 1 (Apr. 1920): 19.
72. Another example: Overton was on intimate terms with William Maclin, whom Jackson had assaulted during the height of his 1803 feud with Sevier. See William Maclin to John Overton, Jan. 22, 1804, AC 803-2, Murdock Collection, John Overton Papers.

73. Note Robertson County resident Thomas Johnson's statement to John Sevier in 1796, for example. Hoping that Andrew Jackson would go to Congress, he wrote, "I am happy to hear that Mr. Claiborne resigns to Mr. Jackson the ensuing Election, for it was the promise of that part of the state to give [middle Tennessee] one Representative." Johnson to Sevier, Sept. 4, 1796, GP-2, Reel 3, Q-46, John Sevier Papers, First Administration. See also Abernethy, *From Frontier to Plantation;* Remini, *Course of American Empire;* Walker, "Tennessee, 1796–1821"; and Toomey, "Prelude to Statehood."

74. Historians over the last decades have come to realize that Jeffersonian Republicanism was an umbrella for two competing visions of progress. For more on this division within the ranks of Jeffersonian Republicans, see Ellis, "Market Revolution," 149–76; and John Lauritz Larson, *Internal Improvement: National Public Works and the Promise of Popular Government in the Early United States* (Chapel Hill: Univ. of North Carolina Press, 2001). See also Charles Sellers, *The Market Revolution: Jacksonian America, 1815–1846* (New York: Oxford Univ. Press, 1991); and Harry L. Watson, *Liberty and Power: The Politics of Jacksonian America* (New York: Hill and Wang, 1990).

75. Newman, *Parades and the Politics of the Street,* 7.

76. "A Farmer" to the *Impartial Review and Cumberland Repository,* May 23, 1807.

77. "A Friend of the People" to the *Carthage Gazette,* Feb. 20, 1809. See also "Low Blooded Hag" to the *Carthage Gazette,* June 15, 1809.

78. *Carthage Gazette,* Mar. 13, 1809.

79. *Carthage Gazette,* June 12, 1811.

80. Robert Foster to the *Impartial Review and Cumberland Repository,* July 23, 1807.

81. *Carthage Gazette,* Apr. 10, 1809. Sampson Williams and Joel Dyer did likewise. The former made it clear in the *Gazette* that he was running on a platform of creating circuit courts in lieu of the existing district courts. The latter, despite concerns about electioneering, came out in favor of an arbitration law and an abolition of courts of errors and appeals. *Gazette,* Mar. 13, 1809. For more on the question of judicial reform, see chapter 4, this volume.

82. Thomas Harris, Circular to his Constituents, Nov. 23, 1809, *Early American Imprints: Series II,* no. 17711.

83. *Carthage Gazette,* July 17, 1811.

84. Bureau of the Census, *Second Census of the United States* and *Fourth Census of the United States.* See also Goodstein, *Nashville, 1780–1860,* appendix table 1.

85. Bruce H. Mann, *Republic of Debtors: Bankruptcy in the Age of American Independence* (Cambridge: Harvard Univ. Press, 2002), 36. See also Arnow, *Flowering of the Cumberland,* chap. 4.

Chapter 4

1. "A" to the *Tennessee Gazette,* Feb. 18, 1801.

2. François André Michaux, "Travels to the West of the Allegheny Mountains, September 24, 1801–March 1, 1803," in *Early Western Travels, 1748–1846,* ed. Reuben Goldthwaites (Cleveland: Arthur H. Clark, 1904), 3:251–52. See also the description of the Cumberland pro-

vided by Francis Asbury in his journal. Francis Asbury, *The Journal and Letters of Francis Asbury*, vol. 2, *The Journal, 1794–1816*, ed. Elmer T. Clark, J. Manning Potts, and Jacob S. Payton (Nashville: Abingdon Press, 1958), 258.

3. Although these were the major commodities produced by Middle Tennesseans, they were by no means the only one to turn a profit. Farmers and entrepreneurs also engaged in a lucrative corn and whiskey trade, while the herders of the earlier period gave way to more systematic hog farming.

4. With this expansion, Tennessee's speculators finally cashed in. The entire justification behind speculation had been the expectation that commercial agriculture would make the land valuable. Without question, by 1810 land was worth far more than it had been only twenty years earlier. As to the process of settlement, historian Daniel Dupre has noted that southwestern frontier societies initially were driven by three groups: squatters, settlers, and speculators. These three groups certainly operated within Middle Tennessee, although life in the Cumberland district ensured that squatters did not neatly precede their settler counterparts, as Dupre found in Alabama; rather, the two groups arrived simultaneously, even as speculators gained political and economic control over the region. See Daniel Dupre, *Transforming the Cotton Frontier: Madison County, Alabama, 1800–1840* (Baton Rouge: Louisiana State Univ. Press, 1997), 11–13.

5. See Rohrbough, *Trans-Appalachian Frontier*, chaps. 2 and 3; Gregory Nobles, "Breaking into the Backcountry: New Approaches to the Early American Frontier, 1750–1800," *William and Mary Quarterly* 46, no. 4 (Winter 1989): 654–62. See also Aron, *How the West Was Lost;* Friend, "Inheriting Eden"; Eslinger, *Citizens of Zion;* Dupre, *Transforming the Cotton Frontier;* Cumfer, "Idea of Mankind Is So Various"; and Stephen Ash, *Middle Tennessee Society Transformed: War and Peace in the Upper South, 1860–1870* (Baton Rouge: Louisiana State Univ. Press, 1988).

6. Allan Kulikoff, *The Agrarian Origins of American Capitalism* (Charlottesville: Univ. of Virginia Press, 1992), 46.

7. For more on this question, see Chaplin, *Anxious Pursuit*, esp. chaps. 1 and 2.

8. Richard Beeman noted a similar problem on the Virginia frontier. See Beeman, *Evolution of the Southern Backcountry*, end of chap. 1.

9. See Toomey, "Prelude to Statehood," 215–20.

10. Stephen B. Weeks, "Tennessee: A Discussion of the Sources of its Population and the Lines of Immigration," *Tennessee Historical Magazine* 2, no. 4 (Dec. 1916): 246–57.

11. Carter, *Territorial Papers* 4:404–5.

12. Barter currency during the territorial period included (most prominently) animal skins, surplus produce, and, as we shall see, slaves. See Toomey, "Prelude to Statehood." Lardner Clark first set up shop in the Cumberland region in 1783, offering goods on credit and for these various barter commodities. Not overly successful in his profession, Clark closed up shop and was gone from Middle Tennessee by the mid-1790s. See Rohrbough, *Trans-Appalachian Frontier*, chap. 2. In the 1790s, Andrew Jackson and David Allison would run a general store that maintained a sizable clientele list. See Lewis Laska, "'The Dam'st Situation Ever Man Was Placed In': Andrew Jackson, David Allison, and the Frontier Economy of 1795–1796," *Tennessee Historical Quarterly* 54, no. 4 (Winter 1995): 336–47.

13. The 1805–6 cession of land by the Chickasaws permanently cleared out Middle Tennessee for settlement.
14. Carter, *Territorial Papers* 4:404–5.
15. Bureau of the Census, *Second Census of the United States, Third Census of the United States,* and *Fourth Census of the United States.* These figures do not take into account out-migration.
16. Petition 24-2-1799, Reel 1, TSLA.
17. Joseph Young to his grandfather, Sept. 21, 1802, Subcollection 2, Series 1, Folder 88, Mary H. Kennedy Collection, Southern Historical Collection, Wilson Library, Univ. of North Carolina at Chapel Hill (hereafter cited as Mary H. Kennedy Collection).
18. Hugh Robison to Robert Ramsay, Aug. 26, 1805, J. G. Ramsay Collection, Southern Historical Collection, Wilson Library, Univ. of North Carolina at Chapel Hill (hereafter cited as J. G. Ramsay Collection).
19. Three major roads existed to facilitate migration to the Southwest: (1) the Cumberland Road across Tennessee, (2) Federal Road from Georgia to Natchez, and (3) Natchez Trace from Nashville to Natchez. This would make Nashville and Middle Tennessee the hub for a lot of immigration. Joan Cashin points to the importance of these three roadways in expediting western migration. See Cashin, *A Family Venture: Men and Women on the Southwestern Frontier* (Baltimore: Johns Hopkins Univ. Press, 1991), chap. 3.
20. Arthur Lee to David Campbell, Jan. 30, 1808, Campbell Family Papers.
21. James Norman Smith Memoirs, 1789–1860, 1:86, AC 157, TSLA.
22. Hugh Robison to Robert Ramsay, Aug. 28, 1802, J. G. Ramsay Collection.
23. Thomas Jefferson to John Garland Jefferson, Dec. 17, 1796, *Papers of Thomas Jefferson* 29:222.
24. Robison to Ramsay, Aug. 28, 1802, J. G. Ramsay Collection.
25. Some arrangements were more beneficial than others, to be sure. In 1796, James Bishop, for example, leased 640 acres on the south side of the Cumberland River—ten years for free in return for his services as a surveyor. Cumfer, "Idea of Mankind Is So Various," 522–23. As H. Philip Bacon noted, the typical terms for early tenants were "eight to ten bushels of maize for each acre cleared." This arrangement necessarily meant some level of corn production, but cotton became the quickest way to make a profit. Bacon, "Nashville's Trade at the Beginning of the Nineteenth Century," *Tennessee Historical Quarterly* 15, no. 1 (Mar. 1956): 30.
26. And then, of course, there was the issue of the land office in Franklin. When it opened in 1785, there appeared yet another obstacle for the stream of migrants entering both the eastern and Cumberland districts. See Williams, *History of the Lost State;* Abernethy, *From Frontier to Plantation;* and Finger, *Tennessee Frontiers.*
27. Stephen Aron, for example, has noted that Daniel Boone was one of thousands whose land titles faced continual overlapping claims. Aron, *How the West Was Lost,* 84.
28. Frederick Stump to John Overton, Dec. 12, 1792, as noted in Toomey, "Prelude to Statehood," 212.
29. North Carolina Land Warrant No. 121, No. 678, Reel 1, Box 1, B-17, THS Miscellaneous Files.

30. Friend, "Inheriting Eden," 45. See also Watlington, *Partisan Spirit*, chap. 1.
31. See White, *Messages of the Governors of Tennessee* 1:213–14.
32. William P. Anderson to John Coffee, May 15, 1807, AC 814, Box 5, Folder 2, Dyas Collection, John Coffee Papers.
33. G. W. Campbell to Albert Gallatin, Oct. 2, 1807, Brown-Ewell Family Papers, Filson Historical Society, Louisville, Ky. (hereafter cited as Brown-Ewell Family Papers).
34. "A Friend of the People" to the *Carthage Gazette*, Feb. 20, 1809.
35. "Manlius" to the *Impartial Review and Cumberland Repository*, Sept. 3, 1808.
36. James Norman Smith Memoirs 1:65.
37. Ibid., 1:65, 94. Smith's problem reflects what for the state legislature was a consistent source of trouble: fraudulent claims. Stockley Donelson seemed to catch the brunt of the people's wrath, as no less than five petitions regarding his behavior made their way to the Tennessee House of Representatives between 1807 and 1809. See, for example, Petition 12-1-1807, Reel 1, TSLA.
38. *Impartial Review and Cumberland Repository*, Dec. 10, 1807.
39. "A" to the *Tennessee Gazette*, Feb. 18, 1801.
40. Goodstein, *Nashville, 1780–1860*, chap. 1.
41. Petition 9-1-1806, Reel 3, TSLA.
42. G. W. Campbell Letter Book, Brown-Ewell Family Papers.
43. Elizabeth H. Peeler, "The Policies of Willie Blount as Governor," *Tennessee Historical Quarterly* 1, no. 4 (Dec. 1942): 312.
44. Preemption claims were already well established by the early 1790s. Squatters had particularly good luck remaining on Indian lands, but it also included other lands. In 1807, land commissioners for the state, for example, legitimized forty-three out of fifty-five preemption claims for western Tennessee. Report of land commissioners, *Journal of the Senate*, Oct. 12, 1807, quoted in Cumfer, "Idea of Mankind Is So Various," 513.
45. Petition 10-2-1806, Reel 3, TSLA. This would remain a complaint throughout the early years of statehood. In 1812, for example, a similar petition made its way to the legislature. See Petition 21-1-1812, Reel 3. And then there were the complaints of direct fraud by individuals, most prominently Stockley Donelson. See Petition 22-1808-1, Reel 3.
46. Kulikoff, *Agrarian Origins of American Capitalism*, 44.
47. Ash, *Middle Tennessee Society Transformed*, 16. As Allan Kulikoff has noted, Tennesseans' proclivity toward commercial production indicates the extent to which the "frontier economy was embedded in commercial markets." Kulikoff, *Agrarian Origins of American Capitalism*, 24, 20.
48. In some areas, migration rates were as high as 70 percent. Goodstein, *Nashville, 1780–1860*; and Remini, *Course of American Empire*. Admittedly, much of this argument is based on conjecture. Unfortunately for scholars, all of Tennessee's 1800 and 1810 census returns have been destroyed, as have the vast majority of tax lists for this early period. This fact, combined with the massive in- and out-migration, makes it difficult to re-create a significant picture of the lowest sorts in the region.
49. Kulikoff, *Agrarian Origins of American Capitalism*, 22.
50. Arnow, *Flowering of the Cumberland*, 331.

51. William Coghlan to Thomas Jefferson, Apr. 10, 1811, in *The Papers of Thomas Jefferson: Retirement Series*, vol. 3, ed. J. Jefferson Looney (Princeton, N.J.: Princeton Univ. Press, 2006), 548-9. Jefferson received regular requests for loans and charity. See *The Papers of Thomas Jefferson: Retirement Series*, vols. 1, 2, and 3, ed. J. Jefferson Looney (Princeton, N.J.: Princeton Univ. Press, 2004–).
52. Barthelemi Tardiveau to Hector St. John de Crevecouer, Oct. 7, 1789, Barthelemi Tardiveau Miscellaneous Files, Filson Historical Society, Louisville, Ky.
53. *Knoxville Gazette*, Jan. 14, 1792.
54. Michaux, "Travels to the West of the Allegheny Mountains," 252–53.
55. Hugh Robison to Robert Ramsay, Aug. 28, 1802, J. G. Ramsay Collection.
56. Thomas Jefferson to Archibald Fisher, May 4, 1810, *Papers of Thomas Jefferson: Retirement Series* 2:359–60.
57. Michaux, "Travels to the West of the Allegheny Mountains," 257.
58. Middle Tennesseans understood the national market as inclusive primarily of New Orleans, New York, and Baltimore. See, for example, the *Impartial Review and Cumberland Repository*, Dec. 13, 1805, Jan. 18, 1806, and Jan. 3, 1807.
59. Finger, *Tennessee Frontiers*, 185.
60. Acts of the General Assembly, 1803, quoted in Albert C. Holt, "The Economic and Social Beginnings of Tennessee," *Tennessee Historical Magazine* 7, no. 4 (Jan. 1922): 277–78.
61. *Tennessee Gazette*, Mar. 20, 1805.
62. *Impartial Review and Cumberland Repository*, Nov. 15, 1806.
63. Michaux, "Travels to the West of the Allegheny Mountains," 252.
64. H. Denison to John Hillsman, Oct. 30, 1800, No. 678, Reel 2, Box 4, D-46, THS Miscellaneous Files.
65. *Tennessee Gazette*, June 24, 1801.
66. *Tennessee Gazette*, Feb. 8, 1804. The *Impartial Review and Cumberland Repository* reported New Orleans prices at $23.00 in January and $26.50 in May 1806. By November the price had gone back to $15.00 and remained at that level well into 1807. See, for example, the *Impartial Review and Cumberland Repository*, Mar. 28, 1807.
67. This particular price was quoted from general cotton values in Great Britain. *Tennessee Gazette*, July 5, 1806. Britain was a particularly important market; as an anonymous merchant noted, "Tennessee cotton is in considerable repute now in that market." *Impartial Review and Cumberland Repository*, May 16, 1807. As regards the issue of watching foreign markets: Thomas Easton, editor of the *Impartial Review*, wrote, "In the present convoluted state of the world it is incumbent on every individual in the community to have an eye on the political affairs of the country, and watch with a careful eye, the transactions of foreign governments." *Impartial Review and Cumberland Repository*, Dec. 8, 1809. See also *Impartial Review and Cumberland Repository*, Mar. 21, Apr. 11, May 9, June 6, 1807; Aug. 11, Sept. 1, Dec. 7, 1808; and Mar. 16, Dec. 8, 1809.
68. *Impartial Review and Cumberland Repository*, Jan. 14, 1808. For more on Middle Tennessee and the embargo, see chapter 5, this volume.
69. See, for example, John R. Eaton to General Winchester, Sept. 19, 1811, No. 794, Reel 1, Box 1, Folder 5, James Winchester Papers, TSLA (hereafter cited as James Winchester Papers). See also Finger, *Tennessee Frontiers*, 185.

70. The *Impartial Review and Cumberland Repository*, for example, quoted prices from "$8–15," depending on quality, on December 8, 1809. It remained steady over the next two years. See the *Impartial Review and Cumberland Repository*, May 3, 1811.
71. "A Cotton Planter" to the *Impartial Review and Cumberland Repository*, Nov. 12, 1807.
72. Cotton's value also remained one of the three major mediums of exchange in Middle Tennessee, along with cash and slaves. See, for example, King, Carson, and King's advertisement on January 1, 1803, in the *Tennessee Gazette:* "COTTON; THE subscribers takes this method of informing their friends, customers and the public in general that they have on hand a general assortment of MERCHANDIZE, which they will dispose of on reasonable terms for cotton."
73. Finger, *Tennessee Frontiers*, 185.
74. Willoughby Williams, "Recollections of Nashville in Early Days," 9, Reel 6, Box 11, N-19, THS Miscellaneous Files.
75. Bureau of the Census, *Second Census of the United States*. Tennessee's home production was similar—if not as expansive—to what was going on in Massachusetts and other areas of the United States as the country turned toward an industrial revolution. See Lisa Tolbert, *Constructing Townscapes: Space and Society in Antebellum Tennessee* (Chapel Hill: Univ. of North Carolina Press, 1999), 133–35. See also Christopher Clark, *Roots of Rural Capitalism: Western Massachusetts, 1780–1860* (Ithaca, N.Y.: Cornell Univ. Press, 1990); and Jeanne Boydston, *Home and Work: Housework, Wages and the Ideology of Labor in the Early Republic* (Oxford: Oxford Univ. Press, 1990).
76. Rohrbough, *Trans-Appalachian Frontier*, chap. 2.
77. Acts of the General Assembly, Oct. 20, 1797, quoted in Albert C. Holt, "The Economic and Social Beginnings of Tennessee," *Tennessee Historical Magazine* 8, no. 1 (Apr. 1924): 26.
78. Petition 1-2-1799, Reel 1, TSLA.
79. Elizabeth Topp Reminiscences, River Traffic Volume, AC-173, Reel 1, Topp Family Papers, TSLA (hereafter cited as Topp Family Papers).
80. Petition 13-2-1806, Reel 3, TSLA.
81. William Carvin to John Coffee, July 10, 1801, Box 5, Folder 9, Dyas Collection, John Coffee Papers. In 1805 Charles Cabanis announced that he would buy tobacco at "three dollars fifty cents per hundredweight." *Tennessee Gazette*, Dec. 7, 1805. In 1806 the *Impartial Review* listed prices between $6.50 and $3.00. *Impartial Review and Cumberland Repository*, Jan. 23, May 17, Nov. 29, 1806.
82. On January 3, 1807, the *Impartial Review* reported prices at two dollars, but within two weeks it had returned to three dollars. It remained at that level for the next several months. *Impartial Review*, Mar. 28, 1807. On 1811: *Impartial Review and Cumberland Repository*, May 3, 1811.
83. Petition 2-1-1809, reel 3, TSLA.
84. Aaron D. Purcell, "A Spirit of Speculation: David Burford, Antebellum Entrepreneur of Middle Tennessee," *Tennessee Historical Quarterly* 64, no. 2 (Summer 2005): 90–109.
85. William Blount to John Gray Blount, Nov. 7, 1797, in *John Gray Blount Papers*, vol. 3, *1796–1802*, ed. Alice B. Keith (Raleigh, N.C.: State Department of Archives and History, 1965), 174-86.

86. Bureau of the Census, *Second Census of the United States*. Given their expansive cotton and tobacco markets, it is no surprise that Davidson and Sumner Counties maintained the most slaves, at 3,087 and 1,284, respectively.
87. Bureau of the Census, *Fourth Census of the United States*. In 1810 the largest slave counties were Davidson and Williamson, at 6,305 and 3,985, respectively, with Sumner close behind at 3,734. Distribution in 1820 follows the same pattern: Davidson County held 7,899 slaves and Williamson held 6,972.
88. Bureau of the Census, *Fourth Census of the United States,* and Bureau of the Census, *Fifth Census of the United States,* 1830 (Washington, D.C.: Gales and Seaton, 1831). The lower percentage of Middle Tennessee slaves relative to the total Tennessee population in 1830 is accounted for by the emergence of slavery in West Tennessee. Whereas in 1820 two western counties held 239 slaves, by 1830, fifteen counties held a total of 26,542, or 19 percent of the statewide slave population.
89. See Dupre, *Transforming the Cotton Frontier,* 27. The destruction of the 1800 and 1810 censuses for Tennessee mean that it is not clear how many slaves these men held. The 1820 numbers, however, indicate that they fell well within the traditional understanding of "planter."
90. Jackson in the *Impartial Review and Cumberland Repository,* Apr. 14, 1808.
91. James Iredell, *Laws of the State of North Carolina* (Edenton, N.C., 1791), 85–95, Rare Books Room, Katherine R. Everett Law Library, University of North Carolina School of Law. See also Marvin Michael Kay and Lorin Lee Cary, *Slavery in North Carolina, 1748–1775* (Chapel Hill: Univ. of North Carolina Press, 1995). Some of the more brutal punishments included whipping, castration, branding, ear cropping, and, in some cases, a combination of these. Perhaps the most notorious part of the 1741 code established that slaves who gave false witness in their defense at a trial had "one ear nailed to the Pillory, and there stand for the Space of an Hour, and the Said Ear to be cut off, and thereafter the other Ear nailed in like manner, and cut off, at the Expiration of one hour; and moreover, to order every such Offender thirty-nine lashes, well laid on, on his or her bare Back, at the Common Whipping-post." Iredell, *Laws of the State of North Carolina,* 94.
92. Iredell, *Laws of the State of North Carolina,* 91–94.
93. Cumfer, "Idea of Mankind Is So Various," 537. See also Eslinger, *Citizens of Zion,* 41; and Eslinger, "Shape of Slavery on the Kentucky Frontier," 1–23. For more on Indians' use of stolen slaves and property to acquire capital, see chapter 1, this volume.
94. Goodstein, "Black History on the Nashville Frontier," 401–20. See also Goodstein, *Nashville, 1780–1860,* chap. 4.
95. Hugh Williamson to John Gray Blount, Nov. 25, 1792, *John Gray Blount Papers* 2:218–19, as quoted in Toomey, "Prelude to Statehood," 246.
96. Last will and testament of James Moore King, Sept. 25, 1814, Folder A-1, James Moore King Collection, Senator Albert Gore Sr. Research Center, Middle Tennessee State Univ., Murfreesboro. Another example: In 1809 John Overton offered to take slaves in payment for land for "a likely Negro boy of good condition, of the age of 15 years for my interest" on a land deal. Overton to Edward Scott, Apr. 1, 1809, Microfilm, No. 812. Reel 1, Box 3, Folder 12, Claybrooke Collection. On William Moore: *Carthage Gazette,* Oct. 13, 1809.

See also Overton to John Coffee, Jan. 25, 1807, AC 814, Reel 5, Box 11, Folder 9, Dyas Collection, John Coffee Papers. See also George Washington Campbell's offer to sell land on Stone's River "for a good price in cash & Negroes." Campbell to John Coffee, July 12, 1809, Box 5, Folder 8, Dyas Collection, John Coffee Papers.

97. *Carthage Gazette,* Aug. 17, 1809.
98. Cumfer, "Idea of Mankind Is So Various," 543.
99. John Trimble to Robert Whyte, Sept. 14, 1803, I-C-4 AC no. 41, Folder 3, Robert Whyte Papers, TSLA. By 1818 Whyte was making a good sum of money on his trading. George Bell, for example, offered sixty-five hundred dollars for a "Negro blacksmith, cooper, and three mulatto women." Bell to Whyte, Mar. 4, 1818, AC 41, Folder 3, Robert Whyte Papers, TSLA.
100. Petition 18-1-1809, reel 3, TSLA. See also James Reynolds's and John McFarlane's petition, 21-1-1809; and Stephen Pate's petition, 9-2-1801, reel 3, TSLA.
101. *Impartial Review and Cumberland Repository,* Feb. 21, 1807.
102. For more on urban slavery, see Richard Wade, *Slavery in the Cities: The South, 1820–1860* (New York: Oxford Univ. Press, 1964). See also Midori Takagi, *Rearing Wolves to Our Own Destruction: Slavery in Richmond, 1782–1865* (Charlottesville: Univ. of Virginia Press, 1999).
103. Joseph Coleman, mayor, to the *Impartial Review and Cumberland Repository,* July 4, 1807.
104. Ibid. See also Petition 8-2-1799, Petition 12-2-1809-1 (signed by 157 Maury County residents), and Petition 15-3-1813 from Davidson County, reels 1, 3, and 4, TSLA; and Goodstein, "Black History on the Nashville Frontier," 414–15.
105. The proceeds from this auction went to the city. Records of the Board of Commissioners for the Town of Nashville, 1802, MF 678, Reel 6, Box 11, N-11, THS Miscellaneous Files.
106. William Lloyd Imes, "The Legal Status of Free Negroes and Slaves in Tennessee," *Journal of Negro History* 4, no. 3 (July 1919): 258.
107. Goodstein, "Black History on the Nashville Frontier," 414.
108. *Carthage Gazette,* Nov. 9, 1811. See also the announcement of Francis Gildart in the *Gazette,* Dec. 14, 1811.
109. *Impartial Review and Cumberland Repository,* May 24, 1806.
110. *Impartial Review and Cumberland Repository,* Jan. 10, Dec. 31, 1807.
111. William B. Wood to James Madison, June 19, 1811, in *The Papers of James Madison: Presidential Series,* vol. 3, *3 November 1810–4 November 1811,* ed. J. C. A. Stagg (Charlottesville: Univ. of Virginia Press, 1996), 343–44.
112. *Carthage Gazette,* Apr. 5, 1811.
113. *Tennessee Gazette Extraordinary,* May 11, 1803, AC 678, Reel 8, Box 15, T-39, THS Miscellaneous Files. Regarding Nashville and slaves, see Goodstein, *Nashville, 1780–1860,* chap. 4.
114. Mary Jane Thomas, *Old Days in Nashville, Tenn.* (Nashville: Publishing House Methodist Episcopal Church, South, 1897), 22.
115. He would remain in business for another thirty years. Williams, *Recollections of Nashville in Early Days,* 8. See also Goodstein, "Black History on the Nashville Frontier," 412.
116. These petitions came from Davidson and Smith Counties, respectively. Petitions 65-1815-1 and 24-1822-1, 2, TSLA. Abstracted on Race and Slavery Petitions Project, University of North Carolina at Greensboro, http://library.uncg.edu/slavery_petitions/.

117. Lovett, *African-American History of Nashville*, 4.
118. Petitions 145-1825 and 181-1825-1, 9, TSLA. Abstracted on Race and Slavery Petitions Project.
119. There is a large and ever-growing historiography emphasizing the democratic nature of the Second Great Awakening. See, for example, Nathan Hatch, *The Democratization of American Christianity* (New Haven, Conn.: Yale Univ. Press, 1987?); Robert Abzug, *Cosmos Crumbling: American Reform and the Religious Imagination* (Oxford: Oxford Univ. Press, 1994); and John B. Boles, *The Great Revival: Beginnings of the Bible Belt* (Lexington: Univ. Press of Kentucky, 1972). Historian Donald Mathews argues that the evangelical impulse grew as much out of social strains "of a nation on the move into new political, economic, and geographical areas" as out of an inherent democratic impulse. See Mathews, "The Second Great Awakening as an Organizing Process, 1780–1830: An Hypothesis," *American Quarterly* 21 (1969): 27. See also Eslinger, *Citizens of Zion*. In Tennessee it was both: While democracy certainly directed evangelical activity, the social strains brought on by economic and demographic changes helped define the parameters of this democratization.
120. Wilson Creek Primitive Baptist Church Records, MF 90, TSLA.
121. Mount Olivet Baptist Church Records, Jan. 27, 1802, MF 511, TSLA.
122. The Conference Business of the Baptist Church under the Care of James Whitsitt, on Mill Creek, Davidson County, Record Book, 1797–1814, TSLA.
123. John B. McFerrin, *History of Methodism in Tennessee* (Nashville: Publishing House of the Methodist Episcopal Church, South, 1886), iii, 64, 68, 81.
124. See John and Milley to Michael Shofner, Apr. 3, 1822, No. 4067, Michael Shofner Papers, Southern Historical Collection, Wilson Library, Univ. of North Carolina at Chapel Hill (hereafter cited as Michael Shofner Papers). See also Terry Mehlman, "From Seeder Rales to Iron Rails: John Shofner, Yeoman Farmer in an Age of Change, 1831–1857" (master's thesis, Univ. of North Carolina at Chapel Hill, 1999); and Tolbert, *Constructing Townscapes*, 133–35.
125. 1816 Davidson County Tax List, No. 678, Reel 2, Box 4, D-11, THS Miscellaneous Files, TSLA; Bedford County Census, 1820, TSLA.
126. As to in-migration: James Norman Smith noted when he moved from North Carolina, "There were a great many Movers on the Road—I would stop at almost all wagons to Enquire where they were moving from and where to." James Norman Smith Memoirs 2:67. An announcement from the town council in 1804 further speaks to the issue of migration and its attendant evils: In pointing to the need to enforce Sabbath laws, they wrote that "divine service is interrupted in the town of Nashville by the ratling of waggons, profane swearing and drunkenness." *Tennessee Gazette*, Mar. 28, 1804. And in commenting on a rash of assault cases, "Agricola" noted they would "continue to be frequent as long as whiskey is the common beverage of the people. But whenever malt liquors, beer, ale and porter shall prevail as the common drink men will cease to make brutes of themselves and we shall not hear of one assault and battery where we now hear twenty." *Impartial Review and Cumberland Repository*, May 19, 1808. For more on lower-class rowdiness, see Elliot Gorn, "'Gouge and Bite; Pull Hair and Scratch': The Social Significance of Fighting in the Southern Backcountry," *American Historical Review* 90, no. 1 (Feb. 1985): 18–43.

127. Cato, *Tennessee Gazette,* July 29, 1801.
128. Petition 6-1-1801, Reel 1, TSLA. Among the more prominent names on the petition were Robert Searcy, William Anderson, Robert Hays, and James Robertson, all of whom would consistently appear in positions of both political and economic power, as either planters, commercial agents, bankers, or a combination of the three.
129. *Tennessee Gazette,* Mar. 27, 1805.
130. *Tennessee Gazette,* Sept. 4, 1805.
131. Petition 11-2-1799-1b, Reel 1, TSLA.
132. Holt, "Economic and Social Beginnings of Tennessee," Apr. 1924, 44; Petition 14-01-1801, Reel 1, TSLA.
133. *Impartial Review and Cumberland Repository,* Sept. 20, 1806. The major merchants also engaged in land speculation. One of the most prominent was the firm Deadrick and Tatum, which brokered deals both large and small throughout Middle Tennessee. See, for example, William Brown's 1805 journal regarding their sales in and around Palmyra. AC-173, Reel 1, Topp Family Papers. Other large firms included Baird and Boyce, which advertised that they sold "steel and axes, bar-iron, tin wares, cutlery, Anvils, etc." *Impartial Review and Cumberland Repository,* Dec. 10, 1807. The firm Anderson and Weir advertised as selling "General Merchandize" and purchasing cotton (*Tennessee Gazette,* June 24, 1801). There were also advertisements for silver smiths (*Tennessee Gazette,* June 24, 1801), waggoners and bar-iron salesmen (*Carthage Gazette,* Mar. 13, 1809), brick layers and makers (*Impartial Review and Cumberland Repository,* Sept. 17, 1807), whiskey (*Impartial Review and Cumberland Repository,* Sept. 17, 1807), and rifle barrels (*Impartial Review and Cumberland Repository,* July 4, 1807). And in a visible marker of the emerging element of refinement, Daniel White advertised silk and velvet bonnets, "elegant ribbons, Havannah segars, and English toys consisting of alabaster babies, complete tea services in wood and Pewter, Organs, Swords, tambourines and coaches," among other wares (*Impartial Review and Cumberland Repository,* Sept. 20, 1806). This does not get into the obvious cotton and tobacco merchants or the numerous advertisements for more general stores.
134. See, for example, Adam McGuire's regular advertisements for "Blue, Red, Green, Black and Yellow Dying" in the *Tennessee Gazette,* Apr. 17, 1805.
135. For more on these issues, see chapter 1, this volume.
136. Petition 25-1-1799, Reel 1, TSLA.
137. A Citizen to the *Impartial Review and Cumberland Repository,* Aug. 10, 1807. The question of opening the Tombigbee and Mobile was later addressed by the Tennessee congressional delegation at the behest of the state legislature. See their letter to President Madison, published in the *Carthage Gazette,* May 4, 1810. For more on the question of virtue and national improvements, see Larson, *Internal Improvement.*
138. Asbury, *Journal and Letters* 2:308; and Finger, *Tennessee Frontiers,* 186–90.
139. Parker's Road Bill, Sept. 1804, *Early American Imprints: Series II,* no. 6988.
140. Thomas Claiborne to the *Tennessee Gazette,* Aug. 8, 1804.
141. Holt, "Economic and Social Beginnings," Jan. 1922, 284–85. As "A Farmer" put it in 1807, "Commerce, if carried on from a port on Mobile River, would in a few years raise a commercial town there of no small consequence; it would be more within the reach

and management of commercial men in this country." *Impartial Review and Cumberland Repository*, June 6, 1807.

142. Cumfer, "Idea of Mankind Is So Various," 535.
143. Although from a slightly later period, see, for example, John Williams's petition in 1815, 60-1815-1. See also David Allen's petition, 49-1815-1, Reel 5, TSLA.
144. Petition 25-1-1799, Reel 1, TSLA.
145. "A Citizen" to the *Impartial Review and Cumberland Repository*, Aug. 10, 1807. For more on the early drive for federal internal improvements, see Larson, *Internal Improvement*. Larson points to a general level of self-interest in the development of internal improvement schemes, and this certainly plays out in Middle Tennessee. In August 1802, for example, an exasperated Governor Archibald Roane complained that "the Court of Williamson County would not agree to lay off the [Natchez] Road contemplated by the President than any other route than thro' Franklin." Roane to Overton, Aug. 7, 1802, AC 803-2, Murdock Collection, John Overton Papers.
146. *Carthage Gazette*, Mar. 6, 1809. Only a year later the *Gazette* announced a meeting for Smith County to write a petition to the legislature instructing them to request "the interposition of the general government in removing the difficulty and embarrassments which at present obstruct a free communication with the Ocean, by Way of the Tombigbee and the Mobile." *Carthage Gazette*, Nov. 16, 1810.
147. *Carthage Gazette*, Mar. 6, 1809.
148. *Carthage Gazette*, Nov. 16, 1810; Folmsbee, "Sectionalism and Internal Improvements," chap. 2.
149. *Impartial Review and Cumberland Repository*, Mar. 21, Oct. 15, 1807; and Peeler, "Policies of Willie Blount," 315. This point reflects Richard Ellis's assertion that state banks were critical to expanding the market economy. See Ellis, "Market Revolution," 156.
150. "An Act to Incorporate a Banking Association, By the Name of THE NASHVILLE BANK," *Impartial Review and Cumberland Repository*, Feb. 4, 11, 1808.
151. Ibid.
152. Another bank would not appear in Tennessee for four years, and it was in Knoxville. Between 1815 and 1819, however, the state chartered another thirteen banks. As we shall see in chapter 6, they would all become hopelessly entangled in the Panic of 1819. Interestingly, the merchant class eventually lost hegemonic control of the bank. At its founding the bank board was peopled exclusively by Nashville merchants. A year later lawyer John Dickinson came on board, and only ten years later the board was half-lawyer. This pattern would repeat itself for every other Middle Tennessee bank. According to Anita Goodstein, this mix was an indication that banks linked professionals with merchants, who combined provided the impetus for the region's dynamic growth. Goodstein, *Nashville, 1780–1860*, 25.
153. Williams, *Recollections of Nashville in Early Days*, 29–31.
154. Ibid.
155. Arthur to David Campbell, Jan. 30, 1808, Campbell Family Papers.
156. "General Instructions for A. L. Campbell in 1801, by his employer and brother-in-law John McFarlane," Arthur Lee Campbell Papers.

157. Robison to Robert Ramsay, Aug. 28, 1802, J. G. Ramsay Collection.
158. Letter of "A" to the *Tennessee Gazette,* Feb. 18, 1801.
159. *Carthage Gazette,* Aug. 24, 1810.
160. *Impartial Review and Cumberland Repository,* May 14, 1807.
161. George Richardson to Thomas Jefferson, Dec. 22, 1809, *Papers of Thomas Jefferson: Retirement Series* 2:88–89.
162. Michaux, "Travels to the West of the Allegheny Mountains," 252.
163. An excellent example of Lexington merchants were George and Samuel Trotter, who both took Nashville cotton loads and acted as wholesaler for general goods. See Friend, "Inheriting Eden," 151–52.
164. International trade left New Orleans as well. As early as 1805 and 1806, J. Lyon advertised his brig *Industry* as one regularly running Middle Tennessee produce to Liverpool via New Orleans. *Tennessee Gazette,* Mar. 6, 1805.
165. For more on bills of sale, see Peter Temin, *The Jacksonian Economy* (New York: W. W. Norton, 1969), 33–35.
166. Gavin Wright, *The Political Economy of the Cotton South: Households, Markets and Wealth in the Nineteenth Century* (New York: W. W. Norton, 1978), 66–67.
167. "Aristedes," "Reflections on Political Economy and the Prospect Before Us," *Tennessee Gazette and Mero District Advertiser,* Oct. 12, 1803.
168. Joshua Wilson to Joseph Hamilton, July 17, 1806, Reel 1, Box 3, Folder 12, No. 1257, Mary H. T. Orr Papers, TSLA.
169. Robert Akin to James Winchester, Feb. 17, 1808, No. 794, Reel 1 Box 1, Folder 3, James Winchester Papers.
170. Thomas Knox to Robert Ramsay, Mar. 20, 1810, No. 1568, Subseries 1, Folder 1.1, J. G. Ramsay Collection. Knox made a similar statement in January of that year, writing that there was "a grate [sic] famin for the want of money in our Country." Knox to Ramsay, Jan. 17, 1810, J. G. Ramsay Collection.
171. Thomas Knox to Robert Ramsay, Jan. 17, 1810, No. 1568, Subseries 1, Folder 1.1, J. G. Ramsay Collection.
172. "L" to the *Rural Visitor,* reprinted in the *Carthage Gazette,* June 19, 1811. See also Abram Murrey to the *Carthage Gazette,* Apr. 3, 1809.

Chapter 5

1. Arthur to David Campbell, July 16, 1810, Campbell Family Papers.
2. Newman, *Parades and the Politics of the Streets,* 7–9. See also Waldstreicher, *In the Midst of Perpetual Fetes.*
3. Newman, *Parades and the Politics of the Streets,* 7.
4. Their concerns increasingly reflected John Larson's contention that "few Americans truly lived outside the market or intended never to exploit their opportunities for profit, but some people saw their economic options embedded in structures of power and social relations that might be threatened by the rise of more starkly capitalistic institutions." Larson, *Internal Improvement,* 72. See also Eslinger, *Citizens of Zion,* 55.

5. Norman Risjord and Gordon DenBoer, "The Evolution of Political Parties in Virginia, 1782–1800," *Journal of American History* 60, no. 4 (Mar. 1974): 961–84. See also Risjord, *Chesapeake Politics, 1781–1800* (New York: Columbia Univ. Press, 1978). Similarly, in 1786 and 1787 impoverished farmers shut down western Massachusetts courts, where creditors were suing to foreclose farm mortgages; also behind their attack were concerns over issues of taxation and land in that state, Vermont, New Hampshire, and Connecticut. Alan Taylor has called this the "New England Regulation." Taylor, *Liberty Men and Great Proprietors*, 5. For more on Shays's Rebellion, see David P. Szatmary, *Shays' Rebellion: The Making of an Agrarian Insurrection* (Amherst: Univ. of Massachusetts Press, 1980); and Leonard Richards, *Shays's Rebellion: The American Revolution's Final Battle* (Philadelphia: Univ. of Pennsylvania Press, 2002). See also Richard Ellis, *The Jeffersonian Crisis: Courts and Politics in the Young Republic* (New York: Oxford Univ. Press, 1971); and Onuf, *Origins of the Federal Republic*. For more on western frontier unrest, see Thomas Slaughter, *The Whiskey Rebellion: Frontier Epilogue to the American Revolution* (Oxford: Oxford Univ. Press, 1986); Terry Bouton, "A Road Closed: Rural Insurgency in Post-Independence Pennsylvania," *Journal of American History* 87, no. 3 (Dec. 2000): 855–87; and Saul Cornell, *The Other Founders: Anti-Federalism and the Dissenting Tradition in America, 1788–1828* (Chapel Hill: Univ. of North Carolina Press, 1999).
6. Aron, *How the West Was Lost*, 82–89; Eslinger, *Citizens of Zion*, 65–67; and Watlington, *Partisan Spirit*, chap. 3. See also Ellis, *Jeffersonian Crisis*, 134–38.
7. "Manlius" to the *Impartial Review and Cumberland Repository*, Sept. 3, 1808.
8. Kulikoff, *Agrarian Origins of American Capitalism*, 45; Eslinger, *Citizens of Zion*, 68; and Aron, *How the West Was Lost*.
9. *Black's Law Dictionary* defines "fieri facias," which literally means "cause it to be done," as a "judicial writ directing a sheriff to satisfy a judgment from debtor's property." "Venditioni exponas" literally means "you expose to sale." *Black's Law Dictionary* defines it as "a writ of execution requiring a sale to be made, directed to a sheriff when he has levied upon goods under a writ of fieri facias, but returned that they remained unsold for want of buyers." Henry Campbell Black, *Black's Law Dictionary*, 6th ed. (St. Paul, Minn.: West Group, 1990), 627, 1555. See, for example, *Tennessee Gazette*, May 27, 1801; *Carthage Gazette and Friend of the People*, Oct. 13, 1809; and *Impartial Review and Cumberland Repository*, June 27, 1807. Connected to this were the consistent lists of people with outstanding taxes on land. They were there because of a 1799 law that commissioned Benjamin Bradford, editor of the *Tennessee Gazette*, and, later, George Roulstone of the *Impartial Review and Cumberland Repository* to publish the lists. Petitions 8-2-1806 and 15-1-1807, Reel 3, TSLA.
10. See, for example, John Spencer's petition in 1809. A Maury County landowner, he had his property taken away from him because he had not heard that tax day had been moved forward and therefore was in arrears. The unsympathetic sheriff took his land anyway, and Spencer petitioned for a state-mandated exception. Petition 30-1-1809, Reel 3, TSLA.
11. For more on speculators' efforts at removal, see chapter 4, this volume.
12. Kulikoff, *Agrarian Origins of American Capitalism*, 44.

13. Goodstein, *Nashville, 1780–1860*, chap. 2. See also James Ely Jr., "The Legal Practice of Andrew Jackson," *Tennessee Historical Quarterly* 38, no. 4 (Winter 1979): 421–35; and Remini, *Course of American Empire*. After 1800 local newspapers were filled with public announcements of debt cases, and at times these included such formerly prominent names as David Allison, who, in the 1790s, had been a partner of Jackson's and a close ally of William Blount's. See the *Tennessee Gazette*, Apr. 13, June 22, 1803, Feb. 8, 1804, and Jan. 2, 1805.
14. Single justices tended to hear civil cases with sums less than twenty dollars and petty crimes such as swearing. Toomey, "Prelude to Statehood," chap. 2. If Donald Winters is correct, then the Tennessee yeoman in the antebellum period was more economically adept than the image created either by contemporary Fredrick Law Olmsted or by historian Frank Owsley. Using census data from 1850 and 1860, he notes that gains in holdings and improved economic positions were central to the Tennessee yeoman experience. Winters, "'Plain Folk' of the Old South Reexamined: Economic Democracy in Tennessee," *Journal of Southern History* 53, no. 4 (Nov. 1987): 584.
15. Toomey, "Prelude to Statehood," chap. 2; Goodstein, *Nashville, 1780–1860*. See also Beeman, *Evolution of the Southern Backcountry*, chap. 2; and Rohrbough, *Trans-Appalachian Frontier*, 126–27.
16. Goodstein, *Nashville, 1780–1860*, 12–14; see also chap. 1.
17. Ely, "Legal Practice of Andrew Jackson," 426.
18. James Ely Jr., "Andrew Jackson as a Tennessee State Court Judge, 1798–1804," *Tennessee Historical Quarterly* 40, no. 2 (Summer 1981): 146.
19. *Impartial Review and Cumberland Repository*, Sept. 1, 1808.
20. Ibid.
21. Petition 16-1-1806, Reel 3, TSLA.
22. Ibid.; Petition 6-1-1809, Reel 3, TSLA.
23. In 1809, seventy-four petitioners addressed the situation by asking that the legislature "grant longer time. Otherwise there are good numbers of Citizens having Just Claims will be materially injured." Petition 6-1-1809, Reel 3, TSLA.
24. Benton's position is similar to that of "radical reformers" of Kentucky and other areas of the early Republic: those people who wanted a cheap, simple, easily available and speedy system of administering justice that could ensure equality and provide security with only a minimum of oversight from the legal profession. Ellis, *Jeffersonian Crisis*, 121.
25. *Impartial Review and Cumberland Repository*, Feb. 11, 1808. See also "Simm" to the *Carthage Gazette*, Feb. 20, 1809. The real John Oldcastle, Lord Cobham, was executed in 1417 for attempting to overthrow King Henry V and the church hierarchy. See Peter Corbin and Douglas Sedge, eds., *The Oldcastle Controversy: Sir John Oldcastle, Part I and the Famous Victories of Henry V* (New York: Manchester Univ. Press, 1991).
26. *Impartial Review and Cumberland Repository*, Mar. 17, 1808.
27. *Impartial Review and Cumberland Repository*, June 4, 1808.
28. Ibid.

29. *Impartial Review and Cumberland Repository,* Apr. 21, 1808; and *Carthage Gazette,* Apr. 5, 1811.
30. *Carthage Gazette,* Feb. 6, 1809; *Impartial Review and Cumberland Repository,* July 21, 1808; *Impartial Review and Cumberland Repository,* May 9, 1808; and the Oldcastle series, 1808, *Impartial Review and Cumberland Repository.*
31. Continuing, "Slim" pointed out that political retrenchment would solve Middle Tennessee's legal dilemma: "'The electioneering system ought to undergo a complete reform. Is it not a bare faced absurdity to see every man who pays taxes, or a militia man, together with emigrants not more than two or three years in the country, walk into the courthouse and pass a vote! I call that the *mad Jefferson plan!*" *Carthage Gazette,* Apr. 5, 1811.
32. Ibid.
33. *Carthage Gazette,* Mar. 6, 1809. "Detector" continued that he was not antilawyer per se. Rather, he argued, his "object is only to call the attention of the farmers, and invite them to reflect that it is their duty and interest to oppose the election of any lawyer to a legislative capacity because the interest of a lawyer and farmer do not agree—the farmer lives by honest industry; the lawyers, by broils and lawsuits; the interest of the farmer is peace and plain laws; the interest of the lawyer is quarrels and obscure, mysterious and intricate laws."
34. *Nashville Clarion,* July 9, 1811, quoted in Tom Kanon, "'James Madison, Felix Grundy, and the Devil': A Western War Hawk in Congress," *Filson History Quarterly* 75 (Fall 2001): 446.
35. "A Freeholder" to the *Impartial Review and Cumberland Repository,* May 3, 1811.
36. "Honestus" to the *Impartial Review and Cumberland Repository,* Nov. 24, 1808.
37. *Impartial Review and Cumberland Repository,* Feb. 8, 1808.
38. "Friend of the People" to the *Carthage Gazette,* Feb. 13, 1809.
39. *Impartial Review and Cumberland Repository,* July 14, 1808.
40. *Impartial Review and Cumberland Repository,* July 21, 1808. Interestingly, only Davidson County condemned the measure—the one county where entrepreneurial elements were particularly strong and where lawyers held sway as much as merchants. *Impartial Review and Cumberland Repository,* Sept. 1, 1808.
41. *Nashville Clarion,* reprinted in the *Carthage Gazette,* Jan. 25, 1809.
42. Ibid.
43. *Carthage Gazette,* Apr. 10, Dec. 15, 1809.
44. Representative Thomas Harris in the *Carthage Gazette,* Dec. 15, 1809. In an election in which every candidate supported judicial reform, Harris's victory did not come without controversy. See chapter 2, this volume, for Williams's attempt to overturn the election.
45. Acts of Tennessee, 1809, chap. 49, quoted in White, *Messages of the Governors of Tennessee* 1:313. Benton's proposal was remarkably similar to Felix Grundy's Kentucky proposal of 1802. See Ellis, *Jeffersonian Crisis,* 150.
46. Thomas Harris, Circular to his Constituents, Nov. 23, 1809. See also White, *Messages of the Governors of Tennessee* 1:313.
47. *Impartial Review and Cumberland Repository,* June 9, 1808; Ellis, *Jeffersonian Crisis,* 151–52.
48. Thomas Harris, Circular to his Constituents, Nov. 23, 1809.
49. *Carthage Gazette,* July 28, 1808. See also the "Junius" dialogues in the *Nashville Clarion.*

50. Thomas Harris, Circular to his Constituents, Nov. 23, 1809.
51. The two Supreme Court judges were Hugh Lawson White and George Washington Campbell; the five circuit judges were former senator William Cocke, James Trimble, Nathaniel Williams, Thomas Stuart, and Parry W. Humphreys. White, *Messages of the Governors of Tennessee* 1:314.
52. AC 814, Dyas Collection, John Coffee Papers.
53. Jonathan Atkins, *Parties, Politics and the Sectional Conflict in Tennessee, 1832–1861* (Knoxville: Univ. of Tennessee Press, 1997), chap. 1.
54. Perhaps historian George Dangerfield put it best when he pointed out that although speculators and investors got into trouble during economic contractions, "it is not unsafe to assume that the chief burden was borne by those farmers" whose loans no longer were renewed. Dangerfield, *The Era of Good Feelings* (New York: Harcourt, Brace, 1952), 186.
55. Exports to Britain alone grew from 118,368 tons of goods in 1805 to 154,467 tons in 1806. Account of Imports, American States, 1805; Ledgers of Imports Under Countries, Customs 17/27, 1806; Accounts of Imports, American States, 1806; Ledgers, Customs 17/28, 1807, all in Public Record Office, London.
56. Donald Hickey, *The War of 1812: A Forgotten Conflict* (Urbana: Univ. of Illinois Press, 1990), 18. See also Richard Buel Jr., *America on the Brink: How the Political Struggle Over the War of 1812 Almost Destroyed the Young Republic* (New York: Palgrave, 2005); J. C. A. Stagg, *Mr. Madison's War: Politics, Diplomacy and Warfare in the Early American Republic, 1783–1830* (Princeton, N.J.: Princeton Univ. Press, 1983); Harry Coles, *The War of 1812* (Chicago: Univ. of Chicago Press, 1965); and Roger Brown, *The Republic in Peril: 1812* (New York: Norton, 1971).
57. GP-4, Box 1, Folder 12, John Sevier Papers, Second Administration.
58. *Carthage Gazette,* Mar. 6, 1809.
59. Thomas Harris, Circular to his Constituents, Nov. 23, 1809.
60. *Carthage Gazette,* Feb. 13, 1809.
61. Petition 24-1-1809, Reel 3, TSLA.
62. Polly Young to Thomas Young, July 18, 1811, Subcollection 2, Series 1, Folder 91, Mary H. Kennedy Collection.
63. *Carthage Gazette,* Feb. 20, 1809.
64. Ibid.
65. *Nashville Clarion,* Feb. 7, 1809; *Carthage Gazette,* Mar. 6, 1809.
66. GP-4, Box 1, Folder 12, John Sevier Papers, Second Administration.
67. Ibid.
68. Ibid. Showing that the specie problem was not limited merely to Tennessee, these petitioners also pointed out that in "many of the adjacent states from whence the State of Tennessee is chiefly populated, the usual course of Civil Law has been suspended." Another 1809 petition to Governor Sevier argued similarly. Looking for examples of debtor protection, they noted that surrounding states "are protected from ruin by the just and benevolent interference of public authority." GP-4, Box 1, Folder 12, John Sevier Papers, Second Administration.
69. GP-4, Box 1, Folder 12, John Sevier Papers, Second Administration.

70. *Carthage Gazette,* Mar. 6, 1809.
71. Ibid.
72. Ibid.
73. Petition 24-1-1809, Reel 3, TSLA.
74. *Impartial Review and Cumberland Repository,* July 14, 1808.
75. *Impartial Review and Cumberland Repository,* July 28, 1808. See also *Carthage Gazette,* Feb. 1809; and *Nashville Clarion,* July 5, 1808.
76. "A Citizen" to the *Impartial Review and Cumberland Repository,* Aug. 11, 1808.
77. See, for example, John Rhea to the *Carthage Gazette,* May 25, 1810.
78. "An Observer" to the *Impartial Review and Cumberland Repository,* Nov. 17, 1808.
79. See Lawrence A. Peskin, "How the Republicans Learned to Love Manufacturing: The First Parties and the 'New Economy,'" *Journal of the Early Republic* 22, no. 2 (Summer 2002): 235–62. See also Larson, *Internal Improvement.*
80. Petition 19-1809-1, Reel 3, TSLA.
81. John Rhea to the *Carthage Gazette,* May 25, 1810.
82. *Carthage Gazette,* Mar. 6, 1809.
83. Friend of the People to the *Carthage Gazette,* Feb. 13, 1809.
84. Ibid.
85. *Carthage Gazette,* Mar. 6, 1809.
86. Oldcastle to the *Impartial Review and Cumberland Repository,* June 4, 1808. As regards the 1809 law: Laws of Tennessee, 1809, 7th General Assembly, 2nd sess., chap. 2; 8th General Assembly, 1st sess., chap. 46, TSLA. See also Thomas Harris, Circular to his Constituents, Nov. 23, 1809.
87. *Impartial Review and Cumberland Repository,* July 30, 1807.
88. Ibid. See also the *Carthage Gazette,* July 6, 1810.
89. *Gazette,* Feb. 6, 1809.
90. Representative Thomas Harris in the *Carthage Gazette,* Dec. 15, 1809.
91. Republican Meeting of Nashville, Tennessee to James Madison, Sept. 11, 1809, in *The Papers of James Madison: Presidential Series,* vol. 1, *March–30 September 1809,* ed. Robert A. Rutland and Thomas A. Mason (Charlottesville: Univ. of Virginia Press, 1984), 372–73.
92. Ibid.
93. Abram Murrey to the *Carthage Gazette,* Apr. 3, 1809.
94. Quoted from Waldstreicher, *In the Midst of Perpetual Fetes,* 276.
95. Over the years several historians have asserted that Tennesseans also desired war as a means of obtaining Canada. Certainly there is evidence to support this position, as Samuel Overton's announcement made clear. In 1813 he wrote to his father that "Kentucky has taken the ground, that Canada is not to be given up by negotiators for peace; and Tennessee, I think, is disposed to second her in the proposition." Samuel to John Overton, Dec. 2, 1813, AC 803-2, Murdock Collection, John Overton Papers. For an older but interesting view of frontier relations and the War of 1812, see Julius Pratt, *Expansionists of 1812* (New York: Macmillan, 1925).
96. *Carthage Gazette,* June 29, 1810.

97. Andrew Jackson to George Roulstone, enclosing letters from Jackson to Dickson and Dickson to Jackson, Sept. 29, 1801, *Papers of Andrew Jackson* 1:256–59.
98. *Carthage Gazette,* July 6, 1810.
99. *Nashville Clarion,* reprinted in the *Carthage Gazette,* Mar. 14, 1812. A few months later they were given a prominent place on the Fourth of July toast list: William Porter paid homage to that "revolutionary corps, may their steady and inflexible example of true patriotism, be emulated throughout the U. States." *Carthage Gazette,* July 8, 1812.
100. *Carthage Gazette,* Apr. 1, 1812.
101. *Carthage Gazette,* July 8, 1812. Only one toast received more support: the one to President Madison. Nine cheers were given in response to "The president of the United States, firm and vigilant at his post, we will support him." See the *Carthage Gazette,* June 29, 1810.
102. See, for example, James Norman Smith's report of an Indian assault on the frontier, James Norman Smith Memoirs. *Impartial Review and Cumberland Repository,* Mar. 16, 1809; *Nashville Clarion,* July 3, Oct. 15, 1811. See also Walker, "Tennessee, 1796–1821," 239–40. British instigation of Indian attack was a longstanding issue in Tennessee, of course. See, for example, the *Knoxville Gazette* of April 10, 1795, which reprinted accusations dating to 1788.
103. Peeler, "Policies of Willie Blount." See also William Woods to James Madison, Aug. 10, 1812, in *The Papers of James Madison: Presidential Series,* vol. 5, *10 July 1812–7 February 1813,* ed. J. C. A. Stagg, et al. (Charlottesville: Univ. of Virginia Press, 2004), 137–39.
104. For more on the drive to remove Indian tribes during this period, see chapter 5, this volume.
105. Walker, "Tennessee, 1796–1821," 240.
106. *Carthage Gazette,* Nov. 16, 1811.
107. Andrew Jackson to Willie Blount, June 5, 1812, in *The Papers of Andrew Jackson,* vol. 2, *1804–1814,* ed. Harold D. Moser and Sharon Macpherson (Knoxville: Univ. of Tennessee Press, 1985), 301.
108. Ibid. Tennessee seemed to be similar to frontier sentiment throughout the United States. See, for example, Ohioans' perception of Indian-British relations. Ratcliffe, *Party Spirit in a Frontier Republic,* chap. 6. See also Hickey, *War of 1812;* Coles, *War of 1812;* and John K. Mahon, *The War of 1812* (Gainesville: Univ. of Florida Press, 1972).
109. David Campbell to John Steele, Jan. 12, 1812, Arthur Lee Campbell Papers.
110. Kanon, "Kidnapping of Martha Crawley," 3–24.
111. *Wilson's Knoxville Gazette,* June 19, 1812.
112. *Nashville Clarion,* May 23, 1812.
113. John Sevier to James Madison, May 12, 1809, *Papers of James Madison: Presidential Series* 1:182–83.
114. Kanon, "James Madison, Felix Grundy, and the Devil," 433–68.
115. For more on Grundy and the panic relief debate, see chapter 6, this volume.
116. David Campbell to John Steele, Jan. 12, 1812, Arthur Lee Campbell Papers.
117. *Nashville Clarion,* July 7, 1812.

118. Ibid.
119. Tennessee's emphasis on Indians reinforces David Waldstreicher's contention that the war helped western residents transform Indian fighting from a source of frontier chaos to an act of patriotic virtue. Waldstreicher, *In the Midst of Perpetual Fetes*, 289.
120. Karl Davis, "'Remember Fort Mims': Reinterpreting the Origins of the Creek War," *Journal of the Early Republic* 22, no. 4 (Winter 2002): 611–12.
121. In some cases, news outlets reported that as many as 600 people had been killed. The actual number was between 75 and 120. See Davis, "Remember Fort Mims," 632–33.
122. *Nashville Clarion*, Sept. 21, 1813; *Nashville Whig*, Sept. 21, 1813.
123. Walker, "Tennessee, 1796–1821," 292.
124. Hickey, *War of 1812*, 148.
125. Walker, "Tennessee, 1796–1821," 293.
126. By contrast, only forty-one Americans were killed, with another two hundred wounded. Finger, *Tennessee Frontiers*, 233–35.
127. See, for example, the *Boston Gazette*, May 9, 1814.
128. *Nashville Clarion*, June 10, 1812; Sept. 1813.
129. *Nashville Whig*, July 27, 1813, as quoted in Kanon, "Kidnapping of Martha Crawley," 16.
130. Finger, *Tennessee Frontiers*, 234–35; Hickey, *War of 1812*, 151.
131. Waldstreicher, *In the Midst of Perpetual Fetes*, 294. Historians agree that the Hartford Convention destroyed the Federalist Party as a national political force. See Buel, *Securing the Revolution*; Fischer, *Revolution in American Conservatism*; Linda Kerber, *Federalists in Dissent: Imagery and Ideology in Jeffersonian America* (Ithaca, N.Y.: Cornell Univ. Press, 1970); and Shaw Livermore, *The Twilight of Federalism: The Disintegration of the Federalist Party, 1815–1830* (Princeton, N.J.: Princeton Univ. Press, 1962).
132. This reflects many historians' contention that ritual and celebration facilitated cross-regional political links. See, for example, Newman, *Parades and the Politics of the Streets*; Waldstreicher, *In the Midst of Perpetual Fetes*. See also Lewis, *American Union and the Problem of Neighborhood*; Remini, *Course of American Empire*; Masterson, *William Blount*; and Melton, *First Impeachment*.
133. Ellis, "Market Revolution," 149–76; Larson, *Internal Improvement*; and Sellers, *Market Revolution*.
134. *Nashville Clarion and Tennessee Gazette*, June 16, 1818. Harry Watson has noted that similar entrepreneurial sentiments existed in North Carolina. See Watson, *Jacksonian Politics and Community Conflict: The Emergence of the Second Party System in Cumberland County, North Carolina* (Baton Rouge: Louisiana State Univ. Press, 1981); and Harry Watson, "Slavery and Development in a Duel Economy," in *The Market Revolution in America: Social, Religious and Political Expressions, 1800–1880*, ed. Melvyn Stokes and Stephen Conway (Charlottesville: Univ. Press of Virginia, 1996), 43–73.

Chapter 6

1. John Campbell to David Campbell, Nov. 20, 1816, Campbell Family Papers.
2. John to David Campbell, Dec. 29, 1817.
3. Christopher Houston to Samuel Young, Jan. 24, 1815, Subcollection 1, Series 1, Folder 5, Mary H. Kennedy Collection. More specifically, he noted that land around the mouth of the Duck River was "first rate, and may be had there for cash, at 3 dollars, perhaps 2½ or less. There is no poor ground, & the good, is amazing rich."
4. *Nashville Whig*, Mar. 7, 1815.
5. *Nashville Whig*, May 21, 1816. Tobacco prices similarly skyrocketed. As early as February 1815, the tobacco market had improved so much that Richard Papier announced his wish to purchase two hundred hogshead a week through the upcoming month of May. *Nashville Whig*, Feb. 28, 1815. Prices for the weed tended to remain between five and ten dollars prior to the panic. See, for example, the *Nashville Whig*, May 21, 1816; *Nashville Clarion*, Nov. 4, 1817; and *Nashville Clarion*, Sept. 29, 1818. James Winchester observed these prices as well. In 1815 he wrote to John Eaton, "Seven and Eight dollars per cwt. Has been received for [tobacco] on the banks of the Cumberland. If this price continues our planters would soon be in affluent circumstances." Winchester to Eaton, July 6, 1815, Folder 234-z, John R. Eaton Papers, 1794–1815, Southern Historical Collection, Wilson Library, University of North Carolina at Chapel Hill.
6. *Nashville Clarion*, Mar. 31, Apr. 1, Sept. 29, 1818.
7. Dangerfield, *Era of Good Feelings*, 178–79.
8. *Nashville Clarion*, Apr. 7, 1818.
9. Winchester to Overton, Jan. 25, Mar. 6, Nov. 21, 1816, No. 794, Reel 1, Box 1, Folder 2, James Winchester Papers. Overton had mentioned the factory to Winchester as early as August 5, 1814. By 1818 it was fully operational, even turning a 10 percent dividend for its investors. See the *Nashville Clarion*, July 14, 28, 1818.
10. Petition 71-1817-1, Reel 5, TSLA.
11. Thomas Claiborne to David Campbell, Jan. 4, 1816, Campbell Family Papers. By July 1818 the steam mill was up and running, taking orders for one hundred cords of wood and one hundred thousand barrel staves. *Nashville Clarion*, July 21, 1818. For more on the exuberant nationalism of the postwar period, see Larson, *Internal Improvement*; Sellers, *Market Revolution*; and Dangerfield, *Era of Good Feelings*.
12. *Nashville Whig*, July 25, 1815.
13. Asbury, *Journal and Letters* 2:795. Ann Cantrell echoed this sentiment three years later, pointing out, "Intolerable roads and poor accommodations are to be found everywhere." Ann Cantrell to Cynthia Polk, Apr. 1818, MF 1073, Reel 5, Box 26, Folder 1, Yeatman-Polk Collection, TSLA.
14. See, for example, Petitions 14-1815-3, 45-1815-1, 89-1817-3, and 89-1817-4, Reel 5, TSLA.
15. *Nashville Whig*, Mar. 7, 1816.
16. Folmsbee, "Sectionalism and Internal Improvements," 14–15.
17. Jefferson to Campbell, Oct. 15, 1815, Library of Congress.

18. *Nashville Whig*, Mar. 7, 1816. Along with this declaration was an announcement of intent to build a boat signed by five of Nashville's most prominent entrepreneurs: Jenkin Whiteside, Wilkins Tannehill, William Carroll, Christopher Stump, and Alpha Kingsly. Not surprisingly, all of these men except Carroll were or became directors of the Bank of Nashville.
19. Finger, *Tennessee Frontiers*, 199–200. See also Goodstein, *Nashville, 1780–1860*; Folmsbee, "Sectionalism and Internal Improvements"; and George Rogers Taylor, *The Transportation Revolution, 1815–1860* (New York: Harper & Row, 1951).
20. Petition 1819-116, Reel 7, TSLA. Polk looked to get steamboats both on the Duck River, which fed into Columbia in Maury County and on the Cumberland. He would find that geological impediments made steamboat activity along the Duck an impossibility, which meant that Columbia never would develop to the extent of its Davidson County counterpart.
21. Goodstein, *Nashville, 1780–1860*, 35.
22. For more on postwar speculation in the Southwest, see Dupre, *Transforming the Cotton Frontier*; Dangerfield, *Era of Good Feelings*; Larson, *Internal Improvement*, 129–30; Sellers, *Market Revolution*; Abernethy, *From Frontier to Plantation*; and Murray Rothbard, *The Panic of 1819: Reactions and Policies* (New York: Columbia Univ. Press, 1962).
23. Petition 49-1815-1.
24. Christopher Houston to Placebo Houston, Oct. 5, 1816, Subcollection 1, Series 1, Folder 4, Mary H. Kennedy Collection.
25. Christopher Houston to Samuel and Sally Young, July 5, 1817, Folder 4, Mary H. Kennedy Collection.
26. Petition 91-1815-1, Reel 5, TSLA.
27. Petition 29-1819-1, Reel 6, TSLA.
28. Pressure had built on the Chickasaw throughout the early nineteenth century. In September 1808, "Pericles" wrote, "The day is not far distant when we shall be in possession of that country lying between the Tennessee and the Mississippi—at present occupied by Indians. This savage race of inhabitants, enclosed on every side by a civilized and enlightened people, must, in the course of a century, become entirely exterminated." *Impartial Review and Cumberland Repository*, Sept. 15, 1808. In 1809 Governor Willie Blount pushed Tennessee congressmen to remove the Chickasaw from over seven million acres of western land. Peeler, "Policies of Willie Blount," 312. For more on white-Indian perceptions in this period, see Cumfer, "Idea of Mankind Is So Various," chap. 3; and Sheidley, "Unruly Men."
29. *Carthage Gazette*, June 16, 1815; and Petition 14-1815-3, TSLA. See also *Nashville Whig*, Aug. 1, 1815.
30. *Nashville Clarion*, Feb. 17, Aug. 18, 1818. The *Clarion* also, disingenuously, asked, "Are we to see another forty years pass away before the soldiers of the revolution can get their western lands, which are not in any respect useful to the savages, who prevent their occupation?" *Nashville Clarion*, Aug. 18, 1818.
31. The three hundred thousand dollars was to be divided into fifteen payments of twenty thousand dollars. Although Andrew Jackson was the most visible negotiator in the Chickasaw cession, the leader of the push for western land was the shadowy but powerful John

Overton. He, Andrew Jackson, and James Winchester had since the 1790s set their sights on the Chickasaw Bluffs. And given that Jackson's nephew, John Donelson, as well as his close confidante, John Coffee, became the region's surveyors, friends of the general reaped particularly generous benefits in the form of padded surveys. See George Elliot to John Coffee, Mar. 29, 1817, AC 814, Reel 3, Box 7, Folder 1, Dyas Collection, John Coffee Papers. See also William Kelly to Coffee, Apr. 8, 1817, Reel 4, Box 11, Folder 2, Dyas Collection, John Coffee Papers. They also put pressure on the assembly to open the land and recognize old North Carolina claims, which led the assembly in turn to petition Congress to that affect. Petition 15-1817-4, Reel 5, TSLA. See also Finger, *Tennessee Frontiers*, chaps. 10 and 11; and Abernethy, *From Frontier to Plantation*.

32. John Campbell to his father, Dec. 4, 1817; John to David Campbell, Dec. 29, 1817.
33. Christopher Houston to Placebo Houston, Dec. 22, 1818, Subcollection 1, Series 1, Folder 5, Mary H. Kennedy Collection. See also George Washington Campbell to William Polk, Jan. 24, 1818, Brown-Ewell Family Papers; and George to William Foote, Oct. 2, 1816, Foote Family Papers, Filson Historical Society, Louisville, Ky. (hereafter cited as Foote Family Papers).
34. James Campbell to David Campbell, Mar. 8, 1819, Campbell Family Papers. Noting the promising nature of Chickasaw speculation, J. M. Taylor even suggested to William Foote that they obtain old Yazoo claims and use them to procure pieces of the land. Taylor to Foote, Nov. 3, 1816, Foote Family Papers.
35. John Campbell to his father, Dec. 4, 1817.
36. Finger, *Tennessee Frontiers*, 184. Of these fifteen, nine were in Middle Tennessee: the Franklin Tennessee Bank, Gallatin Bank, Carthage Bank, Rogersville Bank, Farmers' and Mechanics Bank of Nashville, Winchester Bank, Columbia Bank, Shelbyville Bank, and Murfreesborough Bank. See "'Tennessee Banks in the Antebellum Period, Part I," *Tennessee Historical Quarterly* 45, no. 2 (Summer 1986): 126–27. Such proliferation reflects Donald Ratcliffe's assertion that increased purchases after 1814 created a demand for loans that could only be provided with paper money. Thus an explosion of wildcat banking occurred. Ratcliffe, *Party Spirit in a Frontier Republic*, 193.
37. Sellers, "Banking and Politics in Jackson's Tennessee," 66–67. See also Thomas P. Abernethy, "The Early Development of Commerce and Banking in Tennessee," *Mississippi Valley Historical Review* 14 (1927–28): 311–25; Thomas P. Abernethy, "Andrew Jackson and the Rise of Southwestern Democracy," *American Historical Review* 33, no. 1 (Oct. 1927): 64–77; and Goodstein, *Nashville, 1780–1860*.
38. John Summerville to Thomas Sumner, May 13, 1819, John Sumner Russwurm Papers, TSLA (hereafter cited as John Sumner Russwurm Papers). A month later he proclaimed that the "distress of the commercial part of the community throughout Europe and the U. States reached Nashville to an extent not anticipated by those who thought they knew most in relation to the solvency of our traders." Summerville to Thomas Sumner, June 3, 1819, John Sumner Russwurm Papers. See also the essay of "A Farmer" in the *Nashville Whig*, July 3, 1819.
39. The locals certainly thought so. See, for example, the open letter from the directors of the Nashville Bank, *Nashville Whig*, June 26, 1819. See also Rothbard, *Panic of 1819*, chap.1; and Ralph Catterall, *The Second Bank of the United States* (Chicago: Univ. of Chicago Press, 1903).

40. As the editor of the *Nashville Clarion* put it in November 1818, "The local banks are obliged to curtail their accommodations, press their collections, and refuse currency to the paper of other banks—in some banks it is found necessary to refuse taking all bank notes." *Nashville Clarion*, Nov. 17, 1818. See also "A Farmer" to the *Nashville Whig*, July 10, 1819. Two months later they were more specific: "The pressure for money to the east, and the great number of failures there, has had the effect of withholding from the market here very large sums of money that would otherwise have been given for produce at this place." *Nashville Clarion*, Jan. 5, 1819. See also the essay of "A Farmer" in the *Nashville Whig*, July 3, 1819; Dangerfield, *Era of Good Feelings*, 286; Rothbard, *Panic of 1819*, chap. 1; Catterall, *Second Bank of the United States;* and Sellers, *Market Revolution*.
41. Christopher to Placebo Houston, Mar. 22, 1822, Mary H. Kennedy Collection.
42. John Summerville to Thomas Sumner, June 3, 1819, John Sumner Russwurm Papers.
43. *Nashville Clarion*, Jan. 26, 1819. See also J. H. Hawkins to Arthur Lee Campbell, June 17, 1818, Arthur Lee Campbell Papers; *Nashville Clarion*, Dec. 8, 1818; Enoch Ensby to B. Gray, Mar. 1, 1819, No. 880, Reel 2, Box 4, Folder 9, Gray Family Papers, TSLA; and Breedlove Bradford to James Winchester, Feb. 4, 1818, in which he quotes New Orleans prices at twenty-eight to thirty-two dollars. No. 797-1, Box 2, Folder 3, James Winchester Papers. For more on the causes of the panic, see Rothbard, *Panic of 1819*, chap. 1; Dangerfield, *Era of Good Feelings;* and Sellers, *Market Revolution*.
44. *Nashville Clarion*, May 17, 1820.
45. *Nashville Clarion*, Jan. 26, 1819.
46. *Nashville Whig*, Mar. 19, 1819.
47. James Houston to Placebo Houston, July 16, 1820, Mary H. Kennedy Papers.
48. Andrew Jackson to Andrew Jackson Donelson, Sept. 17, 1819, MF 403, Reel 1, Containers 1–2, Andrew Jackson Donelson Papers.
49. James to Arthur Campbell, May 15, 1819, Campbell Family Papers.
50. *Nashville Clarion*, June 26, 1819. See also *Nashville Clarion*, Apr. 18, 1820.
51. *Nashville Whig*, June 26, 1819.
52. *Nashville Clarion*, Oct. 10, 1820.
53. "A Farmer" to the *Nashville Whig*, July 3, 1819.
54. "S. N. G." to the *Nashville Clarion*, Mar. 14, 1821.
55. Petition 136-1821-1, Reel 7, TSLA. See also James to David Campbell, July 13, 1819, Campbell Family Papers.
56. John Summerville to Thomas Sumner, Jan. 2, 9, 1817, MF 1197, John Sumner Russwurm Papers.
57. Summerville to Sumner, June 10, 14, 1817, July 16, 21, Aug. 14, 1818, Jan. 20, July 29, 1819, MF 1197, John Sumner Russwurm Papers. For more on the BUS specie suspension, see Catterall, *Second Bank of the United States*.
58. Summerville to Sumner, June 3, 1819, MF 1197, John Sumner Russwurm Papers. As Summerville himself put it in the same letter to Sumner, "From my present view of things I am under no apprehension of any loss in the end, except some part of the premiums usually received, but it will require time to bring matters to a close."

59. Ibid.
60. *Nashville Clarion,* Apr. 18, 1820.
61. "A Farmer" to the *Nashville Whig,* July 3, 1819. The editor of the *Nashville Clarion* agreed. On February 8, 1820, he wrote, "The directors of banks in this place continue to press their debtors with the most unrelenting calls. Between the banks and the courts, the people in debt have a fair prospect of being completely ruined."
62. Petition 1819-106-1, Reel 7, TSLA. A Wilson County grand jury agreed, arguing that in banks "men possess great and dangerous powers, without any responsibility to the people or their representatives." *Nashville Whig,* Oct. 31, 1820, quoted in Sellers, "Banking and Politics in Jackson's Tennessee," 72.
63. *Nashville Whig,* Dec. 8, 1819. Five months later the paper noted, "If ever there was an occasion, when necessity called for legislative interference, to save a whole people from bankruptcy and ruin, the present is surely the time." *Nashville Whig,* May 24, 1820. See also the report of a meeting on June 26, 1819. Interestingly, although more than attuned to local sentiment regarding bankruptcy laws and specie suspension, the Overton-controlled *Whig* generally disdained the former and supported the latter. Its position on this matter helped fuel a heated debate with the editors of the *Nashville Clarion.* See Sellers, "Banking and Politics in Jackson's Tennessee," 67.
64. Petition 47-1819-1, Reel 7, TSLA. A Davidson County grand jury asked for fundamentally the same thing. See the *Nashville Whig,* May 10, 1819.
65. James Campbell to Arthur Campbell, May 26, 1820, Campbell Family Papers. James to David Campbell, Oct. 23, 1821, Campbell Family Papers.
66. Sellers, "Banking and Politics in Jackson's Tennessee," 67–68; and Sioussat, "Some Phases of Tennessee Politics," 51–69. For an in-depth description of proposed relief laws, see Rothbard, *Panic of 1819.* A similar debate emerged in northern Alabama and Kentucky, as Daniel Dupre and Matthew Schoenbachler have shown, that revolved around similar issues. See Dupre, *Transforming the Cotton Frontier;* and Schoenbachler, "The Origins of Jacksonian Politics," Ph.D. diss., Univ. of Kentucky, 1998.
67. This despite the fact that "foreign markets are very dull, and land has fallen nearly one third in this settlement." James Houston to Placebo Houston, July 16, 1820, Mary H. Kennedy Collection.
68. James to John Campbell, Nov. 21, 1820, Campbell Family Papers.
69. Petition 28-1820-1, Reel 7, TSLA.
70. Ibid.
71. Some were incredulous that such a bank could pass the legislature at all. James Campbell noted that he hardly supposed "any thing was intended by [Grundy's bank] further than to recommend to the banks not to press their debts for payment further than was indispensably necessary, a thing which it is obvious they will not do any how." Campbell to his brother, Oct. 28, 1819, Campbell Family Papers.
72. Grundy's bank formally ceased to exist in 1826. See *Nashville Republican and State Gazette,* Nov. 18, 1826; and Abernethy, "Early Development of Commerce and Banking," 320–21.
73. "A Farmer" to the *Nashville Whig,* July 3, 1819.

74. *Nashville Whig*, July 26, 1820.
75. Andrew Jackson to John Donelson, Sept. 2, 1821, No. 678, Reel 4, Box 8, J-24, THS Miscellaneous Files.
76. *Nashville Whig*, June 7, 1820. See also the *Nashville Whig*, May 24, 1820.
77. Robert Allen, Speech on Public Land Debt, *Annals of Congress*, 16th Cong., 2d sess. (Washington, D.C.: Gales and Seaton, 1834–56), 1188. See also *Nashville Clarion*, June 19, 1819.
78. *Nashville Whig*, June 7, 1820.
79. Rothbard, *Panic of 1819*, 49.
80. Ibid., 96.
81. White, *Messages of the Governors of Tennessee* 1:671.
82. Ford MSS, Lenox Library, New York, as quoted in Sioussat, "Some Phases of Tennessee Politics," 60–61. The state supreme court would agree with Jackson in 1821.
83. For more on Polk's early career, see Charles Sellers, *James K. Polk: Jacksonian, 1795–1843* (Princeton, N.J.: Princeton Univ. Press, 1957).
84. *Nashville Clarion*, Feb. 9, 1819.
85. Petition 136-1821-2, Reel 7, TSLA.
86. *Nashville Clarion*, Feb. 1, 1820.
87. *Nashville Whig*, Sept. 8, 1823.
88. Abernethy, *From Frontier to Plantation*, 238. Grundy himself, faced with the fact that his debtor relief platform was losing steam, conceded defeat in 1821. He declared that since 1819, three-fifths of the state's debt had been liquidated, that the economy was reviving, and that the situation was no longer so grave as to warrant sweeping reform. Although he still supported stay laws, and favored the legislature's maintenance of specie suspension until 1826, by January 1822 debtor relief was no longer a viable political option in Middle Tennessee. Rothbard, *Panic of 1819*, 52.
89. *Nashville Whig*, July 3, 1819.
90. James to David Campbell, Aug. 17, 1821, Campbell Family Papers.
91. Andrew Jackson to Andrew Jackson Donelson, Oct. 11, 1822, MF 403, Reel 1, Container 1, Andrew Jackson Donelson Papers.
92. James Campbell to Arthur Campbell, May 15, 1819, Campbell Family Papers.
93. Ibid.
94. James Campbell to his brother, Jan. 9, 1821, Campbell Family Papers.
95. John McLemore to John Coffee, May 10, 1821, AC 814, Reel 5, Box 11, Folder 5, Dyas Collection, John Coffee Papers.
96. James to David Campbell, July 17, 1821, Campbell Family Papers.
97. See also "A Big Fish" to the *Nashville Clarion*, July 4, 1821, as quoted in Gabriel Hawkins Golden, "William Carroll and His Administration: Tennessee's Business Governor," *Tennessee Historical Magazine* 9, no. 1 (Apr. 1925): 18. Ward did make public that he felt banks served a useful commercial purpose, and proposed that all banks in Tennessee, both public and private, consolidate into one entity. Sellers, "Banking and Politics in Jackson's Tennessee," 72. See also letter of James Campbell, Jan. 9, 1821, Campbell Family Papers. For more on Governor Carroll and his political leanings, see Atkins, *Parties, Politics and the*

Sectional Conflict; Paul Bergeron, *Antebellum Politics in Tennessee* (Lexington: Univ. Press of Kentucky, 1982); or Hamer, *Tennessee,* vol. 1.

98. John McAlister to John Overton, July 25, 1821, Letter S03-1, MF 748, John Overton Collection, TSLA.
99. Glashan, *American Governors and Gubernatorial Elections,* 290–97. Votes would again spike statewide in the relatively hotly contested 1827 race, when Sam Houston defeated Newton Cannon 40,017 to 31,244.
100. After all, he argued, although farmers "may complain of the heaviness of the taxes that would be necessary to do it, what are such taxes compared to the expense occasioned by bad roads?" "A Farmer" to the *Nashville Clarion,* Aug. 4, 1818. See also *Nashville Clarion,* Dec. 14, 1819.
101. *Nashville Clarion,* Dec. 29, 1818, Jan. 29, 1819.
102. Petition 1819-145-1, Reel 7, TSLA.
103. *Nashville Whig,* Jan. 12, 19, 1820.
104. See, for example, "Civis" and "Bogtrotter" in the *Nashville Clarion,* Apr. 25, May 2, 1820.
105. John to Edward Campbell, Jan. 13, 1819, Campbell Family Papers.
106. Mathias Murfree to his brother, Nov. 26, 1820, No. 838, Folder 16, Douglas-Maney Family Papers, THS, housed at the TSLA. For more on lotteries in this early period, see Lewis Laska and Severine Brocki, "The Life and Death of the Lottery in Tennessee, 1787–1836," *Tennessee Historical Quarterly* 45, no. 2 (Summer 1986): 95–118.
107. Open letter of the Directors of the Nashville Bank, *Nashville Whig,* June 26, 1819.
108. John Summerville to Thomas Sumner, Mar. 19, 1819, John Sumner Russwurm Papers.
109. *Nashville Whig,* Jan. 22, Feb. 5, 1823; and Thomas Scott to his father, Nov. 15, 1823, Box 4, Folder 4, Leonard F. Chapman Family Papers (Tennessee Historical Society), TSLA (hereafter cited as Leonard F. Chapman Family Papers). The *Whig* accounted for this rise on Feb. 26, 1823: "Taking into view the comparatively small quantity [of cotton] on hand in Europe at the last dates, we are induced to believe that the price of this article will advance during the spring."
110. Hamer, *Tennessee* 1:43.
111. Thomas Scott to his father, Apr. 1, 1825, Box 4, Folder 4, Leonard F. Chapman Family Papers.
112. This element also turned inward and cooled to statewide internal improvements. Where once they pushed schemes however they could, by 1824 they minimized support for endeavors that did not significantly benefit Middle Tennessee. Backers of the region's commercial prosperity simply were loath to lose their "economic advantage" over the other regions of the state by supporting their quests for progress. A good example: The *Whig* congratulated the town of Nashville for erecting a bridge to the benefit of local commercial traffic and generally supported "improvements of our town [and the] progress of civilization." *Nashville Whig,* Aug. 26, 1823.
113. A great indication of the city's political leaning, as Anita Goodstein has shown, was that between 1828 and 1860 only three Democrats were elected as mayor. See Goodstein, *Nashville, 1780–1860,* appendix table 5, 206.
114. John to Edward Campbell, Jan. 13, 1819, Campbell Family Papers.

115. Golden, "William Carroll and His Administration," 23.
116. A good example: Jackson left Overton in charge of all his Chickasaw Bluff dealings. See, for example, John Overton to James Winchester, Apr. 4, 1823, No. 794, Reel 1, Box 1, Folder 9, James Winchester Papers.
117. Regarding support for Henry Clay, historian Charles Sellers has argued that John Overton advanced Jackson's name for the 1824 presidential election only as a means of winning the state for a more "entrepreneurially friendly" Henry Clay. See Sellers, "Jackson Men with Feet of Clay," *American Historical Review* 62, no. 3 (Apr. 1957): 550–51. See also *Nashville Whig*, Apr. 9, 1823. Given Overton's longstanding friendship with Jackson, it was not surprising that the former also feared for the latter's health. See Overton to James Winchester, Jan. 25, 1822, No. 794, Reel 1, Box 1, Folder 9, James Winchester Papers. Among the more prominent Adamsites were James Jackson, whom Jackson called a "compleat convert to Clay's american system [and] a thorough tariff man"; John Williams, Hugh Lawson White's brother-in-law; and Boyd McNairy, Judge John McNairy's son. Jackson had leaned upon Judge McNairy when he arrived in Tennessee in 1788, but they had a falling out in the late 1790s and never made up. Harold D. Moser, ed., *The Papers of Andrew Jackson*, vol. 6, *1825–1828* (Knoxville: Univ. of Tennessee Press, 2002), 373, 317–18, 509. See also Remini, *Course of American Empire*.
118. Cannon represented the counties as state representative, state senator, and congressional representative over the course of his career. Although not consistent in his voting, Cannon did go along with Clay's American system on multiple occasions. He also consistently advocated state aid for education and internal improvements. See John E. Harkins, "Newton Cannon, Jacksonian Nemesis," *Tennessee Historical Quarterly* 43, no. 4 (Winter 1984): 355–75.
119. B. T. Martin to Frank McGavock, Dec. 26, 1827, MF 742, Francis McGavock Papers, TSLA.
120. For more on Jackson's presence in Tennessee writ large, see Atkins, *Parties, Politics and the Sectional Conflict*; Bergeron, *Antebellum Politics in Tennessee*; and Robert Remini, *Andrew Jackson and the Course of American Democracy* (New York: Harper and Row, 1980).
121. Sellers, *James K. Polk*, 98. See also Joseph M. Pukl Jr., "James K. Polk's Early Congressional Campaigns of 1825 and 1827," *Tennessee Historical Quarterly* 39, no. 4 (Winter 1980): 445–48.
122. On Middle Tennessee's antebellum economic diversity, see Ash, *Middle Tennessee Society Transformed*; Atkins, *Parties, Politics and the Sectional Conflict*; Abernethy, *From Frontier to Plantation*; and Finger, *Tennessee Frontiers*.
123. Edmond Dillahunty to Robert Caruthers, Sept. 29, 1823, Robert Caruthers Papers, Southern Historical Collection, Wilson Library, University of North Carolina at Chapel Hill.
124. Christopher to Placebo Houston, Apr. 8, 1822, Mary H. Kennedy Collection.
125. Dupre, *Transforming the Cotton Frontier*. See also J. Mills Thornton, *Politics and Power in a Slave Society: Alabama, 1800–1860* (Baton Rouge: Louisiana State Univ. Press, 1978).
126. Aron, *How the West Was Lost*, chap. 5. See also Craig Friend, *Along Maysville Road: The Early American Republic in the Trans-Appalachian West* (Knoxville: Univ. of Tennessee Press, 2005).
127. See, for example, Atkins, *Parties, Politics and the Sectional Conflict*; Bergeron, *Antebellum Politics in Tennessee*; Ash, *Middle Tennessee Society Transformed*; and Sellers, *James K. Polk*.

Epilogue

1. For more on slave life during the territorial period, see the introduction and chapter 4 to this volume. See also Cumfer, "Idea of Mankind Is So Various"; Toomey, "Prelude to Statehood"; and Walker, "Tennessee, 1796–1821."
2. For more on slavery in the antebellum South, see Eugene Genovese, *Roll, Jordan, Roll: The World the Slaves Made* (New York: Vintage Books, 1972); Robert Fogel and Stanley Engerman, *Time on the Cross: The Economics of Negro Slavery* (New York: Univ. Press of America, 1984); Herbert Gutman, *The Black Family in Slavery in Freedom, 1750–1925* (New York: Vintage, 1976); James Oakes, *The Ruling Race: A History of American Slaveholders* (New York: Vintage Books, 1983); James Oakes, *Slavery and Freedom: An Interpretation of the Old South* (New York: Norton Press, 1990); and Fox-Genovese and Genovese, *Fruits of Merchant Capital*.
3. See chapter 4, this volume.
4. See Thornton, *Politics and Power in a Slave Society*. An 1816 Davidson County tax list, an 1824 Sumner County tax list, and specific research into legislative members makes clear that all regional representatives between 1796 and 1824 owned at least one or two slaves, and in many cases many more. Davidson County Tax List, No. 678, Reel 2, Box 4, d-11, THS Miscellaneous Files, TSLA. See also White, *Messages of the Governors of Tennessee*, vol. 1, Appendix: Members of the General Assembly of Tennessee. See also Atkins, *Parties, Politics and the Sectional Conflict*, 8.
5. Pierre L. van den Berghe, *Race and Racism: A Comparative Perspective* (New York: Wiley and Sons, 1967). See also Fredrickson, *Black Image in the White Mind*.
6. As we have seen, in 1800, 13,584 slaves lived in Tennessee. Within ten years the number had grown to 35,000, and by 1820 it had risen to approximately 67,000. In 1830, 141,603 slaves comprised 21 percent of the total population. Of these, 97,174, or 69 percent, lived in Middle Tennessee. Given that 379,644 people resided in the region, it meant 26 percent were bondsmen. Bureau of the Census, *Third Census of the United States, Fourth Census of the United States*, and *Fifth Census of the United States*. In 1810 the largest slave counties were Davidson and Williamson, at 6,305 and 3,985, respectively, with Sumner close behind at 3,734. In 1820 distribution followed the same pattern: Davidson County held 7,899 slaves and Williamson held 6,972. The lower percentage of Middle Tennessee slaves relative to the total Tennessee population in 1830 is accounted for by the emergence of slavery in West Tennessee. Whereas in 1820 two western counties held 239 slaves, by 1830 fifteen counties held a total of 26,542, or 10 percent, of the statewide slave population. See also Asa Earl Martin, "The Anti-Slavery Societies of Tennessee," *Tennessee Historical Magazine* 1 (Dec. 1915): 261–81. For more on Haiti and Gabriel's Rebellion, see C. L. R. James, *The Black Jacobins: Touissant L'Ouverture and the San Domingo Revolution* (New York: Vintage Press, 1963); and Douglas Egerton, *Gabriel's Rebellion: The Virginia Slave Conspiracies of 1800 and 1802* (Chapel Hill: Univ. of North Carolina Press, 1993).
7. *Tennessee Acts*, 1799, chap. 9.
8. Kay and Cary, *Slavery in North Carolina*, 64; *Tennessee Acts*, 1799, chap. 9.
9. Elizabeth Fortson Arroyo, "Poor Whites, Slaves, and Free Blacks in Tennessee, 1796–1861," *Tennessee Historical Quarterly* 55, no. 1 (Spring 1996): 60.

10. John Haywood and Robert Cobb, *The Statute Laws of Tennessee of a General and Public Nature* (Knoxville, 1831), 1:315. See also Caleb Perry Patterson, *The Negro in Tennessee, 1790–1865* (New York: Negro Universities Press, 1968), 46.
11. Petition 18-1-1806, Reel 3, TSLA. See also Walker, "Tennessee, 1796–1821," 170. Patrols had existed during the territorial period, to be sure. They generally were composed of "searchers" who were to detect illegal weapons in slave quarters and return to masters any slaves without written passes. Other parts of the North Carolina statute on patrols remained the same: Tennessee still exempted patrollers from muster, jury, and road service. See H. M. Henry, "The Slave Laws of Tennessee," *Tennessee Historical Magazine* 2 (Sept. 1916): 179, 181.
12. MF 678, Reel 8, Box 14, s-70, THS Miscellaneous Files.
13. *Tennessee Gazette*, Oct. 3, 1804. See also "'And Ten Dollars Extra, for Every Hundred Lashes Any Person Will Give Him, to the Amount of Three Hundred': A Note on Andrew Jackson's Runaway Slave Ad of 1804 and on the Historian's Use of Evidence," *Tennessee Historical Quarterly* 36, no. 4 (Winter 1977): 468–78.
14. *Impartial Review and Cumberland Repository*, Feb. 21, 1807.
15. Petition 26-1815-2, Reel 5, TSLA.
16. Zion Presbyterian Church Records, MF 125, TSLA.
17. Andrew Jackson to Andrew Jackson Donelson, July 3, 1821, No. 403, Reel 1, Container 1, Andrew Jackson Donelson Papers.
18. John Campbell to Edward Campbell, Jan. 13, 1819, Campbell Family Papers.
19. Goodstein, *Nashville, 1780–1860*, 80; Bureau of the Census, *Second Census of the United States* and *Third Census of the United States*.
20. Goodstein, *Nashville, 1780–1860*, chap. 4.
21. As they did so, it became clear that the free black population was composed mostly of single men and transients. In Davidson County only nineteen out of seventy people identified with free passes were women; only five were families. Goodstein, "Black History on the Nashville Frontier," 411.
22. Chase Mooney, "Slavery in Davidson County" (master's thesis, Vanderbilt Univ., 1936), 19. Such treatment was known already to have happened. In 1802 Betty Lucust learned that her free seventeen-year-old daughter had been taken to New Orleans and auctioned. A few years later, two of her other children were bound as orphans in Kentucky. Cumfer, "Idea of Mankind Is So Various," 388–89.
23. See chapter 4, this volume.
24. Petition 65-1815-1, Reel 5, TSLA; Petition 24-1822-1,2, Reel 7, TSLA.
25. Petition 130-1819-1, Reel 7, TSLA; Petition 203-1833-1, Reel 13, TSLA.
26. Walker, "Tennessee, 1796–1821," 210–11. See also *Tennessee Public Acts*, 1833, chap. 64, TSLA.
27. See, for example, John Summerville to Thomas Sumner, June 30, 1819, John Sumner Russwurm Papers.
28. John Summerville to Thomas Sumner, May 13, 1819, John Sumner Russwurm Papers.
29. Mooney, "Slavery in Davidson County," chap. 3.
30. *Carthage Gazette*, Aug. 20, 1816.

31. Text taken from Kristofer Ray, "Missouri Compromise," in *Encyclopedia of Minorities in American Politics* (Phoenix: Oryx Press, 1999), 111. For more on Missouri, see Glover Moore, *The Missouri Controversy, 1819–1821* (Lexington: Univ. Press of Kentucky, 1953); Sellers, *Market Revolution;* and Ashworth, *Slavery, Capitalism and Politics.*
32. Andrew Jackson to Andrew Jackson Donelson, 1818, MF 403, Reel 1, Container 1, Andrew Jackson Donelson Papers.
33. *Nashville Whig,* July 5, 1820.
34. Every single branch and member hailed from East Tennessee. Martin, "Anti-Slavery Societies," 264–80.
35. E. E. Hoss, "Elihu Embree, Abolitionist," *American Historical Magazine* 2, no. 1 (Apr. 1897): 116–32.
36. Mooney, "Slavery in Davidson County," 69.
37. Asbury, *Journal and Letters* 2:580.
38. Asa Earl Martin, "Anti-Slavery Activities of the Methodist Episcopal Church in Tennessee," *Tennessee Historical Magazine* 2, no. 2 (June 1916): 102–5. The amount of time allowed by the church depended upon the time necessary to determine a purchase price. Walker, "Tennessee, 1796–1821," 193–95.
39. Martin, "Anti-Slavery Societies," 273.
40. Summerville to Sumner, June 30, 1819, John Sumner Russwurm Papers.
41. *Nashville Republican,* Oct. 29, 1833. See also Imes, "Legal Status of Free Negroes and Slaves," 265.
42. Christine Leigh Heyrman, *Southern Cross: The Origins of the Bible Belt* (Chapel Hill: Univ. of North Carolina Press, 1997). See also Martin, "Anti-Slavery Activities," 99.
43. Martin, "Anti-Slavery Activities," 106-7.
44. Ibid., 107.
45. See, for example, Charles C. Trabue, "The Voluntary Emancipation of Slaves in Tennessee as reflected in the State's Legislation and Judicial Decisions," *Tennessee Historical Magazine* 4, no. 1 (Mar. 1918): 50.
46. Petitions 144-1825-1-3, 145-1825-1, and 181-1825-1, Reel 9, TSLA.
47. Patterson, *Negro in Tennessee,* 49.
48. J. Merton England, "The Free Negro in Ante-Bellum Tennessee," *Journal of Southern History* 9 (Feb. 1943): 37–49.
49. Laws of Tennessee, 1831, chap. 102, TSLA. See also Arthur Howington, "'A Property of Special and Peculiar Value': The Tennessee Supreme Court and the Law of Manumission," *Tennessee Historical Quarterly* 44, no. 3 (Fall 1985): 315–16. Although the legislature modified the law in 1833 and 1842, by the end of the antebellum period the 1831 version was back in place.
50. *Tennessee Public Acts,* 1831, chap. 102, TSLA. The law made it into the public press as well. See *National Banner and Nashville Whig,* Dec. 20, 1831. See also Arthur F. Howington, "'Not in the Condition of a Horse or an Ox': Ford v. Ford, the Law of Testamentary Manumission, and the Tennessee's Courts' Recognition of Slave Humanity," *Tennessee Historical Quarterly* 34, no. 3 (Fall 1975): 253.
51. Mooney, "Slavery in Davidson County," 16.

52. *Tennessee Public Acts,* 1831, chap. 103, TSLA.
53. The last gasp of the antislavery movement came in the 1834 constitutional convention. Although they put up a serious debate, their defeat effectively ended any chance of manumission in antebellum Tennessee. See Walker, "Tennessee, 1796–1821"; and Mooney, "Slavery in Davidson County."
54. Hamer, *Tennessee* 1:462.
55. Mooney, "Slavery in Davidson County," chap. 2.
56. Peeler, "Policies of Willie Blount," 327; and Ford, "Making the 'White Man's Country' White," 725.
57. Ford, "Making the 'White Man's Country' White," 731.
58. See van den Berghe, *Race and Racism.* See also Fredrickson, *Black Image in the White Mind.*
59. See, for example, Andrew Jackson's remarks about southern responses to Missouri. Andrew Jackson to Andrew Jackson Donelson, 1818, MF 403, Reel 1, Container 1, Andrew Jackson Donelson Papers.
60. Andrew Jackson to Andrew Jackson Donelson, Oct. 23, 1822, Andrew Jackson Donelson Papers. For an example of his purchase practices, see Jackson to Donelson, Apr. 12, 1822, Andrew Jackson Donelson Papers. The charge of slave trader would haunt Jackson in the 1828 pro-Adams presidential literature in Tennessee.
61. *Nashville Clarion,* May 5, 1818.
62. John and Milley to Michael Shofner, Apr. 3, 1822, No. 4067, Michael Shofner Papers. See also Mehlman, "From Seeder Rales to Iron Rails."
63. Turner, "Significance of the Frontier." See also Faragher, *Rereading Fredrick Jackson Turner.*

Bibliography

Primary Material

Newspapers

Boston Gazette.
Carthage Gazette and Friend of the People.
Impartial Review and Cumberland Repository.
Knoxville Gazette.
Nashville Clarion.
Nashville Republican.
Nashville Whig.
Tennessee Gazette.

Tennessee State Library and Archives

Blount, Willie. Papers.
Carroll, William. Papers.
Chapman, Leonard F. Family Papers. (Tennessee Historical Society).
Claybrooke Collection (Tennessee Historical Society).
The Conference Business of the Baptist Church under the Care of James Whitsitt, on Mill Creek, Davidson County. Record Book, 1797–1814.
Davidson County Tax Lists, 1805, 1815.
Davidson County Wills and Inventories.
Donelson, Andrew Jackson. Papers.
Douglas-Maney Family Papers.
Draper Collection (microfilm edition).
Dyas Collection, John Coffee Papers (Tennessee Historical Society).
Gray Family Papers.
Grundy, Felix. Papers.
Hardeman Family Papers.
Jackson, Andrew. Papers.
Journal of the Senate, 1804.
Laws of Tennessee, 1801, 1809, 1831.
Legislative Petitions.
McGavock, Francis. Papers.
McMinn, Joseph. Papers.
Militia Election Returns.
Mount Olivet Baptist Church Records.
Murdock Collection, John Overton Papers.
Numerical List of Regiments of the Militia of Tennessee, 1796–1836.
Orr, Mary H. T. Papers.
Overton, John. Collection.
The Recollections of John Hillsman, Esq., an Aged Gentleman Residing a Few Miles from Knoxville, in 1849.
Williams, Willoughby. "Recollections of Nashville in Early Days."

Roane, Archibald. Papers.
Russwurm, John Sumner. Papers.
Smith, James Norman. Memoirs, 1789–1860.
Sevier, John. Papers. First Administration.
Sevier, John. Papers. Second Administration.
Sumner County Tax Lists, 1824.
Tennessee Counties: Dates of Formation and Parent Counties.
Tennessee Historical Society Miscellaneous Files.
Tennessee House Journal, 1829.
Tennessee Public Acts, 1799, 1815, 1819, 1825, 1831, 1833.
Topp Family Papers.
Whyte, Robert. Papers.
Williamson County Tax Lists, 1805.
Wilson Creek Primitive Baptist Church Records.
Winchester, James. Papers.
Yeatman-Polk Collection.
Zion Presbyterian Church Records.

Southern Historical Collection, Wilson Library, University of North Carolina at Chapel Hill
Brown, Hamilton. Papers.
Caruthers, Robert. Papers.
Conner, Juliana Margaret. Diary.
Eaton, John R. Papers.
Grundy, Felix. Papers.
Kennedy, Mary H. Collection.
Kimberly, John. Papers.
Lytle, William. Papers.
Polk and Yeatman Collection
Ramsay, J. G. Collection.
Shofner, Michael. Papers.

Rare Books, Manuscripts, and Special Collections, William R. Perkins Library, Duke University
Campbell Family Papers
Henley, David. Papers.
Sevier, John. Papers.

Filson Historical Society, Louisville, Kentucky
Barthelemi, Tardiveau. Miscellaneous Files.
Blount, William. Papers.
Brown-Ewell Family Papers.
Bullitt Family Papers—Oxmoor Collection.
Campbell, Arthur. Papers.
Campbell, Arthur Lee. Papers.
Foote Family Papers.
Preston Family Papers—Joyes Collection.
Shelby, Isaac. Papers.

Library of Congress
Thomas Jefferson Papers Series 9: Collected Manuscripts, 1783–1822.

Senator Albert Gore Sr. Research Center, Middle Tennessee State University, Murfreesboro
James Moore King Collection.

North Carolina State Library and Archives, Raleigh
Governor's Papers: Samuel Ashe, 1796–1798. Vol. 21.
Laws of North Carolina, 1782, chap. 3

Rare Books Room, Katherine R. Everett Law Library, University of North Carolina School of Law
Iredell, James. *Laws of the State of North Carolina.* Edenton, N.C., 1791.

Public Record Office, London
Account of Imports, American States, 1805, 1806.
Ledgers, Customs 17/28, 1807.
Ledgers of Imports Under Countries, Customs 17/27, 1806.

Published Primary Material

Abbot, William W., et al., eds. *The Papers of George Washington: Presidential Series.* Vols. 2, 4. Charlottesville: Univ. of Virginia Press, 1993.

Asbury, Francis. *The Journal and Letters of Francis Asbury.* Vol. 2, *The Journal, 1794–1816,* edited by Elmer T. Clark, J. Manning Potts, and Jacob S. Payton. Nashville: Abingdon Press, 1958.

Baily, Francis. *Journal of a Tour in Unsettled Parts of North America, in 1796 and 1797.* Carbondale: Southern Illinois Univ. Press, 1969.

Bassett, James Spencer, ed. *The Correspondence of Andrew Jackson.* Vol. 1. Washington, D.C.: Carnegie Institution, 1926.

Boyd, Julian P., et al., eds. *The Papers of Thomas Jefferson.* 32 vols. to date. Princeton, N.J.: Princeton Univ. Press, 1950–.

Cappon, Lester, ed. *The Adams-Jefferson Letters: The Complete Correspondence Between Thomas Jefferson and Abigail and John Adams.* Chapel Hill: Univ. of North Carolina Press, 1959.

Carter, Clarence E., ed. *The Territorial Papers of the United States.* Vol. 4. Washington, D.C.: GPO, 1936.

Clark, William, ed. *State Records of North Carolina.* Vol.17, *1781–1785.* Wilmington, N.C.: Broadfoot, 1994.

Corbin, Peter, and Douglas Sedge, eds. *The Oldcastle Controversy: Sir John Oldcastle, Part I and the Famous Victories of Henry V.* New York: Manchester Univ. Press, 1991.

Gibbs, George, ed. *Memoirs of the Administrations of Washington and John Adams, Edited from the Papers of Oliver Wolcott, Secretary of the Treasury.* Vol. 1. New York, 1846.

Glashan, Roy R., ed. *American Governors and Gubernatorial Elections, 1775–1978.* Westport, Conn.: Meckler Books, 1979.

Goldthwaites, Reuben, ed. *Early Western Travels, 1748–1846.* Vol. 3. Cleveland: Arthur H Clark, 1904.

Haywood, John, and Robert Cobb. *The Statute Laws of Tennessee of a General and Public Nature.* Vol. 1. Knoxville, 1831.

Journal of the Proceedings of the House of Representatives of the Territory of the United States South of the River Ohio, 1795. Knoxville, 1795.

Keith, Alice B., ed. *The John Gray Blount Papers.* Vols. 1–3. Raleigh, N.C.: State Department of Archives and History, 1952–65.

King, Charles, ed. *The Life and Correspondence of Rufus King.* Vol. 1. New York: G. P. Putnam's Sons, 1971.

Kline, Mary-Jo, ed. *The Political Correspondence and Public Papers of Aaron Burr.* Vol. 1. Princeton, N.J.: Princeton Univ. Press, 1983.

"Letters of Jefferson, etc." *Virginia Magazine of History and Biography* 12, no. 1 (Jan. 1905): 259–64.

Looney, J. Jefferson, ed. *The Papers of Thomas Jefferson: Retirement Series.* Vols. 1–3. Princeton, N.J.: Princeton Univ. Press, 2004–.

Lowrie, Walter, and Arthur St. Clair, eds. *American State Papers: Indian Affairs*. Vol. 1. Washington, D.C.: GPO, 1932.

Morris, Eastin. *Tennessee Gazetteer, or Topographical Dictionary*. Nashville: W. Haskell Hunt, 1834.

Moser, Harold, et al., eds. *The Papers of Andrew Jackson*, Vols. 1–6. Knoxville: Univ. of Tennessee Press, 1982–.

Robertson, James. "Correspondence of James Robertson." *American Historical Magazine* 1–4 (1896–99).

Sevier, John. "Journal of John Sevier." *Tennessee Historical Magazine* 5, no. 3 (Oct. 1919): 156–94.

———. "Journal of John Sevier." *Tennessee Historical Magazine* 5, no. 4 (Jan. 1920): 232–64.

———. "Journal of John Sevier." *Tennessee Historical Magazine* 6, no. 1 (Apr. 1920): 18–68.

Smith, Daniel. "The Journal of Daniel Smith, September 25, 1779." *Tennessee Historical Magazine* 1, no. 1 (Mar. 1915): 40–65.

Smith, Daniel, and Willie Blount. *Tennessee Beginnings, Combining a Short Description of the Tennessee Government (by Daniel Smith) 1793; The Constitution of the State of Tennessee, 1796; and A Catechetical Exposition of the Constitution of the State of Tennessee, by Willie Blount, 1803*. Spartanburg, S.C.: Reprint Company, 1976.

Stagg, John C. A., gen. ed. *The Papers of James Madison: Presidential Series*. Vols. 1–5. Charlottesville: Univ. of Virginia Press, 1984–.

Three Pioneer Documents: John Donelson's Journal, Cumberland Compact, and the Minutes of the Cumberland Court. Nashville: Tennessee Historical Society, 1964.

U.S. Bureau of the Census. *Second Census of the United States*. 1800. Washington, D.C.: Gales and Seaton, 1801.

———. *Third Census of the United States*. 1810. Washington, D.C.: Gales and Seaton, 1811.

———. *Fourth Census of the United States*. 1820. Washington, D.C.: Gales and Seaton, 1821.

———. *Fifth Census of the United States*. 1830. Washington, D.C.: Gales and Seaton, 1831.

U.S. Congress. *The Congressional Register; or, History of the Proceedings and Debates of the First House of Representatives of the United States of America: Namely New-Hampshire, Massachusetts, Connecticut, New-York, New-Jersey, Pennsylvania, Delaware, Maryland, Virginia, South-Carolina and Georgia. Being the Eleven States that Have Ratified the Constitution of the United States. Containing an Impartial Account of the Most Interesting Speeches and Motions; and Accurate Copies of Remarkable Papers Laid Before and Offered to the House*. New York: Harrison and Purdy, 1789–97.

———. *The Debates and Proceedings in the Congress of the United States; with an Appendix Containing Important State Papers and Public Documents*. 4th Cong., 1st sess. Washington, D.C.: Gales and Seaton, 1834.

White, Robert, ed. *Messages of the Governors of Tennessee*. Vol. 1, *1796–1821*. Nashville: Tennessee Historical Commission, 1952.

Internet Sources

American Antiquarian Society and Readex Corporation. *Early American Imprints: Series I* and *Early American Imprints: Series II*. www.readex.com.

Documenting the American South. University Library, University of North Carolina at Chapel Hill. http://docsouth.unc.edu.

Library of Congress. American Memory. http://memory.loc.gov/ammem/index.html.

Officer, Lawrence H. "Exchange rate between the United States dollar and the British pound, 1791–2004." Economic History Services (EH.Net). http://www.eh.net/hmit/exchangerates/pound.php (2004).

Race and Slavery Petitions Project. University of North Carolina at Greensboro. http://library.uncg.edu/slavery_petitions/

The Tennessee Encyclopedia of History and Culture. Online edition. Tennessee Historical Society. http://tennesseeencyclopedia.net.

University of Virginia Library Historical Census Browser. Geospatial and Statistical Data Center, Charlottesville. http://fisher.lib.virginia.edu/collections/stats/histcensus (June 2006).

Secondary Sources

Abernethy, Thomas Perkins. "Andrew Jackson and the Rise of Southwestern Democracy." *American Historical Review* 33, no. 1 (Oct. 1927): 64–77.

———. "The Early Development of Commerce and Banking in Tennessee." *Mississippi Valley Historical Review* 14 (1927–28): 311–25.

———. *From Frontier to Plantation in Tennessee: A Study in Frontier Democracy.* Chapel Hill: Univ. of North Carolina Press, 1932.

———. *The South in the New Nation, 1789–1820.* Baton Rouge: Louisiana State Univ. Press, 1961.

Abzug, Robert. *Cosmos Crumbling: American Reform and the Religious Imagination.* Oxford: Oxford Univ. Press, 1994.

Ammon, Harry. *The Genet Mission.* New York: W. W. Norton, 1973.

Anderson, Benedict. *Imagined Communities: Reflections on the Origins and Spread of Nationalism.* London: Verso Press, 1983.

Anderson, Fred. *Crucible of War: The Seven Years' War and the Fate of Empire in British North America, 1754–1766.* New York: Knopf, 2000.

Appleby, Joyce. *Capitalism and a New Social Order: The Republican Vision of the 1790s.* New York: New York Univ. Press, 1984.

———. *Inheriting the Revolution: The First Generation of Americans.* Cambridge: Harvard Univ. Press, 2000.

Arnow, Harriet Simpson. *Flowering of the Cumberland.* New York: Macmillan, 1963.

———. *Seedtime on the Cumberland.* New York: Macmillan, 1960.

Aron, Stephen. *How the West Was Lost: The Transformation of Kentucky from Daniel Boone to Henry Clay.* Baltimore: Johns Hopkins Univ. Press, 1996.

———. "Lessons in Conquest: Towards a Greater Western History." *Pacific Historical Review* 2 (1994): 125–47.

Arroyo, Elizabeth Fortson. "Poor Whites, Slaves, and Free Blacks in Tennessee, 1796–1861." *Tennessee Historical Quarterly* 55, no. 1 (Spring 1996): 57–65.

Ash, Stephen V. *Middle Tennessee Society Transformed: War and Peace in the Upper South, 1860–1870.* Baton Rouge: Louisiana State Univ. Press, 1988.

Ashworth, John. *Agrarians and Aristocrats: Party Political Ideology in the United States, 1837–1846.* New York: Cambridge Univ. Press, 1983.

———. *Slavery Capitalism and Politics in the Antebellum Republic.* Vol. 1, *Commerce and Compromise.* New York: Cambridge Univ. Press, 1995.

Atkins, Jonathan. *Parties, Politics and the Sectional Conflict in Tennessee, 1832–1861.* Knoxville: Univ. of Tennessee Press, 1997.

Ayers, Edward. *Vengeance and Justice: Crime and Punishment in the Nineteenth Century American South.* Oxford: Oxford Univ. Press, 1984.

Bacon, H. Philip. "Nashville's Trade at the Beginning of the Nineteenth Century." *Tennessee Historical Quarterly* 15, no. 1 (Mar. 1956): 30–36.

Bailyn, Bernard. *The Ideological Origins of the American Revolution.* Cambridge: Harvard Univ. Press, 1967.

———. *Voyagers to the West: A Passage in the Peopling of American on the Eve of the Revolution.* New York: Vintage Press, 1986.

Banner, Stuart. *How the Indians Lost Their Land: Law and Power on the Frontier.* Cambridge: Harvard Univ. Press, Belknap Press, 2005.

Banning, Lance. *The Jeffersonian Persuasion: Evolution of a Party Ideology.* Ithaca, N.Y.: Cornell Univ. Press, 1978.

Baptist, Edward. *Creating an Old South: Middle Florida's Plantation Frontier Before the Civil War.* Chapel Hill: Univ. of North Carolina Press, 2002.

Beard, William E. "Joseph McMinn, Tennessee's Fourth Governor." *Tennessee Historical Quarterly* 4, no. 2 (Summer 1946): 154–66.

Beeman, Richard. "Deference, Republicanism and the Emergence of Popular Politics in Eighteenth-Century America." *William and Mary Quarterly* 49, no. 3 (July 1992): 401–30.

———. *The Evolution of the Southern Backcountry: A Case Study of Lunenburg County, Virginia, 1746–1832.* Philadelphia: Univ. of Pennsylvania Press, 1984.

———. *The Varieties of Political Experience in Eighteenth-Century America.* Philadelphia: Univ. of Pennsylvania Press, 2004.

Beeman, Richard, Stephen Botein, and Edward Carter II, eds. *Beyond Confederation: Origins of the Constitution and American National Identity.* Chapel Hill: Univ. of North Carolina Press, 1987.

Ben-Atar, Doron, and Barbara Oberg, eds. *Federalists Reconsidered.* Charlottesville: Univ. of Virginia Press, 1998.

Bergeron, Paul. *Antebellum Politics in Tennessee.* Lexington: Univ. Press of Kentucky, 1972.

Bergeron, Paul, Stephen Ash, and Jeanette Keith. *Tennesseans and Their History.* Knoxville: Univ. of Tennessee Press, 1999.

Bibliography

Berlin, Ira. *Many Thousands Gone: The First Two Centuries of Slavery in North America.* Cambridge: Harvard Univ. Press, 1998.

———. *Slaves Without Masters: The Free Negro in the Antebellum South.* New York: Pantheon, 1974.

Black, Henry Campbell. *Black's Law Dictionary.* 6th ed. St. Paul, Minn.: West Group, 1990.

Bloom, Jo Tice. "Establishing Precedents: Dr. James White and the Southwest Territory." *Tennessee Historical Quarterly* 54, no. 4 (Winter 1995): 324–35.

Boles, John B. *The Great Revival: Beginnings of the Bible Belt.* Lexington: Univ. Press of Kentucky, 1972.

Bolton, Charles C. *Poor Whites of the Antebellum South: Tenants and Laborers in Central North Carolina and Northeast Mississippi.* Durham, N.C.: Duke Univ. Press, 1994.

Booraem, Hendrick. *Young Hickory: The Making of Andrew Jackson.* Dallas: Taylor Trade, 2001.

Bouton, Terry. "A Road Closed: Rural Insurgency in Post-Independence Pennsylvania." *Journal of American History* 87, no. 3 (Dec. 2000): 855–87.

Bowman, Albert Hall. *The Struggle for Neutrality: Franco–American Diplomacy During the Federalist Era.* Knoxville: Univ. of Tennessee Press, 1974.

Boydston, Jeanne. *Home and Work: Housework, Wages and the Ideology of Labor in the Early Republic.* New York: Oxford Univ. Press, 1990.

Bradburn, Douglas. *The Citizenship Revolution: Revolutionary Politics, Nationhood, and the Making of the American Body Politic, 1787–1804.* Charlottesville: Univ. of Virginia Press, forthcoming.

Brown, John P. *Old Frontiers: The Story of the Cherokee Indians from the Earliest Times to the Date of Their Removal to the West, 1838.* Kingsport, Tenn.: Southern Publishers, 1938.

Brown, Roger. *The Republic in Peril: 1812.* New York: Norton, 1971.

Broussard, James H. *The Southern Federalists, 1800–1816.* Baton Rouge: Louisiana State Univ. Press, 1978.

Buel, Richard, Jr. *America on the Brink: How the Political Struggle Over the War of 1812 Almost Destroyed the Young Republic.* New York: Palgrave Macmillan, 2005.

———. *Securing the Revolution: Ideology in American Politics, 1789–1815.* Ithaca, N.Y.: Cornell Univ. Press, 1972.

Burstein, Andrew. *America's Jubilee, July 4, 1826: A Generation Remembers the Revolution After Fifty Years of Independence.* New York: Vintage Books, 2001.

Bushman, Richard. *The Refinement of America: Places, Houses, Cities.* New York: Vintage Books, 1993.

Carr, John. *Early Times in Middle Tennessee.* Nashville: E. Stevenson & F. A. Owen, 1857.

Carwardine, Richard. *Evangelicals and Politics in the Antebellum Republic.* New Haven, Conn.: Yale Univ. Press, 1993.

Cashin, Joan. *A Family Venture: Men and Women on the Southwestern Frontier.* Baltimore: Johns Hopkins Univ. Press, 1991.

Catterall, Ralph. *The Second Bank of the United States.* Chicago: Univ. of Chicago Press, 1903.

Cayton, Andrew. *Frontier Indiana.* Bloomington: Indiana Univ. Press, 1997.

———. "'Separate Interests' and the Nation-State: The Washington Administration and the Origins of Regionalism in the Trans-Appalachian West." *Journal of American History* 79, no. 1 (June 1992): 39–67.

Cayton, Andrew, and Fredrika Teute. *Contact Points: American Frontiers from the Mohawk Valley to the Mississippi, 1750–1830.* Chapel Hill: Univ. of North Carolina Press, 1998.

Chaplin, Joyce. *An Anxious Pursuit: Agricultural Innovation and Modernity in the Lower South, 1830–1815.* Chapel Hill: Univ. of North Carolina Press, 1993.

Clark, Christopher. *Roots of Rural Capitalism: Western Massachusetts, 1780–1860.* Ithaca, N.Y.: Cornell Univ. Press, 1990.

Clayton, Lawrence, Vernon Knight Jr., and Edward Moore, eds. *The De Soto Chronicles: The Expedition of Hernando de Soto to North America in 1539–1543.* 2 vols. Tuscaloosa: Univ. of Alabama Press, 1993.

Clayton, W. W. *History of Davidson County, Tennessee.* Philadelphia: J. L. Lewis, 1880.

Coles, Harry. *The War of 1812.* Chicago: Univ. of Chicago Press, 1965.

Cooper, William J. *Liberty and Slavery: Southern Politics to 1860.* New York: McGraw-Hill, 1983.

Cornell, Saul. *The Other Founders: Anti-Federalism and the Dissenting Tradition in America, 1788–1828.* Chapel Hill: Univ. of North Carolina Press, 1999.

Cronon, William. *Changes in the Land: Indians, Colonists and the Ecology of New England.* New York: Hill and Wang, 1983.

Cumfer, Cynthia. "Local Origins of National Indian Policy: Cherokee and Tennessean Ideas about Sovereignty and Nationhood, 1790–1811." *Journal of the Early Republic* 23, no. 1 (Spring 2003): 21–46.

Dangerfield, George. *The Awakening of American Nationalism, 1815–1828.* New York: Harper Collins, 1965.

———. *The Era of Good Feelings.* New York: Harcourt, Brace, 1952.

Davis, Karl. "'Remember Fort Mims': Reinterpreting the Origins of the Creek War." *Journal of the Early Republic* 22, no. 4 (Winter 2002): 611–36.

Driver, Carl. *John Sevier: Pioneer of the Old Southwest.* Chapel Hill: Univ. of North Carolina Press, 1932.

Dupre, Daniel. *Transforming the Cotton Frontier: Madison County, Alabama, 1800–1840.* Baton Rouge: Louisiana State Univ. Press, 1997.

Egerton, Douglas R. *Gabriel's Rebellion: The Virginia Slave Conspiracies of 1800 and 1802.* Chapel Hill: Univ. of North Carolina Press, 1993.

———. "Markets Without a Market Revolution: Southern Planters and Capitalism." *Journal of the Early Republic* 16, no. 2 (Summer 1996): 207-22.

Elkins, Stanley, and Eric McKitrick. *The Age of Federalism: The Early American Republic, 1788–1800.* Oxford: Oxford Univ. Press, 1993.

———. "A Meaning for Turner's Frontier, Part 1: Democracy in the Old Northwest." *Political Science Quarterly* 69, no. 3 (Sept. 1954): 321–53.

———. "A Meaning for Turner's Frontier, Part 2: The Southwest Frontier and New England." *Political Science Quarterly* 69, no. 4 (Dec. 1954): 565–602.

Bibliography

Ellis, Joseph. *Founding Brothers: The Revolutionary Generation.* New York: Knopf, 2000.

Ellis, Richard. *The Jeffersonian Crisis: Courts and Politics in the Young Republic.* Oxford: Oxford Univ. Press, 1971.

England, J. Merton. "The Free Negro in Ante-Bellum Tennessee." *Journal of Southern History* 9, no. 1 (Feb. 1943): 37–49.

Eslinger, Ellen. *Citizens of Zion: The Social Origins of Camp Meeting Revivalism.* Knoxville: Univ. of Tennessee Press, 1999.

———. "The Shape of Slavery on the Kentucky Frontier, 1775–1800." *Register of the Kentucky Historical Society* 92, no. 4 (Winter 1994): 1–23.

Faragher, John Mack. *Sugar Creek: Life on the Illinois Prairie.* New Haven, Conn.: Yale Univ. Press, 1986.

———, ed. *Rereading Fredrick Jackson Turner: The Significance of the Frontier in American History and Other Essays.* New York: Henry Holt, 1994.

Fehrenbacher, Don E. *The Slaveholding Republic: An Account of the United States Government's Relations to Slavery.* New York: Oxford Univ. Press, 2001.

Feller, Daniel. *The Public Lands in Jacksonian Politics.* Madison: Univ. of Wisconsin Press, 1984.

Fields, Barbara Jeanne. *Slavery and Freedom on the Middle Ground: Maryland During the Nineteenth Century.* New Haven, Conn.: Yale Univ. Press, 1985.

Finger, John R. *Tennessee Frontiers: Three Regions in Transition.* Bloomington: Indiana Univ. Press, 2001.

———. "Tennessee Indian History: Creativity and Power." *Tennessee Historical Quarterly* 54, no. 4 (Winter 1995): 286–305.

Fischer, David Hackett. *Albion's Seed: Four British Folkways in America.* Oxford: Oxford Univ. Press, 1989.

———. *The Revolution of American Conservatism: The Federalist Party in the Era of Jeffersonian Democracy.* New York: Harper, 1965.

Fischer, David Hackett, and James C. Kelly. *Bound Away: Virginia and the Westward Movement.* Charlottesville: Univ. of Virginia Press, 2000.

Flexner, Stuart, ed. *The Random House Dictionary.* Rev. ed. New York: Random House, 1988.

Fogel, Robert, and Stanley Engerman. *Time on the Cross: The Economics of Negro Slavery.* New York: Univ. Press of America, 1984.

Ford, Lacey. "Making the 'White Man's Country' White: Race, Slavery, and State-Building in the Jacksonian South." *Journal of the Early Republic* 19, no. 4 (Winter 1999): 713–37.

———. *Origins of Southern Radicalism: The South Carolina Upcountry, 1800–1860.* Oxford: Oxford Univ. Press, 1988.

Fox-Genovese, Elizabeth, and Eugene Genovese. *The Fruits of Merchant Capital: Slavery and Bourgeois Property in the Rise and Expansion of Capitalism.* Oxford: Oxford Univ. Press, 1983.

Fredrickson, George M. *The Black Image in the White Mind: The Debate on Afro-American Character and Destiny, 1817–1914.* New York: Harper and Row, 1971.

Freehling, William. *The Road to Disunion: Secessionists at Bay, 1776–1854.* New York: Oxford Univ. Press, 1990.

Freeman, Joanne B. *Affairs of Honor: National Politics in the New Republic.* New Haven, Conn.: Yale Univ. Press, 2001.

———. "Dueling as Politics: Reinterpreting the Burr-Hamilton Duel." *William and Mary Quarterly* 53, no. 2 (Apr. 1996): 289–318.

———. "The Election of 1800: A Study in the Logic of Political Change." *Yale Law Journal* 108, no. 8 (June 1999): 1959–94.

———. "Slander, Poison, Whispers and Fame: Jefferson's 'Anas' and Political Gossip in the Early Republic." *Journal of the Early Republic* 15, no. 1 (Spring 1995): 25–58.

Friend, Craig T. *Along Maysville Road: The Early American Republic in the Trans-Appalachian West.* Knoxville: Univ. of Tennessee Press, 2005.

———. *The Buzzel About Kentuck: Settling the Promised Land.* Lexington: Univ. Press of Kentucky, 1998.

Genovese, Eugene. *The Political Economy of Slavery: Studies in the Economy and Society of the Slave South.* New York: Vintage, 1961.

———. *Roll, Jordan, Roll: The World the Slaves Made.* New York: Vintage Books, 1972.

Gilje, Paul. *The Road to Mobocracy: Popular Disorder in New York City, 1763–1834.* Chapel Hill: Univ. of North Carolina Press, 1987.

Golden, Gabriel Hawkins. "William Carroll and His Administration" *Tennessee Historical Magazine* 9, no. 1 (Apr. 1925): 9–30.

Goodstein, Anita Shafer. "Black History on the Nashville Frontier, 1780–1810." *Tennessee Historical Quarterly* 38, no. 4 (Winter 1979): 401–20.

———. *Nashville, 1780–1860: From Frontier to City.* Gainesville: Univ. Press of Florida, 1989.

Gorn, Elliot. "'Gouge and Bite, Pull Hair and Scratch': The Social Significance of Fighting in the Southern Backcountry." *American Historical Review* 90, no. 1 (Feb. 1985): 18–43.

Greenberg, Kenneth. *Honor and Slavery: Lies, Duels, Noses, Masks, Dressing as a Woman, Gifts, Strangers, Humanitarianism, Death, Slave Rebellions, the Proslavery Argument, Baseball, Hunting and Gambling in the Old South.* Princeton, N.J.: Princeton Univ. Press, 1996.

Habermas, Jürgen. *The Structural Transformation of the Public Sphere: An Inquiry into a Category of Bourgeois Society.* Translated by Thomas Burger. Cambridge: Harvard Univ. Press, 1989.

Hadden, Sally. *Slave Patrols: Law and Violence in Virginia and the Carolinas, 1700–1865.* Cambridge: Harvard Univ. Press, 2001.

Hagy, James W. "Democracy Defeated: The Frankland Constitution of 1785." *Tennessee Historical Quarterly* 40, no. 3 (Fall 1981): 239–56.

Hamer, Philip. *Tennessee: A History.* Washington, D.C.: American Historical Association, 1933.

Harkens, John E. "Newton Cannon, Jackson Nemesis." *Tennessee Historical Quarterly* 43, no. 3 (Winter 1984): 355–75.

Hatch, Nathan. *The Democratization of American Christianity.* New Haven, Conn.: Yale Univ. Press, 1989.

Hay, Robert P. "John Fitzgerald: Presidential Image-maker for Andrew Jackson in 1823." *Tennessee Historical Quarterly* 22, no. 2 (Summer 1983): 138–50.

Bibliography

Haywood, John. *The Civil and Political History of the State of Tennessee from Its Earliest Settlement up to the Year 1796*. 1823. Reprint, Knoxville: Tenase, 1969.

Henry, H. M. "The Slave Laws of Tennessee." *Tennessee Historical Magazine* 2, no. 3 (Sept. 1916): 175–203.

Heyrman, Christine Leigh. *Southern Cross: The Beginnings of the Bible Belt*. Chapel Hill: Univ. of North Carolina Press, 1998.

Hickey, Donald. *The War of 1812: A Forgotten Conflict*. Urbana: Univ. of Illinois Press, 1990.

Hinderaker, Eric. *Elusive Empires: Constructing Colonialism in the Ohio Valley, 1673–1800*. New York: Cambridge Univ. Press, 1997.

Hoffman, Ronald J., and Peter Albert. *Launching the "Extended Republic": The Federalist Era*. Charlottesville: Univ. of Virginia Press, 1996.

Holt, Albert C. "The Economic and Social Beginnings of Tennessee." *Tennessee Historical Magazine* 7, no. 4 (Jan. 1922): 251–313.

———. "The Economic and Social Beginnings of Tennessee." *Tennessee Historical Magazine* 8, no. 1 (Apr. 1924): 24–86.

Holt, Michael F. *The Political Crisis of the 1850s*. New York: W. W. Norton, 1978.

———. *The Rise and Fall of the American Whig Party: Jacksonian Politics and the Onset of the Civil War*. Oxford: Oxford Univ. Press, 1999.

Holton, Woody. *Forced Founders: Indians, Debtors, Slaves and the Making of the American Revolution in Virginia*. Chapel Hill: Univ. of North Carolina Press, 1999.

Horn, James, Jan Ellen Lewis, and Peter S. Onuf, eds. *The Revolution of 1800: Democracy, Race, and the New Republic*. Charlottesville: Univ. of Virginia Press, 2002.

Horsman, Reginald. "The British Indian Department and the Resistance to General Anthony Wayne, 1793–1795." *Mississippi Valley Historical Review* 49, no. 2 (Sept. 1962): 269–90.

———. "The Dimensions of an 'Empire for Liberty': Expansion and Republicanism, 1775–1825." *Journal of the Early Republic* 9, no. 1 (Spring 1989): 1–20.

Horwitz, Morton. *The Transformation of American Law, 1780–1860*. Cambridge: Harvard Univ. Press, 1977.

Hoss, E. E. "Elihu Embree, Abolitionist." *American Historical Magazine* 2 (Apr. 1897): 116–32.

Howington, Arthur F. "'Not in the Condition of a Horse or an Ox': Ford v. Ford, the Law of Testamentary Manumission, and the Tennessee Courts' Recognition of Slave Humanity." *Tennessee Historical Quarterly* 34, no. 3 (Fall 1975): 249–63.

———. "'A Property of Special and Peculiar Value': The Tennessee Supreme Court and the Law of Manumission." *Tennessee Historical Quarterly* 44, no. 3 (Fall 1985): 302–17.

Imes, William Lloyd. "The Legal Status of Free Negroes and Slaves in Tennessee." *Journal of Negro History* 4, no. 3 (July 1919): 255–72.

James, C. L. R. *The Black Jacobins: Touissant L'Ouverture and the San Domingo Revolution*. New York: Vintage Press, 1963.

Jordan, Winthrop. *White over Black: American Attitudes Towards the Negro, 1550–1812*. Chapel Hill: Univ. of North Carolina Press, 1968.

Kanon, Tom. "'James Madison, Felix Grundy, and the Devil': A Western War Hawk in Congress." *Filson History Quarterly* 75, no. 3 (Fall 2001): 433–68.

———. "The Kidnapping of Martha Crawley and Settler-Indians Relations Prior to the War of 1812." *Tennessee Historical Quarterly* 64, no. 1 (Spring 2005): 2–23.

Kars, Marjoleine. *Breaking Loose Together: The Regulator Rebellion in Pre-Revolutionary North Carolina.* Chapel Hill: Univ. of North Carolina Press, 2002.

Kastor, Peter J. "'Equitable Rights and Privileges': The Divided Loyalties in Washington County, Virginia, During the Franklin Separatist Crisis." *Virginia Magazine of History and Biography* 105, no. 2 (Spring 1997): 193–226.

Kay, Marvin Michael, and Lorin Lee Cary. *Slavery in North Carolina, 1748–1775.* Chapel Hill: Univ. of North Carolina Press, 1995.

Kerber, Linda. *Federalists in Dissent: Imagery and Ideology in Jeffersonian America.* Ithaca, N.Y.: Cornell Univ. Press, 1970.

Keyssar, Alexander. *The Right to Vote: The Contested History of Democracy in the United States.* New York: Basic Books, 2000.

Klein, Rachel. *Unification of a Slave State: The Rise of the Planter Class in the South Carolina Backcountry, 1760–1808.* Chapel Hill: Univ. of North Carolina Press, 1991.

Koschnik, Albrecht. "The Democratic Societies and the Limits of the American Public Sphere, circa 1793–1795." *William and Mary Quarterly* 58, no. 2 (July 2001): 615–36.

Kulikoff, Allan. *The Agrarian Origins of American Capitalism.* Charlottesville: Univ. of Virginia Press, 1992.

Larson, John Lauritz. *Internal Improvement: National Public Works and the Promise of Popular Government in the Early United States.* Chapel Hill: Univ. of North Carolina Press, 2001.

Laska, Lewis L. "'The Dam'st Situation Ever Man Was Placed In': Andrew Jackson, David Allison, and the Frontier Economy of 1795–1796." *Tennessee Historical Quarterly* 54, no. 4 (Winter 1995): 336–47.

Laska, Lewis, and Severine Brocki. "The Life and Death of the Lottery in Tennessee, 1787–1836." *Tennessee Historical Quarterly* 45, no. 2 (Summer 1986): 95–118.

Laver, Harry S. "Rethinking the Social Role of the Militia: Community-Building in Antebellum Kentucky." *Journal of Southern History* 68, no. 4 (Nov. 2002): 777–816.

Lewis, James. *The American Union and the Problem of Neighborhood: The United States and the Collapse of the Spanish Empire, 1790–1829.* Chapel Hill: Univ. of North Carolina Press, 1998.

Livermore, Shaw. *The Twilight of Federalism: The Disintegration of the Federalist Party, 1815–1830.* Princeton, N.J.: Princeton Univ. Press, 1962.

Lomask, Milton. *Aaron Burr.* New York: Farrar, Strauss and Giroux, 1979.

Lovett, Bobby J. *The African-American History of Nashville, Tennessee, 1780–1930: Elites and Dilemmas.* Fayetteville: Univ. of Arkansas Press, 1997.

Magrath, C. Peter. *Yazoo: Law and Politics in the New Republic: The Case of Fletcher v. Peck.* New York: W. W. Norton, 1967.

Mahon, John K. *The War of 1812.* Gainesville: Univ. Press of Florida, 1972.

Bibliography

Mann, Bruce H. *Republic of Debtors: Bankruptcy in the Age of American Independence.* Cambridge: Harvard Univ. Press, 2002.

Martin, Asa Earl. "Anti-Slavery Activities of the Methodist Episcopal Church in Tennessee." *Tennessee Historical Magazine* 2, no. 2 (June 1916): 98–109.

———. "The Anti-Slavery Societies of Tennessee." *Tennessee Historical Magazine* 1, no. 4 (Dec. 1915): 264–81.

Masterson, William. *William Blount.* Baton Rouge: Louisiana State Univ. Press, 1954.

Mathews, Donald. *Religion in the Old South.* Chicago: Univ. of Chicago Press, 1977.

———. "The Second Great Awakening as an Organizing Process, 1780–1830: An Hypothesis." *American Quarterly* 21 (1969): 23–43.

McCoy, Drew R. *The Elusive Republic: Political Economy in Jeffersonian America.* Chapel Hill: Univ. of North Carolina Press, 1980.

McCurry, Stephanie. *Masters of Small Worlds: Yeoman Households, Gender Relations, and the Political Culture of the Antebellum South Carolina Low Country.* Oxford: Oxford Univ. Press, 1995.

McDonald, Forrest. *The Presidency of George Washington.* Lawrence: Univ. of Kansas Press, 1974.

McFerrin, John B. *History of Methodism in Tennessee.* Nashville: Publishing House of the Methodist Episcopal Church, South, 1886.

McKenzie, Robert. *One South or Many? Plantation Belt and Upcountry in Civil War–Era Tennessee.* New York: Cambridge Univ. Press, 1994.

McLoughlin, William G. *Cherokee Renascence in the New Republic.* Princeton Press, 1986.

Melton, Buckner F., Jr. *Aaron Burr: Conspiracy to Treason.* New York: Wiley and Sons, 2002.

———. *The First Impeachment: The Constitution's Framers and the Case of Senator William Blount.* Macon, Ga.: Mercer Univ. Press, 1998.

Moore, Glover. *The Missouri Controversy, 1819–1821.* Lexington: Univ. Press of Kentucky, 1953.

Morgan, Edmund S. *American Slavery, American Freedom: The Ordeal of Colonial Virginia.* New York: W. W. Norton, 1975.

Morris, Christopher. *Becoming Southern: The Evolution of a Way of Life, Warren County and Vicksburg, Mississippi, 1770–1860.* New York: Oxford Univ. Press, 1995.

Murrin, John. "The Jeffersonian Triumph and American Exceptionalism." *Journal of the Early Republic* 20, no. 1 (Spring 2000): 1–25.

Newman, Simon. *Parades and the Politics of the Street: Festive Culture in the Early American Republic.* Philadelphia: Univ. of Pennsylvania Press, 2000.

Nobles, Gregory. "Breaking into the Backcountry: New Approaches to the Early American Frontier, 1750–1800." *William and Mary Quarterly* 46, no. 4 (Winter 1989): 641–70.

Novak, William J. *The People's Welfare: Law and Regulation in Nineteenth-Century America.* Chapel Hill: Univ. of North Carolina Press, 1996.

Oakes, James. *The Ruling Race: A History of American Slaveholders.* New York: Vintage Books, 1983.

———. *Slavery and Freedom: An Interpretation of the Old South.* New York: Norton Press, 1990.

O'Brien, Greg. *Choctaws in a Revolutionary Age, 1750–1830.* Lincoln: Univ. of Nebraska Press, 2002.

———. "The Conqueror Meets the Unconquered: Negotiating Cultural Boundaries on the Post-Revolutionary Southern Frontier." *Journal of Southern History* 67, no. 1 (Feb. 2001): 39–72.

Onuf, Peter S. *Jefferson's Empire: The Language of American Nationhood.* Charlottesville: Univ. of Virginia Press, 2000.

———. *The Origins of the Federal Republic: Jurisdictional Controversies in the United States, 1775–1787.* Philadelphia: Univ. of Pennsylvania Press, 1983.

———. *Statehood and Union: A History of the Northwest Ordinance.* Bloomington: Indiana Univ. Press, 1987.

Parton, James. *Life of Andrew Jackson.* Vol. 1. New York: Mason Brothers, 1861.

Pasley, Jeffrey. *The Tyranny of Printers: Newspaper Politics in the Early American Republic.* Charlottesville: Univ. of Virginia Press, 2001.

Pasley, Jeffrey, Andrew Robertson, and David Waldstreicher, eds. *Beyond the Founders: New Approaches to the Political History of the Early American Republic.* Chapel Hill: Univ. of North Carolina Press, 2004.

Patterson, Caleb Perry. *The Negro in Tennessee, 1790–1865.* New York: Negro Universities Press, 1968.

Peeler, Elizabeth H. "The Policies of Willie Blount as Governor, 1809–1815." *Tennessee Historical Quarterly* 1, no. 4 (Dec. 1942): 309–27.

Perdue, Theda. *Cherokee Women: Gender and Culture Change, 1700–1835.* Lincoln: Univ. of Nebraska Press, 1998.

Perkins, Elizabeth. *Border Life: Experience and Memory in the Revolutionary Ohio Valley.* Chapel Hill: Univ. of North Carolina Press, 1998.

Perry, Lewis. *Boats Against the Current: American Culture Between Revolution and Modernity, 1820–1860.* New York: Oxford Univ. Press, 1993.

Peskin, Lawrence A. "How the Republicans Learned to Love Manufacturing: The First Parties and the 'New Economy.'" *Journal of the Early Republic* 22, no. 2 (Summer 2002): 235–62.

Powell, William S. *North Carolina Through Four Centuries.* Chapel Hill: Univ. of North Carolina Press, 1989.

Pratt, Julius. *Expansionists of 1812.* New York: Macmillan, 1925.

Pukl, Joseph M. "James K. Polk's Early Congressional Campaigns of 1825 and 1827." *Tennessee Historical Quarterly* 39, no. 4 (Winter 1980): 440–58.

Purcell, Aaron D. "A Spirit of Speculation: David Burford, Antebellum Entrepreneur of Middle Tennessee." *Tennessee Historical Quarterly* 54, no. 2 (Summer 2005): 90–109.

Putnam, A. W. *History of Middle Tennessee; or, Life and Times of Gen. James Robertson.* Nashville, 1859.

Ramsay, J. G. M. *Annals of Tennessee to the End of the Eighteenth Century.* 1853. Reprint, Knoxville: East Tennessee Historical Society, 1967.

Ratcliffe, Donald. *Party Spirit in a Frontier Republic: Ohio, 1790–1821.* Columbus: Ohio State Univ. Press, 1999.

Bibliography

———. *The Politics of Long Division: The Birth of the Second Party System in Ohio, 1818–1828.* Columbus: Ohio State Univ. Press, 2000.

Ratner, Lorman. *Andrew Jackson and His Tennessee Lieutenants.* Westport, Conn.: Greenwood Press, 1997.

Ray, Kristofer. "Land Speculation, Popular Democracy and Political Transformation on the Tennessee Frontier, 1780–1800." *Tennessee Historical Quarterly* 61, no. 3 (Fall 2002): 161–81.

———. "Political Culture and the Origins of a Party System in the Southern Ohio Valley: The Case of Early National Tennessee, 1796–1812." *Ohio Valley History* 4, no. 4 (Winter 2004): 3–26.

Reid, John Philip. *A Law of Blood: The Primitive Law of the Cherokee Nation.* New York: New York Univ. Press, 1970.

Remini, Robert. *Andrew Jackson and the Course of American Democracy.* New York: Harper and Row, 1979.

———. *Andrew Jackson and the Course of American Empire, 1767–1821.* New York: Harper and Row, 1977.

———. *Andrew Jackson and His Indian Wars.* New York: Viking Press, 2001.

———. "Andrew Jackson Takes an Oath of Allegiance to Spain." *Tennessee Historical Quarterly* 54, no. 1 (Spring 1995): 2–15.

Richards, Leonard. *Shays's Rebellion: The American Revolution's Final Battle.* Philadelphia: Univ. of Pennsylvania Press, 2002.

———. *The Slave Power: The Free North and Southern Domination, 1780–1860.* Baton Rouge: Louisiana State Univ. Press, 2000.

Risjord, Norman. *Chesapeake Politics, 1781–1800.* New York: Columbia Univ. Press, 1978.

Risjord, Norman, and Gordon DenBoer. "The Evolution of Political Parties in Virginia, 1782–1800." *Journal of American History* 60, no. 4 (Mar. 1974): 961–84.

Rohrbough, Malcolm. *The Land Office Business.* New York: Oxford Univ. Press, 1968.

———. *The Trans-Appalachian Frontier: People, Societies and Institutions, 1775–1850.* New York: Oxford Univ. Press, 1978.

Rothbard, Murray. *The Panic of 1819: Reactions and Policies.* New York: Columbia Univ. Press, 1962.

Ryan, Mary. *Cradle of the Middle Class: The Family in Oneida County, New York, 1790–1865.* New York: Cambridge Univ. Press, 1981.

Saunt, Claudio. *A New Order of Things: Property, Power and the Transformation of the Creek Indians, 1733–1816.* New York: Cambridge Univ. Press, 1999.

Schweikart, Larry. "Tennessee Banks in the Antebellum Period, Part I." *Tennessee Historical Quarterly* 45, no. 2 (Summer 1986): 119–32.

Schweninger, Loren. "Doctor Jack: A Slave Physician on the Tennessee Frontier." *Tennessee Historical Quarterly* 57, no. 1 (Spring/Summer 1998): 36–41.

Sellers, Charles. "Banking and Politics in Jackson's Tennessee, 1817–1827." *Mississippi Valley Historical Review* 41 (1954–55): 61–84.

———. "Jackson Men with Feet of Clay." *American Historical Review* 62, no. 3 (Apr. 1957): 537–51.

———. *James K. Polk: Jacksonian, 1795–1843*. Princeton, N.J.: Princeton Univ. Press, 1957.

———. *The Market Revolution: Jacksonian America, 1815–1846*. New York: Oxford Univ. Press, 1991.

Shammas, Carol. "How Self-Sufficient was Early America?" *Journal of Interdisciplinary History* 13 (1982): 247–72.

Sharp, James Rogers. *American Politics in the Early Republic: The New Nation in Crisis*. New Haven, Conn.: Yale Univ. Press, 1993.

Shoemaker, Nancy, ed. *Negotiators of Change: Historical Perspectives on Native American Women*. London: Routledge, 1995.

Sioussat, St. George L. "Some Phases of Tennessee Politics in the Jackson Period." *American Historical Review* 14, no. 1 (Oct. 1908): 51–69.

Slaughter, Thomas. *The Whiskey Rebellion: Frontier Epilogue to the American Revolution*. Oxford: Oxford Univ. Press, 1986.

Smith, Kevin E. "Bledsoe's Station: Archeology, History and the Interpretation of the Middle Tennessee Frontier, 1770–1820." *Tennessee Historical Quarterly* 59, no. 3 (Fall 2000): 175–87.

Stagg, J. C. A. *Mr. Madison's War: Politics, Diplomacy and Warfare in the Early American Republic, 1783–1830*. Princeton, N.J.: Princeton Univ. Press, 1983.

Stewart, James Brewer. "The Emergence of Racial Modernity and the Rise of the White North." *Journal of the Early Republic* 18, no. 2 (Summer 1998): 181–217.

Stokes, Melvyn, and Stephen Conway, eds. *The Market Revolution in America: Social, Political and Religious Expressions, 1800–1880*. Charlottesville: Univ. of Virginia Press, 1996.

Stowe, Steven. *Intimacy and Power in the Old South: Ritual in the Lives of the Planters*. Baltimore: Johns Hopkins Univ. Press, 1987.

Sydnor, Charles. *Gentlemen Freeholders: Political Practices in Washington's Virginia*. Chapel Hill: Univ. of North Carolina Press, 1952.

Symonds, Craig. "The Failure of America's Indian Policy on the Southwestern Frontier, 1785–1793." *Tennessee Historical Quarterly* 35, no. 1 (Spring 1976): 29–45.

Szatmary, David P. *Shays' Rebellion: The Making of an Agrarian Insurrection*. Amherst: Univ. of Massachusetts Press, 1980.

Takagi, Midori. *"Rearing the Wolves to our Own Destruction": Slavery in Richmond, Virginia, 1782–1865*. Charlottesville: Univ. of Virginia Press, 1999.

Taylor, Alan. *Liberty Men and Great Proprietors: The Revolutionary Settlement on the Maine Frontier, 1760–1820*. Chapel Hill: Univ. of North Carolina Press, 1990.

———. *William Cooper's Town: Power and Persuasion on the Early American Frontier*. New York: Knopf, 1995.

Taylor, George Rogers. *The Transportation Revolution, 1815–1860*. New York: Harper Torch Books, 1951.

Temin, Peter. *The Jacksonian Economy*. New York: W. W. Norton, 1969.

Bibliography

Thomas, Mary Jane. *Old Days in Nashville, Tenn.* Nashville: Publishing House Methodist Episcopal Church, South, 1897.

Thornton, J. Mills. *Politics and Power in a Slave Society: Alabama, 1800–1860.* Baton Rouge: Louisiana State Univ. Press, 1978.

Tillson, Albert J. "The Militia and Popular Political Culture in the Upper Valley of Virginia, 1740–1775." *Virginia Magazine of History and Biography* 94, no. 3 (July 1986): 285–306.

Tolbert, Lisa C. *Constructing Townscapes: Space and Society in Antebellum Tennessee.* Chapel Hill: Univ. of North Carolina Press, 1999.

Trabue, Charles. "The Voluntary Emancipation of Slaves in Tennessee as Reflected in the State's Legislation and Judicial Decisions." *Tennessee Historical Magazine* 4, no. 1 (Mar. 1918): 50–68.

Travers, Len. *Celebrating the Fourth: Independence Day and the Rites of Nationalism in the Early Republic.* Amherst: Univ. of Massachusetts Press, 1997.

Turner, Frederick Jackson. "The Significance of the Frontier in American History." *Annual Report of the American Historical Association for the Year 1893.* Washington, D.C., 1894.

van den Berghe, Pierre. *Race and Racism: A Comparative Perspective.* New York: Wiley and Sons, 1967.

Wade, Richard. *Slavery in the Cities: The South, 1820–1860.* New York: Oxford Press, 1964.

Waldstreicher, David. *In the Midst of Perpetual Fetes: The Making of American Nationalism, 1776–1820.* Chapel Hill: Univ. of North Carolina Press, 1997.

Watlington, Patricia. *The Partisan Spirit: Kentucky Politics, 1779–1792.* Chapel Hill: Univ. of North Carolina Press, 1972.

Watson, Harry. "Conflict and Collaboration: Yeoman, Slaveholders and Politics in the Antebellum South." *Social History* 10, no. 3 (Oct. 1985): 273–98.

———. *Jacksonian Politics and Community Conflict: The Emergence of the Second American Party System in Cumberland County, North Carolina.* Baton Rouge: Louisiana State Univ. Press, 1981.

———. *Liberty and Power: The Politics of Jacksonian America.* New York: Hill and Wang, 1990.

Watts, Steven. *The Republic Reborn: War and the Making of Liberal America, 1790–1820.* Baltimore: Johns Hopkins Univ. Press, 1987.

Weeks, Stephen. "Tennessee: A Discussion of the Sources of Its Population and the Lines of Immigration." *Tennessee Historical Magazine* 2, no. 2 (June 1916): 245–53.

Weiman, David. "Peopling the Land by Lottery?: The Market in Public Lands and the Regional Differentiation of Territory on the Georgia Frontier." *Journal of Economic History* 51 (Dec. 1991): 835–60.

Wells, Ann Harwell. "Lafayette in Nashville, 1825." *Tennessee Historical Quarterly* 34, no. 1 (Spring 1975): 19–31.

West, Carroll Van. "The Democratic and Whig Political Activists of Middle Tennessee." *Tennessee Historical Quarterly* 42, no. 1 (Spring 1983): 3–17.

———. *The Tennessee Encyclopedia of History and Culture.* Nashville: Rutledge Hill Press, 1998.

White, Richard. *The Middle Ground: Indians, Empires and Republics in the Great Lakes Region, 1650–1815.* New York: Cambridge Univ. Press, 1991.

Wilentz, Sean. *The Rise of American Democracy: Jefferson to Lincoln.* New York: Norton, 2005.

Williams, Samuel Cole. "The Admission of Tennessee into the Union." *Tennessee Historical Quarterly* 4, no. 4 (Winter 1945): 391–419.

———. "The Clarksville Compact of 1785." *Tennessee Historical Quarterly* 3, no. 3 (Sept. 1944): 236–47.

———. *History of the Lost State of Franklin.* Johnson City, Tenn.: Watauga Press, 1924.

Winters, Donald L. "'Plain Folk' of the Old South Reexamined: Economic Democracy in Tennessee." *Journal of Southern History* 53, no. 4 (Nov. 1987): 565–86.

Wood, Gordon. *Creation of the American Republic, 1776–1787.* Chapel Hill: Univ. of North Carolina Press, 1969.

———. *The Radicalism of the American Revolution.* New York: Vintage, 1991.

Wright, Gavin. "Old South, New South, Sunbelt South." Delivered as the Alfred Chandler Lecture, Univ. of North Carolina at Chapel Hill, March 2000.

———. *The Political Economy of the Cotton South: Households, Markets and Wealth in the Nineteenth Century.* New York: Norton Press, 1978.

Wyatt-Brown, Bertram. *The Shaping of Southern Culture: Honor, Grace, and War, 1760s–1880s.* Chapel Hill: Univ. of North Carolina Press, 2001.

———. *Southern Honor: Ethics and Behavior in the Old South.* New York: Oxford Univ. Press, 1982.

Young, Alfred F., ed. *Beyond the American Revolution: Explorations in the History of American Radicalism.* Dekalb: Northern Illinois Univ. Press, 1993.

THESES AND DISSERTATIONS

Cumfer, Cynthia. "'The Idea of Mankind Is So Various': An Intellectual History of Tennessee, 1768–1810." Ph.D. diss., Univ. of California at Los Angeles, 2001.

Dovenbarger, Daniel. "Land Speculation in Early Middle Tennessee: Laws and Practice." Master's thesis, Vanderbilt Univ., 1981.

Folmsbee, Stanley J. "Sectionalism and Internal Improvements in Tennessee, 1796–1845." Ph.D. diss., Univ. of Pennsylvania, 1939.

Friend, Craig Thompson. "Inheriting Eden: The Creation of Society and Community in Early Kentucky, 1792–1812." Ph.D. diss., Univ. of Kentucky, 1995.

Mehlman, Terry. "From Seeder Rales to Iron Rails: John Shofner, Yeoman Farmer in an Age of Change, 1831–1857." Master's thesis, Univ. of North Carolina at Chapel Hill, 1999.

Miller, Mark. "Richard Henderson: The Making of a Land Speculator." Master's thesis, Univ. of North Carolina at Chapel Hill, 1975.

Mooney, Chase. "Slavery in Davidson County." Master's thesis, Vanderbilt Univ., 1936.

Nichols, David A. "Red Gentlemen and White Savages: Indian Relations and Political Culture after the American Revolution, 1784–1800." Ph.D. diss., Univ. of Kentucky, 2000.

Bibliography

Pate, James. "The Chickamauga: A Forgotten Segment of Indian Resistance on the Southern Frontier." Ph.D. diss., Mississippi State Univ., 1969.

Sayers, Jerry Alan. "Disunited States: The Lost State of Franklin and Frontier State Movements at the Dawn of the American Republic." Master's thesis, Univ. of Virginia, 2002.

Schoenbachler, Matthew. "The Origins of Jacksonian Politics: Central Kentucky, 1790–1840." Ph.D. diss., Univ. of Kentucky, 1998.

Sheidley, Nathaniel. "Unruly Men: Indians, Settlers, and the Ethos of Frontier Patriarchy in the Upper Tennessee Watershed, 1763–1815." Ph.D. diss., Princeton Univ., 1999.

Smith, Trevor A. "Pioneers, Politicians and Patriots: The Tennessee Militia System." Ph.D. diss., Univ. of Tennessee, Knoxville, 2003.

Sturgis, Amy H. "'Charged with Republican Notions': Western Constitutions, 1775–1796." Master's thesis, Vanderbilt Univ., 1995.

Teute, Fredrika. "Land, Liberty and Labor in the Post-Revolutionary Era: Kentucky as the Promised Land." Ph.D. diss., Johns Hopkins Univ., 1988.

Toomey, William Michael. "Prelude to Statehood: The Southwest Territory, 1790–1796." Ph.D. diss., Univ. of Tennessee, Knoxville, 1991.

Walker, William Alphonso. "Tennessee, 1796–1821." Ph.D. diss., Univ. of Texas at Austin, 1959.

West, Carroll Van. "'The Money Our Fathers Were Accustomed To': Banks and Political Culture in Rutherford County, Tennessee, 1800–1850." Ph.D. diss., College of William and Mary, 1982.

Index

Page numbers in **boldface** refer to maps.

A

"A": on Middle Tenn., 57, 63, 80
Adams, John: administration of, 35; and presidential election (1796), 32
Adams, John Quincy, 136
"Agricola": on drunkenness, 184n126; on legal system, 98
agriculture: and innovation, 134. *See also* cotton; tobacco
Akin, Robert, 82
Alabama: cotton in, 138; and Creek land, 114–15; and land speculation, 69
Allen, Robert, 131
Allen, Thomas, 105
Allison, David, 60
American Atlas (1795) (Carey), **85**
American Colonization Society, 146
American Revolution: and Indians, 4; and land warrants, 62; legacy of, 109–10
Anderson, William: and land speculation, 69; as Nashville commissioner, 62
Anderson and Weir, 185n133
antislavery, 142, 147–49
"Aristedes," 81–82
Armstrong, Martin, 27
Armstrong, Col. Martin, 6
Aron, Stephen, 138
Asbury, Bishop Francis, 76–77, 119, 148
Ashe, Samuel, 36, 37
autonomy, 3–4
"Avarice," 98–99
Axley, James, 149

B

Baird, John, 66–67
Baird and Boyce, 185n133
Balch, Alfred, 122
Bank of Nashville, 78–79
Bank of the United States, 123, 124
banks: A. Jackson on, 130, 131–32; and anti-bank sentiment, 132–33; Bank of the United States, 123, 124; and "bank war," 123–24; Carthage Bank, 197n36; Columbia Bank, 197n36; Farmers' and Mechanics Bank of Nashville, 197n36; Franklin Tennessee Bank, 197n36; Gallatin Bank, 197n36; Murfreesborough Bank, 197n36; Nashville Bank, 78–79, 123; and notes, 130; and Panic of 1819, 118, 125–26; petitions against, 125; Rogersville Bank, 197n36; "S. N. G." on, 126; Shelbyville Bank, 197n36; Winchester Bank, 197n36
barter, 60, 102, 177n12
Battle of Fallen Timbers (1794), 33
Battle of New Orleans (1815), 115
Beard, Hugh, 166n54
Beard, John, 162n74
Bedford County, 74; and legal reform, 99–100
Bell, George, 183n99
Benton, Thomas Hart: and courts bill, 100–101; on legal system, 97–98, 99
Betty (Rachel Jackson's maid), 144
Black Bobb's Tavern, 73
Blackman, Edmond, 71
Blackmore, George, 47
blacks, free: and political culture, 141, 142; population, **91**; regulation of, 144–46,

blacks, free (cont.)
    150–51; and slaves, 58, 143, 149; and white community, 73–74
Bledsoe, Anthony, 9
Bledsoe, Isaac: killed, 26; as land speculator, 7–8
Bloody Fellow (Cherokee leader), 22, 30
Blount, William: as governor, 14, 15, 16–17, 20, 22, 70, 96; impeachment of, 35; on Indian raids, 23, 24–25; land claims of, 27; and land fraud, 37; and militia elections, 45; and militia expeditions, 29; seeks federal assistance, 25–26, 28, 30; and statehood, 30–32
Blount, Willie, 50, 53, 78, 110–11, 114; on squatters, 64
"Bogtrotter," 135
Boone, Daniel: image of, 3
boosterism, 77–80
Brown, John, 165n42
Bryan, Henry, 132
Bryan, Sherwood, 73, 145
Buchanan's Station (Cumberland district): Indian raid at, 28
Buffon, Georges Louis Leclerc, Comte de, 168n85
Burford, David, 69
Burr, Aaron, 170n1, 173n45

C

Calhoun, John C., 119
Campbell, Arthur Lee: on Cumberland district, 61; on economic growth, 93; on elections, 52; on land speculation, 10; as merchant, 79–80; on Republican system, xviii, 42
Campbell, David: on Indians, 34, 111; mentioned, 93; on Nashville market, 79; and pro-war sentiment, 112; as territorial judge, 15, 52, 60, 97
Campbell, George Washington, 62, 64, 120, 191n51
Campbell, James, 123, 125, 128, 132–33
Campbell, John: and slaves, 144; on Tenn. land, 117, 122, 123, 135, 136
Campbell, John (of Southwest Virginia), 3–4

Canada, 192n95
canals, 134. *See also* internal improvements
Cannon, Newton, 136, 175n68
Cantrell, Ann, 195n13
Carey, Mathew: *American Atlas* (1795), **85**
Carroll, William, 120, 132, 133–34, 196n18
Carter, John, 51
Carthage Bank, 197n36
Carthage Gazette: on *Chesapeake* affair, 108; on economic growth, 80; on Embargo Act, 54, 55; on Indian relations, 111, 122; on legal system, 99; on progress, 77–78; on slave revolt, 146
Caswell, Richard, 9, 163n6
"Cato," 75
celebrations: Lewis and Clark expedition, 173n45; parades, 49, 113, 173n45. *See also* Fourth of July; toasts
censuses: 1800, 31, 48–49; and cotton manufacturing, 68; enumeration by militias, 44
Cherokee Indians: and American Revolution, 4; boundaries with, 21; economy of, 5; and fictive kinship, 3, 21, 161n57; and Hiwassee land, 129; and land claims, 6, 62; and matrilineal tradition, 158n17; and raids on white settlements, 10, 23; removal of supported, 34–35; seek peace, 20, 33; and Spanish government, 2, 24; treaties with, 3; and Treaty of Holston, 22; and Treaty of Hopewell, 11, 12; and white settlers, xviii–xix, 1, 2, 5
Chesapeake, USS: affair of, 108
Chickamauga Indians: and prosperity, 20; and raids on white settlements, 10, 28; and Spanish government, 24; towns of, raided, 29; and Treaty of Hopewell, 11, 12; and white settlers, xix, 2, 5, 22, 23
Chickasaw Indians: and congressional reservation, 62; removal of supported, 34, 122–23, 196n28; and white settlers, xviii
Choctaw Indians, 122–23
Christian, Christopher, 155n20
"Citizen, A," 105
"Citizen of Mero District, A," 76

Index

"Citizen of Smith County, A," 110
Claiborne, Thomas, 119
Clark, Lardner, 60
Clarksville: as tobacco market, 68
Clarksville Compact (1785), 15–16
Clay, Henry, 119, 136, 137
Clinch River, 22
Cocke, John, 175n68
Cocke, William: as circuit court judge, 191n51; impeachment of, 101; as legislator, 162n74; as U.S. senator, 32, 46
codes: slave, 70, 142, 143
Coffee, John: and Chickasaw lands, 196n31; and Creek Indians, 114; and land speculation, 69; as surveyor, 62
Coghlan, William, 65
colonization, 145–46
Columbia Bank, 197n36
Columbian Highway. *See* Natchez Trace
Columbia Steamboat Company, 121
Confederation government: and ties with white settlers, 15–16; treats with Spain, 11–12; and western claims, 19
Congress, U.S.: and internal improvements, 76–77; and Tenn. statehood, 31–32
Constitution, U.S.: Art. 1, 106–7; and elitist culture, 42; as stabilizing influence, 12; and Tenn. statehood, 32
constitutional convention, 30–31
Constitution of 1834, 150–51
constitution (Tenn.), 131
Continental Army: service in, 6
Continental System, 102
Conway, George, 171n21
corn: price of, 60; raised by Indians, 5, 33; raised in Middle Tenn, 60, 137, 177n3, 178n25
cotton: and cloth production, 66, 68; and debt, 65; H. Robison on, 66; manufactories, 76; market, 67, 75–76, 119; in Nashville, 65, 75–76; at New Orleans, 68; price of, 67, 119, 124–25, 135–36; short staple, 58, 65–69; transported by steamboat, 120–21
cotton gin, 66
"Cotton Planter, A," 67–68

counties (Tenn.): in 1800, **85**; courts in, 96; increase of, 48–49; listed, xxvii. *See also under county names*
Craighead, Thomas, 113–14
Crawford, William H., 136
Crawley, Martha, 111
Creek Indians: kidnap Crawley, 111; and raids on white settlements, 10, 23–24, 28; Red-Sticks, 113–14; removal of supported, 34; seek peace, 33; and Spanish government, 2, 24; steal horses, 23; and suspected British connections, 110–11; and white settlers, xix, 2
Cumberland Compact (1780), 8, 16, 159n41, 160n47
Cumberland Ironworks, 79
Cumberland River: Bledsoe surveys, 7; military district, 6; navigation on, 134; and regional economy, 76; trade on, 39, 55–56, 57–58
Cumberland Road, 178n19

D

Davidson County: and commercial activity, 136; courts in, 7; free blacks in, 145; justices of the peace, 16; militia elections in, 43, 47; petitions from, 128; and slaves, 72; and tobacco production, 68
Davis, Karl, 113
Deadrick, George: and Nashville bank, 78–79
debt: commercial, 64, 79; and cotton, 65, 81–82; and Embargo Act, 103–4, 108; relief, 105–7, 128–29; and specie shortage, 82
debtors, 94, 102–7, 128
Delaware Indians, 33
Democratic party, 115–16
demography: and availability of land, 59–64
Dennison, H., 67
"Detector," 99, 100
Dickinson, John, 186n152
Dickson, William, 69, 110
Dickson County, 48
Doherty, George, 162n74
Donelson, John: and Chickasaw lands, 197n31; as land speculator, 7, 70, 163n6

229

Donelson, Stockley, 14, 27, 37, 69, 179n37
Duck River, 196n20
dueling, 52, 170n8
Dunham, Daniel, 62
Dupre, Daniel, 138, 177n4
Dyer, Joel, 176n81

E

economy: and credit networks, 56; post War of 1812, 119–24. *See also* banks; debt
effigy burning, xxii, 49, 173n45
Ekin, George, 149
elections: A. Campbell on, 52; congressional (1825), 136–37; fraud in, 49; gubernatorial (1801), 50–51; gubernatorial (1803), 51–52, 53; gubernatorial (1821), 133–34; militia, 43–46, 47; petitions regarding, 48; presidential (1796), 31–32; presidential (1800), 41; presidential (1824), 136
Embargo Act (1807): and anti-British sentiment, 108–9; and debt, 103–4, 108; origins of, 102–3; petitions against, 48, 103–5
Embree, Elihu, 147
Erwin, Andrew, 137

F

"Farmer, A": on agricultural improvements, 134; on banks, 126, 127, 130; on legal system, 98
Farmers' and Mechanics Bank of Nashville, 197n36
federalism: in Tenn., 37–38
Federalists: and Blount's governorship, 35; in Congress, 26, 29; criticize A. Jackson, 114; and frontier development, 37; and presidential election (1796), 31–32; and white settlers, 17
Federal Road, 178n19
Fisk, Moses, 121
Fletcher v. Peck, 163n6
Ford, James, 162n74; and brigadier election, 44; and militia appointments, 15
Fort Nashborough: land office at, 6
Foster, A., 67

Foster, Robert, 55
Fourth of July: celebrated, 38, 42, 99, 108, 109, 110, 173n45
Franklin, state of, 9, 77, 162n76
Franklin Tennessee Bank, 197n36
fraud: election, 49; land, 36–37, 61, 179n37
"Friend of the People, A," 99, 104, 106

G

Gallatin, Albert, 62
Gallatin Bank, 197n36
Garrison, William Lloyd, 149
General Jackson (steamboat), 120
General Robertson (steamboat), 121
Genet, Edmond, 25
Genius of Universal Emancipation, 147
geography: and political factions, 54. *See also* Cumberland River
Georgia: Yazoo lands, 21, 24, 163n6, 197n34
Glasgow, James, 27, 37
Glasgow conspiracy, 36–37, 51
Goodall, William, 72
Goodstein, Anita, 70, 96
Great Britain: authority of, on frontier, 4; and Battle of Fallen Timbers, 33; Orders in Council, 102; and relations with Indians, 110–11, 111–12; sentiment against, in Middle Tenn., 108–9; and U.S. loans, 124
Grimes, William, 165n42
Grundy, Felix, 99, 128, 130, 131; and pro-war sentiment, 112, 113

H

Habermas, Jürgen, 154n7
Hague, John, 66
Hamilton, Alexander, 158n27
Hamilton, Joseph, 82
Hanes, John: petition from, 48
Hanging Maw (Cherokee chief), 166n54
Hardin, Joseph, 162n74
Harris, Thomas, 49, 55, 100, 101, 103, 108
Hawkins, Benjamin, 168n89
hemp, 105
Henderson, Richard: land speculation of, 4

Index

herrenvolk society, 142, 150–51
Hillsborough: land office at, 6
Hillsman, John, 67
horses: stolen by Indians, 5, 10, 23, 27–28, 33
House of Representatives, U.S., 32
Houston, Christopher, 117, 121, 122–23, 124, 137
Houston, James, 125
Houston, Placebo, 121, 123
Howard, Benjamin, 35
Humphrey County, 173n44
Humphreys, Parry W., 191n51
hunting: and Indians, 3, 5; and white settlers, 3

I

Impartial Review and Cumberland Repository, 54, 67, 71, 72; advertises goods, 76; bank ad, 78; on economic growth, 81
Indians: A. Jackson on, relations with, 28–29, 111, 114; and American Revolution, 4; *Carthage Gazette* on, 111, 122; and hunting, 3, 5; J. White on, 22–23, 23, 24; *Knoxville Gazette* on, 33; and land titles, 21; *Nashville Clarion* on, 110–11, 111–12; and progress, 33–34; and raids, 23, 24–25, 28; raise corn, 5, 33; and relations with Spain, 24, 33; steal horses, 5, 10, 23; steal livestock, 5, 22, 33; steal slaves, 5, 22; steal white settlers, 22, 23; and surveyors, 22; T. Jefferson on civilizing, 34; traditions, 3; treaties, 3, 4. *See also under tribal names*
Ingram, Benjamin, 145–46
internal improvements, 38; and government funding, 58, 76–77; and legislature, 136; and Nashville, 75; roads and canals, 76–77, 120, 134
Iroquois Indians, 157n8

J

Jackson, Andrew: on banks, 130, 131–32; and Chickasaw lands, 196n31; and Creek War, 114–15; and Donelson land claims, 69; and 1801 gubernatorial election, 50–51; and 1803 gubernatorial election, 51–52, 53; and Indian land claims, 122; on Indian relations, 28–29, 111, 114; as justice, 97; and legacy of Revolution, 110; as major general of militia, 50–51; and militia elections, 44, 45; and militia service, 8; on Missouri Compromise, 147; and Sevier, 45–46, 50–51, 52; and slaves, 144, 151–52; on Spanish government, 12; and speculators, 136; as U.S. Senator, 36, 46; and W. Blount, 15; and War of 1812, 113
Jackson, James, 69, 202n117
Jackson, Washington: and Nashville bank, 78–79
Jay, John: treats with Spain, 11–12
Jefferson, John Garland, 61
Jefferson, Thomas: on civilizing Indians, 34; Coghlan seeks help from, 65; and Embargo Act, 102–3; letters to, from Tenn., 81; and presidential election (1796), 32; as secretary of state, 25, 26; on steamboats, 120; on Tenn., 61
Jefferson County, 147
Jeffersonian-Republicans, 17, 21, 115; and frontier development, 37; and presidential election (1796), 31
Jerry (John Campbell's slave), 144
Johnson, Thomas, 44–45, 47–48
Jones, William, 124
judges: speculators as, xix; territorial, 15, 52, 60, 97
judicial reform, 94, 95–102
justices of the peace, 96

K

Kelly, Alexander, 162n74
Kentucky, 138; and legal reform, 95
King, James Moore, 70
King, Thomas, 119
Kingsly, Alpha, 196n18
kinship roles: and Cherokee Indians, 3, 21, 161n57
Knox, Henry, 21, 23, 24, 27
Knox, Thomas, 82
Knoxville, 96, 97

Knoxville Gazette, 27; on federal assistance, 29; on Indians, 33; on Jackson, 53; prints Paine's *Rights of Man*, 13–14

L

"L": on wealth, 82–83
"Land Grab" (1783), 61
land grants: and federal government, 13; and military districts, 6–7
land speculation: and cost of federal government, 20; and legal title, 94, 95–96, 121; without ownership, 121
land titles: and conflicting claims, 94, 95–96, 121; and effect of Revolution, 4; and Indians, 21, 122
Lanier, John, 144
lawyers: in Middle Tenn., 98–99
Leach, David, 144
Leclerc, George-Louis, 168n85
legislature, 143; and cotton production, 66; and debtor party, 128–29; and internal improvements, 136; and judicial reform, 100–101; as proslavery, 142, 143; regulates free blacks, 145–46, 149–50; territorial, 43; and tobacco production, 68
Leopard, HMS, 108
Lewis, William, 47
Lexington, Ky., 138
Liberia: free blacks settlement at proposed, 145
Lincoln, Benjamin, 19
liquor: and slaves, 72; whiskey, 177n3, 184n126
Littlefield, Edward, 148
Little River, 22
Little Tennessee River, 22
livestock: and impact on indigenous animals, 4; stolen by Indians, 5, 22, 33
loan offices, 129–30
Locklier, Jetro, 73–74, 145
Louisiana Purchase, 53, 67
Loving, William, 150
Lucust, Betty (slave), 204n22
Lundy, Benjamin, 147, 148

Lyon, James, 38
Lytle, William, 26–27, 29

M

McAlister, John, 134
McFarlane, John, 79–80
McFerrin, John, 74
McGillivray, Alexander (Creek leader), 24
McLemore, John, 133
Maclin, William, 175n72
McMinn, Joseph, 50, 162n74
McNairy, Boyd, 202n117
McNairy, John, 15
McQuestion, James, 48
Madison, James: declares war, 112–13; and domestic debt, 158n27; as president, 108–9, 111
Maine, 147
"Manlius": on speculators, 63, 95
Mansker, Kasper, 7, 8
manufacturing: cotton, 68; state support for, 106
Manumission Intelligencer, 147
markets: international, 67
Marshall, John, 163n6
Martin, B. T., 136
Maury County: and commercial activity, 136; and legal reform, 99–100
McFarlane, John, 79–80
Mebane, Alexander, 165n42
merchants: in Middle Tenn., 58, 75–80
Methodist Church, 142, 148–49
Miami Indians, 33
Michaux, André, 8, 25
Michaux, François André, 57, 66, 81
military districts, 6, 7
military warrants, 36
militias: and elections, 43–46, 47; and personal networks, 42–43; surveyors serve in, xix, 7–8
Mill Creek Church, 74
Mississippi River: navigation of, 12, 31, 57; and Spanish control, 10–12, 32; and steamboat traffic, 120

Index

Missouri Crisis, 59, 142, 146–51
Mobile, 77
Mobile River, 78, 185n137, 185n141
Monroe, James, 22–23
Montgomery County: petition from, 48
Mount Olivet Baptist Church, 74
Murfreesborough Bank, 197n36
Murrey, Abram, 109
Muscle Shoals, xxvi, 21, 59, 76, 163n6

N

Napoleon: and Continental System, 102
Napoleonic wars: economic impact of, 67, 68, 82, 102, 107
Nash, William, 47
Nashville: cotton market in, 65, 75–76; J. Campbell on society in, 117; land office, 36; and river navigation, 77; and slaves, 71–73; steamboat traffic to, 120–21
Nashville Bank, 123, 125
Nashville Clarion, 99; criticizes wealthy, 127; on economic growth, 116; on Indian-British relations, 110–11, 111–12
Nashville Steamboat Company, 121
Nashville Whig, 120, 125; and congressional election, 137; on Missouri Compromise, 147
Natchez Trace, 77, 78, 178n19
nationalism, 38, 94; and American identity, 109; and *Chesapeake* affair, 108
Nat Turner's rebellion, 149
"Neckar," 132
New Orleans: as commercial outlet, 2–3, 67; cotton market at, 68; roads to, 77; steamboat traffic to, 120–21
Nichols, James, 48
Nichols, John, 26
Non Intercourse law, 109
North Carolina: General Assembly, xix, 5–6, 11; 1789 land cession, 26, 70; land office, 6; and land warrants, 6, 62; laws of, in Tenn., 96; and ratification of constitution, 12–13; slave code (1741), 70, 143; and Tenn. frontier, 2

Northwest Ordinance (1787): as model of territorial government, xix, 13, 32
Northwest Territory: and Indian alliance, 33

O

"Observer, An," 105
Ohio River, 57; post on, 19; as route to Tenn., 59
Old Tassel (Cherokee chief), 4
Onuf, Peter, 34
Osborn, Charles, 147, 148
Ottawa Indians, 33
Overton, John: and bank debate, 123–24; and case of legal corruption, 53, 99; and *Chesapeake* affair, 108; and Chickasaw lands, 196n31; and cotton market, 119; and slaves, 182n96; surveyor, 8; and W. Blount, 15, 50
Overton, Thomas, 72

P

Packenham, Sir Edward, 115
Paine, Thomas: *Rights of Man*, 13–14
Panic of 1819: and banks, 56, 79, 116, 118, 124–28; and shrinking credit, 117
Papier, Richard, 195n5
Park, Joseph, 78–79
Parker, A.: and road bill, 77
patriotism: and American Revolution, 110
patronage: and Tenn. politics, 41–43
"Pericles," 97, 196n28
petitions: antislavery, 142, 150; against banks, 125, 127, 132; against Chickasaw Indians, 122; and cotton manufactory, 75; against Creek Indians, 114; on Embargo Act, 48, 103–5; to enforce land titles, 121–22; against free blacks, 149; from free blacks, 145; of incorporation, 121; to J. Sevier, 103, 104–5; against loan offices, 129; to protect debtors, 128; requesting federal aid, 76; requesting political action, 48–49; requesting state aid, 77, 78, 106, 120; seeking legal reform, 97, 100; and slaves

233

petitions: antislavery (cont.)
as property, 71; against squatters, 63; from squatters, 64; supporting free blacks, 73; from tobacco farmers, 68, 69
Pickering, Timothy: as secretary of war, 30; on white settlers, 35
Pierce, Isaac, 71
"Pindar," 132
political culture, 93, 101–2, 107–13
Polk, James K., 136–37
Polk, Samuel, 121
Polk, Thomas, 7
Pope, John, 78
population (Middle Tenn.): in 1790, 14; in 1796, 39, 55, 60; in 1800, 87; in 1810, **88, 89**; in 1815, xvii; in 1820, 60, **90, 91**; in 1830, 69; of free blacks, **91**, 145; regional, 60; of slaves, 69, **91**; and territorial status, 13
Porter, Alexander, 78–79
Poyzer, George, 68, 78–79
preemption rights, 64
Preston, William, 35
Prince, Caesar, 155n20
Prince, Robert, 44
print culture, 13–14
progress: and Indian culture, 33–34; and white population, 59
Prophet, The (Tenskwatawa), 110–11
Prosser, Gabriel, 143
public opinion, 54–55
public rituals. *See* celebrations; Fourth of July; toasts
Pugh, Jonathan, 9

R

race: and discrimination, 141–42
Rankin, John, 147, 148
reform: judicial, 94, 95–102
"Reformer, A," 103
religion: and antislavery, 142; and Second Great Awakening, 74
Rentfro, Robert, 73, 145
Republican Party: and popular democracy, 41–42

Rhea, John, 106
Richardson, George, 81
roads, 76–77, 120
Roane, Archibald, 15, 50, 51, 97
Roberson, William, 72
Roberts, Isaac, 49
Robertson, James: and Confederation government, 2, 19; and Indians raids, 24, 25; as land speculator, 7, 27; and militia appointments, 15; and militia election, 45–46; militia expedition of, 29; and slave code (1741), 70
Robertson Judicial District, 49
Robison, Hugh, 60–61, 61, 66, 80
Rogersville Bank, 197n36
Rohrbough, Malcolm, 166n68
Royal Proclamation (1763), 4
Rutherford County, 74; and commercial activity, 136; and legal reform, 99–100
Rutledge, George, 162n74
petitions: antislavery

S

"S. N. G.": on banks, 126
Seagrove, James, 26
settlers, white: and Cherokee Indians, xviii–xix, 1, 2, 5; and Chickamauga Indians, xix, 2, 5, 22, 23; and Chickasaw Indians, xviii; and Confederation government, 15–16; and Creek Indians, xix, 2; and Federalists, 17; and G. Washington, 20; and J. White, 30; and Spain, 1–2; stolen by Indians, 22, 23; and T. Pickering, 35
Sevier, John: and boundary controversy, 35–36; on Chickamauga Indians, 5; as governor of Franklin, 9, 174n65; and 1801 gubernatorial election, 50; and 1803 gubernatorial election, 51–52; on Indian relations, 111, 112; and Jackson, 45–46, 50–51, 52, 53; and land fraud, 36–37; and major general appointment, 51; and militia appointments, 15; militia expedition of, 28; and officer elections, 44–46; petitions to, 103, 104–5; on statehood, 30
Shawnee Indians, 33, 157n8

Shelby, Isaac: as Ky. governor, 24
Shelbyville Bank, 197n36
Shofner, John, 74, 152
"Simm," 100
Sims, Leonard, 148
slavery: ambiguity regarding, 141; centrality of, in Middle Tenn., 151–52; and economic development, 58–59, 74; and federal government, 13; and plantation economy, 69–74
slaves: autonomy of, 71; and 1741 code, 70, 143; colonization of proposed, 145–46; corporal punishment, 144, 150, 182n91; hiring out, 72–73, 141; population of, 69, **87, 89, 91**; and rebellion, 143, 146, 149–50; and religion, 74; sold, 70–71; stolen by Indians, 5, 22, 23
"Slim" (pseudonym), 49–50, 98–99
Smith, Daniel, 12, 14–15, 28
Smith, James Norman, 61, 63, 184n126, 193n102
Smith, John H., 76, 78–79
Smith, William Loughton, 31
Smith County, 48, 55, 69, 80; petitions from, 132
South Carolina, 160n55
Southwest Ordinance (1791), xix
Spaight, Richard, 10
Spain: and Indian relations, 24, 33; and navigation of Mississippi, 10–12, 32; and stolen goods, 22; and white settlers, 1–2
specie: Continental bills, 7; in land transactions, 123; and Panic of 1819, 124; shortage of, 81–82, 94, 102, 103, 118, 125; and state loans, 129
speculators: and bank credit, 131; and congressional reservation, 62; as justices, 96, 97; and military land grants, 6, 7, 61; oppose regulation, 135; and statehood, 31
Speed, John (Indian agent), 24
Spencer, John, 188n10
squatters, 61, 62, 63–64, 96, 122, 177n4
statehood, 30–32
stations, 8, 23, 28, 159n34
status: hereditary, 13
stay laws, 105–7, 128, 131

steamboats, 79, 120–21
Stone, Jacob, 73, 145
Stuart, Thomas, 191n51
Stump, Christopher, 196n18
Stump, Frederick, 61
Sullivan County: free blacks in, 145
Summerville, John, 124, 125–26, 135; on emancipation, 148
Sumner, Thomas, 124, 125–26, 135
Sumner County, 7; elections in, 47; free blacks in, 145; and tobacco production, 68, 69
surveyors: and extralegal local government, 2; and military districts, 6, 7; and overlapping grants, 61, 95; and political power, xviii, xxvi, 14–15; and stations, 8; and U.S. Constitution, 12

T

Tait, William, 78–79
Tallapoosa River, 114
Tallmadge, James, Jr., 146–47
Tannehill, Wilkins, 196n18
Tardiveau, Barthelemi, 66
Tate, John, 72
Tatum, H. O., 36
Taylor, James: on Indians, 29
Taylor, Leroy, 47, 162n74
technology: and innovation, 58
Tecumseh, 110–11
Tenan, Hugh, 165n42
Tennessee Gazette, 41, 50, 51, 57, 67; letter from "Cato," 75
Tennessee Manumission Society, 146, 147
Tennessee River, xxvi, 21, 59, 76, 122–23
Tennessee Yazoo Company, 21
Territory South of the River Ohio: created, 13; land claims in, 26; legislature of, 31
Thomas, Jane, 73
Thomas, John, 73
Thomas, Philip, 155n20
Thompson, Robert, 63
Tipton, John, 45, 162n74
toasts: Fourth of July, 42, 49, 99, 108, 110, 173n52, 193n99; and militias, 8; patriotic, 109, 110

tobacco: and Cumberland River, 36, 55–56, 58; price of, 68–69, 125, 135, 181n81, 195n5; and slavery, xxiv, 59
Tombigbee River, 77, 78, 185n137
traditions: Indian, 3, 158n17
Transylvania Company, 4, 5
treaties: Indian, 3
Treaty of Fort Jackson, 114
Treaty of Fort Stanwix (1768), 4
Treaty of Hard Labor (1768), 4
Treaty of Holston (1791), 22, 23, 24
Treaty of Hopewell (1785), 11, 12, 21
Treaty of Lochaber (1770), 4
Treaty of San Lorenzo (1795), 32, 67
Trimble, James, 191n51
Trimble, John, 71
Turner, Frederick Jackson, 13, 152
turnpikes, 76–77
Tyrrell, William, 37

U

urban growth, 58

V

van den Berge, Pierre L., 150–51
Vans Murray, William, 29–30
Virginia: and judicial reform, 95

W

Walker, William, 47
Ward, Edward: and gubernatorial election, 133–34; and land speculation, 69; on slavery, 152
War of 1812: blacks in, 74; declaration of, 112–13; support for, 38, 109, 113–15
Washington, George: administration of, 10, 14, 16, 20–22, 24; and militia expeditions, 29; on Tenn. settlers, 20
Watauga Association, 8, 9
Wayne, Anthony, 33
Wear, Samuel, 162n74
Western Annual Conference (antislavery), 148, 149
Whig party, 115–16, 136
whiskey, 177n3, 184n126

White, Daniel, 185n133
White, Hugh Lawson, 50, 191n51
White, James: on Indians, 22–23, 23, 24; as legislator, 162n74; on Spanish government, 12; on white settlers, 30
White, Richard, 157n8
whites. *See* settlers, white
Whiteside, Jenkin, 196n18
Whyte, Robert, 71
Wilkinson, James: in Ky., 12
Williams, James B., 121
Williams, John, 202n117
Williams, Nathaniel, 191n51
Williams, Sampson, 49, 100, 176n81
Williams, Willoughby, 68, 73, 79
Williamson, I. H., 19
Williamson County: and commercial activity, 136; and legal reform, 99–100
Wilson, David, 162n74
Wilson, Joshua, 82
Wilson County: free blacks in, 145
Wilson Creek Baptist Church, 74
Winchester, James: and brigadier election, 44, 45; and *Chesapeake* affair, 108; and Chickasaw lands, 196n31; and cotton market, 67, 119; mentioned, 82; and militia appointments, 15; and tobacco prices, 195n5; and War of 1812, 113
Winchester Bank, 197n36
Winchester Judicial District, 49
Winn, R., 72
Wood, William B., 72
Wright, William: and Nashville bank, 78–79
Wyandot Indians, 33

Y

Yandle (Yandell), Wilson, 108
Yazoo lands. *See* Georgia, Yazoo lands
Yeatman, Preston, 79
Yeatman, Thomas, 79
Young, Joseph, 60, 104
Young, Polly, 104

Z

Ziegler Station: Indian raid on, 23
Zion Presbyterian Church, 144